W9-CAM-884

Pamela Kesselring Kelley

HOP CITY ROAD
HOUSE

*A Saga of an American
Family*

Hop City Road House: A Saga of an American Family

Copyright © 2007
Pamela Kesselring Kelley

All rights reserved.
No portion of this book may be reproduced or transmitted in any form, except for brief quotations in printed reviews, without the prior permission of the publisher.

This book is a work of fiction. The story is a product of the author's imagination based on what might have historically occurred during this time and place.

Cover art by Pamela Kesselring Kelley
Photographs by Lonny Kelley

Pamela Kesselring Kelley, Publisher
Houston, Texas
PamelaKKelley@aol.com

ISBN: 978-0-9801732-0-8

First Printing: 2008
Second Printing: 2009

Printed in the United States of America by:
Morris Publishing®
3212 East Highway 30
Kearney, NE 68847
800-650-7888

For Lon and our daughters

In memory of my parents and grandparents

Acknowledgments

I thank my editor Mary Jones for her professional editing and encouragement in writing this story. Thank you for believing that I could do this. A very special thank you to B.J. for reading my rough drafts, lending me books, pushing me forward, and nourishing my characters with Christian love. Thank you, Kris, Linda, and Angela for tolerating my digressions during our watercolor sessions. Thank you, Suzanne, for the early American wedding ceremony research and our happy discussions. Thank you, Alice, for urging me to dig deeper and explain more, so my readers would see the story as clearly as I did.

Thank you, Betsy, for agreeing without a moment's hesitation to read *HCRH* for its spiritual content and to Marianne for sharing your book and the path to self-publishing. To my niece Mari Kesselring, a novice editor with a wonderful literary future, thank you for your comments that gave me the push I needed to finish the story.

To all of our friends who knew us in Ballston and were part of our family's life while we lived on Hop City Road, I hope you enjoy reading my story.

I thank all of my family – siblings, daughters, and grandchildren who listened while I talked of my research. I wish my grandparents could have known how much influence they would have on my life – I wish they might have known my family.

To Kris Meucci Jodon a huge thank you for your time editing and preparation for publishing. The experience of being able to share a project with a good friend only proves again that the fun is in the process. Your participation is deeply appreciated.

I thank my husband Lon for his patience and never ending support. It's finally done! PK

December 29, 2007

INTRODUCTION

Queen Anne's *Golden Book*

After the early explorers discovered the American continents, the powerful kings and queens of Europe were in a race to see who would be first to colonize and control the New World. Every seafaring nation was anxious to plunder the riches from the Americas. Pirates sailed back and forth from the Caribbean to the North Atlantic preying on merchant ships. They would fire their cannons, board the ships, and steal the precious goods from the cargo bays. The English, French, and Spanish navies patrolled the Atlantic Ocean protecting their merchant ships. It was an exciting and a perilous time.

In 1708, an Englishman named Samson Broughton and others requested permission from London's Lords of Trade to purchase land in America from the American Natives. The 700,000 acre Kayaderosseras Patent was inhabited by Mohawk Indians, a tribe of the Iroquois Confederacy. The Mohawks hunted in this beautiful wilderness along the Kayaderosseras Creek.

England's newly crowned Queen Anne was the reigning monarch who must sign the deed of purchase. British surveyors were sent out to what is now Upstate New York to draw up the boundary lines of the Patent. Broughton and the others would pay the Mohawks a very small amount of money for their hunting ground. As soon as the purchase was made, the investors began implementing ways to make their fortunes by selling off parcels of the Kayaderosseras Patent to Englishmen and their families willing to settle in the wilderness.

Queen Anne, a Protestant, was deeply religious and concerned for the welfare of the Protestant Palatinates living in the Germanic Rhine River Valley and the French Huguenots who comprised one third of the French population. In 1709 Queen Anne published the *Golden Book* for the people living in the war ravaged land that bordered France and Germany. The Book promised if they could get to the neutral Dutch city of Rotterdam, she would provide ships for their passage first to London and then to America. The colonists had to sign a contract stipulating that after the production of sufficient naval stores (timber, pitch, and tar) they would be given land on which to build their homes.

The *Golden Book* was widely received and it was estimated at the time that 13,000 Protestants and Huguenots took boats or built rafts and traveled down the Rhine River to Rotterdam. There they boarded empty English naval war ships that had just brought British soldiers to Europe. The Protestants sailed across the North Sea and then up the Thames River to London. The immigration of French and German citizens to America continued for years after the *Golden Book* was published while wars continued in Europe. When Queen Anne died in 1714, she left no heir to the throne. By agreement before her death George I who spoke only German became the king of England. Descendants of the House of Hanover would rule Great Britain for the next two centuries. This story begins in 1744.

Map of the journey to the New Jersey Colony

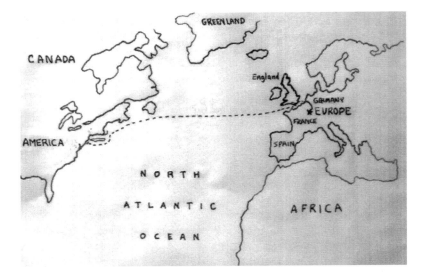

"...the next thing most like living one's Life over again, seems to be a Recollection as durable as possible, the putting it down in writing." –Benjamin Franklin

CHAPTER I

Voyage to America

Phebe's stomach did not feel good. "I think I'm going to be sick again, Samuel."

Samuel didn't feel well either, but he had not heaved over the rail. As he looked to the west, he could just barely see the lead ship. They had boarded the third ship, and seven more stretched out across the horizon bobbing behind them. Before leaving England, he had closely watched the shipyard activity, hoping their vessel would be well-built. He saw returning ships dock and unload their cargo of timber, bales of furs, barrels of grain, and crates of packed goods. All was loaded onto carts and sturdy wagons by the burly men who worked the docks. Samuel quickly discovered that the packed goods were quintals of salted fish the ships had taken on from the British fishing fleets in Newfoundland.

Hauling timber was one thing, but hauling fish left the hold smelly, and their ship was no exception. A short turnaround time for servicing the fleet was a priority as the English traders were anxious to make their profits on the arriving cargo and quickly load and release the vessels back to the colonies for more goods. Consequently, ship cleaning was often poorly done.

Some ships had leaked badly during their return voyage and those must have major repairs. Shipwrights worked long hours and into the night using weak light from lanterns to repair the hulls. New planks replaced damaged timbers and hot tar sealed leaky seams making the ships again seaworthy. Storms during the North Atlantic crossing tore sails and frayed lines. For those ships sailcloth patches were sewn over the tears and new hemp spliced into the long halyards.

Two hundred and eighty colonists, plus paying passengers and the ship's crew, made the voyage aboard Phebe and Samuel's tall mast wooden ship. Samuel had spent days watching the repair procedures and was hoping to be in one of the first ships to leave England. The four months waiting in Blackheath living in a tent had been terrible. The crowded camp conditions and rationed food had taken its toll on the waiting passengers. Some were already weak and sickly even before boarding their ships. He had watched as barrels of food and fresh water were rolled up the gang planks. Sufficient stores of fresh water would be critical if they were to survive the voyage to America. Samuel did not think they had brought enough fresh water on board for the ten week crossing.

Once aboard the ship, the young couple waited again. British officials took weeks to organize and load the ten ships. The plan was for the ships to embark on the voyage within days of each other as sailing in a convoy provided some safety from pirate attacks. They finally left in early spring. The North Atlantic Ocean was ice-free, but the water was cold and the seas rough.

Phebe was sick and unsteady on deck from their ship being tossed about during the last storm. Samuel now prayed for fair weather. Blue skies would lift her spirits as well as those now too weak to climb the ladders and breathe fresh air on deck. Samuel, accustomed to looking to the west to predict the coming weather, today saw only an ominous gray sky.

Holding Phebe's thin waist as they stood at the rail, Samuel recalled their time in London, and he realized that other than now sailing, little had changed. The past weeks aboard the ship proved no better than life in the tent camp in Blackheath. There they had been promised shelter and food, but with so many people they shared what little there was with hundreds of other would-be colonists. They slept six to a tent with two meals a day in overcrowded, unhealthy conditions. The ship was even more crowded and smelly, and the food was much worse.

As a cold wind pieced his thin overcoat, Samuel thought of their plight. He and Phebe had left the beautiful Neckar River Valley of Germany soon after their marriage, and now they were living a nightmare. It was years since Queen Anne's offer to settle German

Palatinates and French Huguenots in America. The wars and famine in Central Europe had continued to encourage still more young people to leave their families in hope of a better future in America's colonies. With their parents fearful blessings, Phebe and Samuel had agreed to make the long voyage, but they had not known of the hardship they would endure.

Samuel, now bored and discouraged, bitterly spoke into the wind, "Too many people read the *Golden Book*."

Phebe only sighed. She'd heard her husband's complaints before. There was nothing she could add that had not already been said. The camp had been bad. Samuel had his savings, but they were not allowed to leave and mingle with the Londoners. Phebe remembered their desperation when she and Samuel left their possessions unguarded and slipped away from the camp. It was but a few blocks to the market where they bought fruit, vegetables, and meat with their small savings. They had hidden behind a hedge and eaten all the food, afraid it would be stolen from them if they ate in camp. Thinking back, she now knew they should have bought food for the voyage.

Sheltered from the wind, the two hungry passengers were wedged between the rail of the upper deck and a small dingy. They were trapped on the rocking stinking ship. The meat was now rancid, and their drinking water foul. Worst of all, they could smell good food cooking for the captain and paying passengers who slept in the small cabins behind them above deck. Samuel and Phebe had but a small corner of an open room with a plank bed two decks below. There was no fresh air at night. The latrines smelled, and they had not washed their bodies or clothes since they had left the tent camp. There was only enough fresh water to drink even with the rain water captured in huge tarps during a storm.

Now shivering, Samuel helped Phebe through the hatch and guided her wobbly legs down the ladder. At least while they were on the ship no one could steal his father's axe and shovel that he kept hidden under their blanket, and Phebe still had her small trunk of clothes, books, and the Bible her mother and father had given them

10

for a wedding present. Her mother had written their birth dates and marriage date on the inside cover.

Phebe Marie Martin
Born September 5, 1727, Heidelberg, Germany

Samuel Joseph Rue
Born June 2, 1724, Mannheim, Germany

Phebe Martin married Samuel Rue
December 13, 1743, Heidelberg, Germany

Phebe prayed each night that her Bible would not record her death before they reached America. She had somehow remained well in the camp, but after being on the ship so long, first waiting for the convoy to be loaded and then sailing in rough seas, she had a fever and knew she was very sick. Samuel brought her up to the fresh air each morning, but since they didn't have heavy woolen coats, it was too cold to stay on deck very long. The man in the next bunk was coughing again, and Phebe prayed she would make it to America before she, too, had the terrible ship's cough.

After ten weeks of sailing west across the Atlantic Ocean, the passengers below deck heard, "Land, land ho!" More shouts were heard, and people stumbled out of their bunks to climb the rough wooden ladders to see for themselves.

Men shouted and women cried as they squinted in the bright sunlight and looked to the west. The stronger ones were now pulling the sick up the ladders out of the bowels of the wretched ship. Some were so weak they had to be held fast to keep from being tossed over the rail as the ship rocked from side to side. Their dreams of hope for a new life swelled in their chests when they saw the coast of North America. Like a shock wave, smiles and weak cheers were heard as each new colonist saw for himself or herself the new land.

For the next few days the colonists seemed to forget their sore and sick bodies as their ship sailed closer to America. On the third day after sighting land, the Rue ship entered a sheltered bay and the water calmed. The captain called his crew to drop sails and anchor beside an island. Small boats were launched from the deck and the colonists climbed down the rope ladders and stepped into the dinghies. As they were rowed ashore, women, clutching their small satchels of possessions, wept in relief.

Samuel went first down the rope ladder with his father's axe and shovel tied to his back. He returned to the deck and lifted Phebe's small trunk and took it down to the waiting boat. Then he returned to the deck and lifted Phebe. She threw her weak arms around his neck and her legs clutched Samuel's waist as he went down the rope ladder for the last time.

When the small boat grounded on the beach, Samuel jumped into the surf and reached for Phebe carrying her to dry land. Only then did he go back for his tools and Phebe's trunk. Phebe took a few steps in the sand and could barely stand up straight, and Samuel, too, felt the ground was moving. They both weakly laughed as they walked crookedly up the beach and then collapsed to their knees thanking God that they were on dry land and finally in America.

Phebe and Samuel Rue, Arrived July 6, 1744, America

The paying passengers and crew sailed on to dock on the mainland. The sick colonists had been rowed to an island just off the coast of the New Jersey Colony. Most were so weak that they fell asleep on the warm sand. Others wondered what they were doing on the beach and not in the harbor that they could clearly see to the west. They had been told they would disembark on the mainland.

Samuel argued with the ship's mate who had rowed them to the beach, but he was warned by the rough sailor not to upset the captain who had orders from the New Jersey Colony not to bring any sick people to the dock. Other passengers were angry, but too weak to protest further. Phebe just stared at her little trunk as it crookedly sat on the sandy beach, and listened while the men argued. She could see the village across the channel. She was coughing and too frightened to speak.

A doctor from the New Jersey Colony was rowed to the island and came ashore soon after their arrival. He looked at the frail and sick immigrants and quarantined the lot. Because so many were ill, the doctor advised, they must all stay on the island until they were well. They would not be allowed to cross the channel for he feared the sickness on the ships would be passed to the people in his Colony.

With compassion in his voice, the doctor told the weary men, women and children, "Indians will come to the island and sell you food today. Eat and sleep and get well."

Phebe turned to Samuel and buried her face in his dirty shirt as she clung to him. Indians. What was to happen to them now? She had heard of the terrible Indian attacks on settlers. Samuel said nothing, but held her shaking body until it stopped trembling. The doctor appeared to be telling the truth, but they had heard so many lies, what was the truth?

As promised, Delaware Indians paddled their canoes to the island to trade with the newcomers. Their canoes were filled with crab, fish, clams, and oysters. As the women hid behind the dunes, the men bought the seafood from the half naked Indian braves. Samuel traded a few coins for enough fish and crabs for himself and Phebe, then, before the Indians had even paddled but a few strokes back to the shore, he and others quickly gathered driftwood and began building fires on the beach. Soon the hungry settlers were roasting crabs in clumps of steaming wet seaweed. Before eating they quickly asked God's blessing for the fresh food he had provided and then stuffed themselves with the fish cooked on sticks held over the hot flames.

With good food at last in their shrunken bellies, the group of weary survivors gathered on the beach that first evening, and together they sang hymns of thanks to God for their safe passage across the Atlantic. They watched the sun set on the American shore and stretched out their tired, thin bodies on the clean sandy beach and slept motionless through the night.

Phebe awoke with a start. *What smelled so awful?* "Samuel, give me your clothes! I can't stand the smell of you another minute, or of myself, for that matter," said Phebe with a hacking cough. "What can we do?"

Samuel grinned. He wasn't sure what he had just heard, but Phebe was already walking down the beach. He followed.

Normally modest people, today Samuel and Phebe walked away from the others, took off their filthy clothes, dropped them on the sandy beach, and waded naked into the water. Phebe felt goose bumps on her arms and coughed. Then bending into the next wave, she let her skinny body down into the salty water and lay back into the gentle surf. Her hair floated about her on the waves. Samuel followed and drew her to him.

Clinging to each other, Samuel, shocked at the sight of her body, confessed, "This has been a terrible journey. It was far worse than I thought it might be." His voice now choked when he saw in the bright sunlight how thin they both were. "If I had known how bad the conditions in the camp and ship were going to be, we would have found another way. Somehow, we would have found another way."

Holding Phebe in his arms and rocking in the waves, Samuel cried. Phebe, herself sobbing, clutched her young husband and through her own tears looked at his handsome face and shaggy wet hair and beard and said, "Life in America will be worth the terrible voyage. It can't be any worse!" and with that truthful fact, they both began to laugh.

Then sitting in the shallow water, they used the beach sand to scrub out the stains and smell from their skin and soaked their clothes. Later, climbing among the sand dunes, Samuel found a place out of the wind for them to rest, dry their clothes, and warm their half-starved bodies.

The women from the ship spent the next days washing their families' clothes. Some, who were too weak to work or swim, just sat in the surf. The salty water stung their bruised and sore skin, but the daily bathing and summer sun gradually soaked away the filth and healed their bodies. Sadly, Samuel and the other men spent some mornings digging graves on the island for those who succumbed. And each day at mid morning the Indians came with fish to sell.

There was great excitement when a second small boat arrived carrying the leader of the New Jersey Colony. He stepped onto the beach, careful not to get too close to the settlers, and yelled over the noisy surf, "You will be welcomed to the colony as soon as you are healthy. Farmers will come in the morning with tools that you can use to build shelters and bundles of flour and suet. You will find a letter in each bundle with the name of the farmer who will give you shelter until you have bought land and built a cabin. Until then, buy food from the Delawares and get well."

With those few words, he waded towards his waiting boat. Then, calling back over his shoulder, he yelled, "If you don't have enough money to buy land, you and your family will be apprenticed to farmers."

The new colonists were shocked at the news. They had all signed agreements that they would be given land in return for their labor cutting timber. Samuel assured Phebe that there must be a mistake. He had his copy of the agreement safely stowed in her trunk; and with his father's axe, he was prepared to work for their land.

Just as promised, the next day materials and tools were left on the beach for the newcomers to use to build huts. A heap of tied bundles were also left on the beach. Samuel read the letter tied in his bundle that Phebe was now sorting. It held a small sack of flour, salt pork, potatoes, onions, carrots, two cups, plates, fork and knife. The note was from a New Jersey farmer named Morley explaining that the food and supplies were in exchange for work they would do for him later when they were allowed to come to the colony. He and his wife would welcome them only when they were well.

Samuel wished he had saved more money. He walked among the men and helped those who could not read the English notes in their sacks. It was a beginning, thought Phebe. But Samuel was

15

worried that he would not have enough money to buy land if there was no longer an agreement. He had thought they would be given land in exchange for his labor. Clearly there had been a misunderstanding.

With the goal of being the first to leave the island, Samuel made sure he and Phebe ate well and swam every day. Her cough kept them awake at night. Phebe napped in their hut during the day or walked the beach looking for a plant to make a tea that might sooth her throat. Cautiously, she had thought of boiling leaves of the strange plants that grew among the dunes, but decided on seaweed tea as none of the plants looked familiar to her and the seaweed had proven safe to eat. Even though she was surrounded by the same people she had known at the camp and on the ship, she pulled away from the other women. The trip had been terrible. It had been hard to leave her family, and she now longed to sit with her sisters and unload this unhappiness that she felt. They would surely understand and comfort her. Her husband was only interested in getting off the island. He was pushing her to swim each day and sometimes hand fed her until she could swallow no more. She felt like a child again, not the confident bride who had worn a beautiful dress and been adored by her family and friends.

This morning her husband and the other men were making fishnets by weaving the long sea grasses that grew in the shallow tidal pools. They copied the woven nets seen in the Indian canoes. While the men fished and caught crabs, she could look forward to making do with the few pots for cooking and baked flat doughy bread in the hot coals of the fire with the other women. Today should be the day men from the mainland brought barrels of fresh drinking water. Phebe always boiled their water first, as she had done on the ship, and she and Samuel drank green tea.

Samuel kept reminding her that they were some of the lucky ones, and so they both helped to feed and nurse the sick. The children seemed to get well faster than their parents and soon were playing on the beach and splashing in the surf. As they regained strength in their

16

arms and legs, their appetites improved. Samuel and the other healthy men were busy fishing for the sick parents as well as themselves.

It was good news when babies were born. The urgency of taking care of an infant displaced some of the sorrows from the deaths aboard ship and the loss of families left behind in Europe. The colonists lovingly carried on family traditions and named their babies after their parents and grandparents. During the evening prayer service the infants were baptized, welcomed, and held for all to see. Their live births were celebrated. These children were Americans at birth, and the colonists gave thanks to God for this promise of new life. As on the first night, the immigrants gathered for hymns and prayers of thanksgiving and watched the sun set on America. They were the survivors.

CHAPTER II

New Jersey Colony

Samuel and Phebe were swimming and digging with their hands in the wet sand for clams, watching as a small boat was rowed to their beach. Two well-muscled men with long hair and homespun shirts got out and started walking among the colonists. The men would grunt and poke each other, with one or the other shaking his head yes or no. Finally after scaring the women with their stern looks and gestures and alarming the defenseless men, they roughly gestured to four of the oldest boys to step forward.

The man with huge blackened hands asked them, "Are you well?"

"Yes," said the lad who was not yet full grown but strong enough to pull his arm free.

"Good, then tell your families that you are coming with us. We have jobs for you in the colony. You bigger lads can earn your keep apprenticed to me. I'm a smithy and need two young apprentices to help with the horses and keep the fires going in my forge. You know, clean out the stalls, feed the nags, and chop firewood. You might even learn how to shoe a horse. My friend here needs help in his butcher shop."

The families of the chosen boys now stepped forward and confronted the strangers, but less worried, listened to the offers.

"You can all come to the colony and be an apprenticed when you are well. We have farmers and shop keepers who will teach you a trade," continued the blacksmith. "You will be welcomed as there is much to do before winter. The crops are ready for harvest and there is fruit to pick."

The anxious families were slow to agree, but the young men were ready to get off the island. They each promised to find their parents as soon as they were all in the colony, and the four boys ran

18

to their huts, gathered their small sacks of extra clothing, and followed the men to the boat.

Soon a second visitor arrived. The colonial doctor was again rowed to the island. Setting up a chair on the beach, he called for only those well enough to work to step forward. Samuel knew he was ready and pulled Phebe to her feet. Half frightened she might cough and be separated from Samuel, she stepped forward planting her bare feet firmly in the sand. The doctor thought them both well, and they ran back to their hut to gather the tools and Phebe's trunk, then waded out to the rowboat to board the small schooner anchored off the island.

The immigrants were met at the New Jersey dock by the farmers who had given them food and cooking tools. As Samuel and Phebe rode in the wagon to Morley's farm, they could at last see the town. Holding hands, they knew their life in America had begun.

That night, somewhat settled in the back room of Morley's house, they slept on a mattress filled with hay under an old quilt. Samuel quickly realized that his father's hired man slept on hay. Now he and Phebe were no better off.

"But Samuel, we're here! Did you see the town and the people? I expected a wilderness, and it's not like that at all. We must write home."

"Yes," he replied, "and find someone to ask about the land that we were promised in exchange for my labor. I shall also have to work for the Morleys to pay them back for this shelter and food we shall eat until we have a cabin of our own."

Phebe excitedly went on, "And I shall be busy, too. I need to learn all I can about New Jersey and see if this is the place where we want to live, or maybe there is some other place in America that will be just right for us. America is so big. Do we want to live this close to the ocean?"

Their prayers that night were filled with thanksgiving. Phebe could not contain her joy at finally being in the Colony. New Jersey was beautiful farming country with rolling hills down to the ocean beaches. The trees were especially beautiful.

"Samuel, the trees cover the land except where there are fields. And did you notice, the people each have a different look to their houses and barns? I heard some German, Dutch, and even some French being spoken and English. I must speak only English now. We must not speak German, but learn to speak English from the Morleys."

Samuel could hear her smile in the darkened room. She was happy. "We will send off that letter to your mother and father tomorrow, Phebe. They need to know that we are safely here. Now try to sleep."

Samuel accompanied Jack Morley with the farmer's first wagon load of potatoes and posted their letter. Just as important, he found the Germantown office that was to provide the land for settlement. The timber camp was in the Hudson River Valley, far from the New Jersey shore. Samuel would have to live at the camp, and Phebe would not be able to come with him. When he returned and talked with Phebe, they decided they would live with Jack and Deborah until he could figure a way to earn money for land near Morley's farm.

Samuel regained his strength as he cut hay and harvested the oats on the Morley's farm. Phebe's arms and face tanned working in the garden. Eating the fresh vegetables and fruits, she had gained back her shape. Her cough was but a bad memory. Sitting in the sun by the back of the Morley's house, she brushed her long hair and could feel its silkiness once again. She smiled. Her body was strong again too. The plentiful fresh milk and eggs had restored her health.

Life in the Colony was happy. Phebe and Jack Morley's wife, Deborah, shared the work running the farm. Phebe had not milked a cow or raised chickens. She could cook, but not grow vegetables. Deborah could sew, but not weave. The women laughed and learned from each other and enjoyed each other's company. The Morley's two young boys raced through the house and welcomed a hug from both their mother and father and this woman and man who lived with them.

Phebe often spoke of the children they might have someday as she said her evening prayers. Samuel, already half asleep, agreed a family would be good, and he too would welcome strong boys to help with the farm work. But Phebe longed for babies, sons and daughters, who would smile and coo and tug at her hair and soon follow her about the house as she kneaded bread and churned butter. Secretly, not wanting to alarm her husband of her new fears, she said her prayers silently to God's ears alone. She worried that she might not have children, but each month Deborah assured her that now that she was well, she would become pregnant. Phebe hoped her friend was right.

Joseph Rue was born on a frosty morning in Samuel and Phebe's unheated room at the back of Morley's house. He was the first child in the Rue family to be an American. During her labor, Phebe had missed her mother and sisters terribly. She remembered watching as her sisters had their babies and knew that her labor was normal, but she missed their presence and longed for their loving care. As her labor quickened, she had held back and was fearful. Deborah had done all she could to help Phebe with the birth, but as this was her first child, Phebe had faced the last contractions with fear.

Now, as Samuel proudly held their infant in his arms, Phebe wanted to share the news of this beautiful baby with her family. She knew they would calm her as she trembled at the thought that little Joseph might die as so many infants had died on the ship. She longed for a room with a chair next to the fire to nurse her infant son. Exhausted and with pain in her heart as well as her body, she fell asleep saying her prayers.

The next morning, Phebe and Samuel were awakened before dawn by the hungry cries of their son. Phebe was tired. She had been up three times during the night – twice to nurse and once awakened to make sure Joseph was warm enough.

Cross and hurting from the birth, she lashed out at her sleeping husband. "Samuel, we are barely surviving. We have no heat, no land, and no house of our own." A great wave of anger rolled over her. "What are we to do? This cannot be how we will spend the rest of our lives. What about a house and a farm of our own?" She repeated, "We were promised land."

She didn't cry at first, only her anger spoke. Then her body slumped onto the hard hay mattress, and the tears raced down her cheeks. And she couldn't look at her young husband as she was so ashamed to have spoken in anger. They had shared the same dream and had been in America just two years. As she nursed her tiny son, more tears poured over her checks and onto her sleeve. Little Joseph had his eyes closed and knew only his mother's food and warmth. Samuel tried to comfort her, but could not. What she said was true. He dressed and went to the barn. He was a tenant farmer.

Deborah Morley knocked on their door and brought Phebe hot tea and biscuits with slices of cold meat and cheese. She sang a gentle ballad as she entered the room and her apron had the smell of fresh flour and yeast. Her hair was caught up with pins, and Phebe could tell she had been up before dawn and was now kneading the bread. Wisps of damp hair encircled her smiling face. This could be me someday, thought Phebe, happily tending my children and my hearth.

"As soon as you feel well enough to get up and move around, come into the kitchen. I have put a good chair by the fire for you to use whenever you wish. I would enjoy your company, as always." Deborah said these words with a warm smile. "Your work can wait; just enjoy these first days with your handsome son."

Later in the day, Deborah brought in an old petticoat to make more little clothes for Joseph, and before the family had eaten, she returned with warm chicken broth and cooked onions, potatoes, and carrots. The Morley's children came with their mother to see the new baby. The children wanted to touch the infant, and the smallest Morley pressed his chubby face to the infant's blanket. Phebe was grateful for Deborah's caring and once again thanked God for placing her with such a good family. Some day she would find a way to return the kindness. That night Phebe opened her Bible and dipped a pen into the black ink.

Joseph Samuel Rue
Born, December 15, 1746, New Jersey Colony

CHAPTER III

New York Colony

The day after Christmas, Samuel left Morley's farm to work miles from New Jersey Colony. He walked to Germantown in the New York Colony and worked in the logging camp for the remainder of the winter. He had signed a contract with the English to cut down timber in the lower Hudson Valley. He slept in the logging camp far from Phebe and little Joseph during the long, dark winter months.

Tall pines, some two feet across, were needed for ship masts. Planking was needed for the hulls and the pine pitch would be boiled into tar. All this Samuel had seen being delivered at the London docks. American timber and naval supplies were floated down the Hudson River and loaded aboard the returning empty passenger ships. Samuel could see the cycle of trade and he knew now that the survival of his family depended on trade with the English. America's natural resources would be the first riches England would take from the colonies.

The work was hard. Samuel labored cutting timber from early winter until early spring. As soon as the ground was free of frost, he collected his earnings, walked back to Phebe and ploughed Morley's fields as if they were his own. They would save Samuel's earnings to purchase land.

Their reunion had been tearful. Samuel had carried Joseph in his arms most of the day. Phebe could see how hard her husband had worked. His long thin body had thickened and his skin was rough from the cold weather. Samuel tried to explain to her the changes in the agreement they had signed, but Phebe could see that the promise of land was now a broken promise. The agreement to work for land had dissolved when the timber in the Hudson River Valley proved not to be good for producing tar and pitch. As a result, England would no

24

longer pay the New York Governor for the naval supplies. The cut timber was still exported, but the profit was less. It would take years before Samuel's earnings would be enough to buy land in America.

But Samuel and Phebe were still optimistic. They were blessed with two more sons, good health, and now lived in a comfortable small cabin behind Morley's house.

William Martin Rue
Born May 17, 1748, New Jersey Colony

And three years later,

Matthew Joseph Rue
Born September 25, 1751, New Jersey Colony

Samuel's joyous return to Morley's farm each spring made the young family happy. With their father home working in the fields, the family was complete. Phebe's days passed quickly working outdoors in the garden and tending the animals. She took their boys with her picking wild strawberries and raspberries along the fence rows. They would wave and shout to their father as he ploughed and planted.

On the Sabbath, Samuel gathered his family and together they walked to church with other Protestant families. They worshiped freely and sang loudly. If it was a sunny warm day, Phebe packed their food in a basket she had woven and they walked to the New Jersey shore. The boys would laugh and play in the shallow surf while their parents rested on the beach.

On the long winter nights when Samuel was living at the timber camp, Phebe sewed or sat weaving at her loom. After her sons had said their prayers, she sang ballads from her childhood. They were songs her mother, whom she now feared she would never see again, had sung to her. As her shuttle flew across her loom in dim candlelight, her thoughts returned to Samuel and their journey to America, and then to their hopes of a good life in a free country and a house and land of their own.

They had never received letters back from their families. Whether their letters had been lost at sea, or lost on the long road back to Heidelberg, they didn't know. What they had learned was that the wars in Europe continued, and the beautiful little villages where they had grown up were in the middle of the conflict.

Phebe was not discouraged about their future in America. Their three young sons kept her busy, and though her heart ached and longed for Samuel's return during the long winter nights, they still shared in their dreams a real house and land of their own. She would speak to her little boys with conviction that some day they would have a house with a big fireplace for cooking and baking, bedrooms for them and maybe sisters.

"We will need a tall, sturdy barn, bigger than farmer Morley's, for cows and hay. We will need a strong horse to pull our wagon, and your father will need oxen to plough our fields. We shall have our own house on our own land," Phebe would tell her boys.

Joseph, now five years old, could close his eyes and see their house. It would be surrounded by green fields and fruit trees. There would be a big vegetable garden, a pond for swimming, and a fast moving stream filled with fish. They would have friends, and they would laugh and play in a big yard.

Samuel and Jack Morley had become good friends. Samuel had watched Jack deal with poor crops and ruined hay from summer storms, and together they had learned how to deal with their losses. Samuel respected the English-born farmer and appreciated how they worked as a team to get the task completed. So when the day finally came that Samuel had enough money to buy land in the New York Colony, he knew he would sorely miss this good friend.

Samuel had found the land for sale near the Hudson River on his long walk home from the timber camp. He had spied the pretty hillside on the west bank of the Hudson. He walked the property and thought the dirt to be just as fertile as the New Jersey farmland, plus the price was right. He had walked, than ran home to share the discovery with his wife. Phebe agreed at once to buy the land, sight unseen.

While Samuel built their cabin, late that summer with the help of some of the men from the logging camp, Phebe stayed at the Morley's farm. She was expecting their fourth child and was praying for a daughter. Not only did she want the company of another female, but she longed to dress a daughter in long skirts and bonnets. Deborah had two sons and the women decided that Phebe's next child should be a daughter, who they could both spoil.

When the Rue's cabin was completed and a field cleared, Samuel returned to New Jersey. Together, the two families loaded all the Rues' furniture and tools, bedding and clothing, everything they owned, into wagons and the procession traveled to the cabin. Upon arrival there was a great commotion, children running madly about, two women organizing the cabin as the two men unloaded the wagons before dark.

In the morning, Samuel proudly showed Jack Morley where he would clear trees for the second field. "We might even try a small orchard of apple trees if we can get the wheat planted in time."

His friend was silent. He knew this moving day must come and was happy for Samuel, but did not share his enthusiasm for the location. Jack Morley looked at the land and saw the deep woods to the north. This was close enough to the frontier for him. And the hillside did not look like a wheat field. And, he added, the best fruit might be peaches, not apples. Samuel took his friend's suggestion into consideration.

Yes, he liked peaches, Samuel thought, but they would need apples for cider and pies. The river valley would shelter his trees from early winter frosts and moderate the heat of the summer. This would be good for fruit trees. Samuel recalled the vineyards and fruit orchards along the Neckar River near his boyhood home. Yes, this would be a good place to live and plant an orchard, and nearby Manhattan would be a good place to sell his fruit.

As they celebrated that moving day, Jack Morley offered to say the blessing. Samuel and Phebe Rue had proven to be good

27

people; the blessing Jack spoke was received with thanksgiving by the Rues. But both Deborah and Jack hid their deepest feelings that day. The Rues were more like family. They knew they would miss this hard-working couple and Jack's blessing told of the trust and friendship the families had shared, but not the sadness of their parting. The women had worked side-by-side tending each other's sick children and bending long hours over the hearth. Both Phebe and Deborah would miss each other. It was good that Jack had spoken the blessing quickly.

The Morleys were English citizens and Anglicans. America had opened doors that Jack Morley readily acknowledged would never have been open to him in England. Unless you were the first born son, you would not inherit land from your father. Whereas in America, not only did you have a choice of farmland, but a ready market for your crops. Jack had begun to sell his surplus to the English traders and was looking for another tenant farmer to work his land. Maybe two tenant farmers, he had confessed to Samuel, as trading was much more to his liking.

The Rues were Protestants. All of the freedoms of owning your own land were equally true and important to Samuel. But as he listened to his friend, Samuel rejoiced knowing his family had the freedom to worship in a Protestant Church in America. Both families agreed that life in America was a great improvement from life in Europe.

After the Morleys left, Joseph and William climbed the ladder into their new sleeping loft. Matthew was too young to sleep with his brothers. It was a long way down from the loft to the floor of the cabin. Phebe surprised her big boys with a new blanket. She had hurriedly finished the boys' woven blanket days before moving to their cabin. She knew she would be too busy to weave with a new baby and three boys and winter quickly approaching. Matthew slept on the small sleeping cot on Samuel's side of the bed, and a small cradle was ready next to Phebe's side.

"A dream come true," said Phebe. She planted a huge kiss on Samuel's rough lips. Samuel gathered her in his arms and kissed her firmly back. Phebe's labor had been swift and the child a daughter. The boys pounced onto their parent's bed and happily climbed on their father's laughing chest.

Patience Marie Rue
September 7, 1754, New York Colony

The cabin was plenty crowded with Samuel, Phebe, Joseph, William, Matthew and Patience. Samuel would add an addition to the cabin in two years after the birth of their second daughter.

Susanna Magdalena Rue
Born April 14, 1756, New York Colony

And five years later Phebe delivered their sixth and she hoped her last child, a daughter they named Lucy, a good American name.

Lucy Greta Rue
Born July 26, 1761, New York Colony

CHAPTER IV

Good times turn bad

Summers along the Hudson River were good times for a farmer and a growing family. The bottom land by the river was cleared of trees, and the Rue cabin was encircled by orchards and grassy fields. Samuel proved to be a good fruit farmer and apple trees proved to be well suited to growing on the hillside. On the flatter slopes, Samuel had planted his grains. His sons were old enough to help clear the fields of stones, and Samuel had brokered the trade of early crops of barley and wheat with English buyers in Manhattan.

In addition, Samuel was now a respected wood carver. In his workshop behind their cabin, his carefully selected wood became graceful chairs and sturdy table legs for handsome tables that found a ready market in colonial homes. As a boy he had watched his father build chairs and tables and now Samuel's skills had improved enough that sales kept him busy during the winter months. The hard money from the sale of his furniture bought the supplies the family needed. And, soon his fruit trees would bear more fruit, and they would have a cash crop from the orchard.

Phebe and her daughters tended the vegetable garden, milked the two cows, churned the butter, baked the bread, plucked the chickens and did all the other endless tasks that preserved food for the family to eat during the winter. When the frost nipped the last of the plants, Patience and Susanna would help their mother clear away the pots and pans from canning and bring out the kettles to dip candles or make soap. Lucy did what she was asked, but it was clear she was the baby of the family and often just played. With cows and chickens, the farm always had fresh eggs and milk. The girls had a stand at the road and made money selling what the family could not eat or store. A woman's work was never really done, but Phebe was always glad when the last onion was stored in the cold cellar and she could get back to her weaving and sewing.

On their days off, the boys would hunt and fish. Matthew was the best shot of the three. He had good eyes and an uncanny sense of which direction the deer or rabbit would leap just before he shot. Matthew kept his father's musket with him at all times and brought home rabbits, pheasants, ducks, and geese. Fishing in the creeks along the Hudson River was good, too, and William was the best fisherman of the family. Many meals were of sturgeon, shad, and herring served with vegetables from the garden. William often stopped on his way home and took a portion of his catch to their neighbor's family, hoping for a chance to visit with their daughter, Sarah. The young man could hardly mask his attraction to their neighbor's daughter with long blond braids and dark brown eyes. Phebe knew that Sarah had captured her second son's heart.

This winter the three brothers had joined a work camp to build a ferry crossing before the ice was out of the Hudson River, a crossing just north of the Rue farm. During the construction of the landings, Joseph had hours to think of what he might do with his life. He enjoyed neither hunting nor fishing. He was not looking forward to being a fruit farmer or a carpenter like his father; instead, he loved to read. He knew he could not make a living reading and the thoughts gave him sleepless nights of worry. But his reading skills were also a blessing.

Being able to read well gave Joseph a jump above some of the men cutting timber. The barge operators often had newspapers from Albany that Joseph could read to the men, and they would discuss the news together. Joseph became knowledgeable of current events and the men looked up to him. Joseph was especially interested in the affairs of the colonies and he knew some of what was happening in the surrounding colonies of Massachusetts and Pennsylvania.

Recently, the barge captain that had taken an interest in Joseph passed on old Albany newspapers to the young man. The headlines spoke of a new tax on the Colonies. The British Parliament passed a Stamp Act. Joseph read that when word of the tax reached Boston in May, the news spread through the remaining twelve colonies like a wildfire. The tax, that would take effect in November, would require a stamp on every written document. Revenue stamps would be required on newspapers, private letters, and all legal documents. The stamp money would be paid to King George. Joseph's news soon spread through the camp to his friends and he agreed to meet at the tavern after work and read the newspaper aloud.

The temperature was just above freezing and the men, upset with the news, were restless. It had been weeks since Joseph had spent some of his earnings, but today, he joined the others and set off for the tavern almost without thinking where he was going. Once at the tavern, Joseph read the paper to his friends and was interrupted by the men's questions and grunts. They all ordered more ale.

"Tax!" Joseph complained loudly. "The British would charge me a tax on a deed. I would have to pay the King to make a land purchase legal." This was too much, Joseph thought, and some of the other men from the work camp, now part of the group at the tavern, agreed.

"The next thing you know, they'll be charging us tax on the food we eat off our plates," said one of the men.

Most of the men loudly agreed and slapped their callused hands on the rough table, but some were silent.

After another drink of ale, Joseph spouted, "I don't owe King George or anyone else in England anything."

Then after his work friends agreed with hearty cheers, Joseph shouted, "I am American, and I guess I'm a rebel like those few in Boston!" Joseph finally had said out loud what he had been thinking for a long time and others had only whispered.

A few of the older men moved away from the group and left the tavern. Joseph didn't notice their leaving, but did realize the next morning that he had made a huge mistake in lashing out at the British King. He vowed to be more careful what he said in public, especially at the tavern.

Samuel had a keen idea of what was happening in the colonies too. On his last trip to Manhattan, he saw fighting in the streets, and British Redcoats taking two young men into custody. There had been trouble like that in Boston.

When his sons returned home from the lumber camp, Samuel encouraged them to start planning for their futures and their own independence from the family. He and Phebe would live the remainder of their lives in the cabin. His wife loved their land and the view of the Hudson River out the front cabin windows. Samuel, himself, jokingly said, he was getting too old to build a house, and it would take too much time away from his wood shop.

Just as important to Phebe was her garden in the summer and her weaving in the winter. Having a big house to heat and clean held no appeal to her. And moving into Germantown was not needed. Being near the main road was enough company for her. She had lived in the cabin with six children, and she and Samuel would do just fine by themselves after their sons and daughters were married. The Rues were settled at last, and at the end of each day they thanked God for the comfortable life they now lived in America.

Phebe fully appreciated their good fortune. Their cabin seemed to be at the crossroads of east-west and north-south roads. People from Boston going to Philadelphia crossed the Hudson River and then passed their farm, while even more people passed by in carriages and on horseback traveling from Albany going to Manhattan. Phebe thrived on the news the travelers brought. She felt like she was in a city and in the country at the same time. And, despite the horrible stories of Indian attacks on isolated farms written in the Albany newspapers, she felt that any threat of an Indian attack on their land was remote.

Phebe also knew that her son, William, was soon to be wed to their good neighbor's daughter Sarah. That knowledge brought her much joy. William was set on buying a fine piece of land not far from their cabin, and that would mean that she would see them often.

William and Sarah planned to build a cabin in the spring with Joseph and Matthew's help and to wed in June. But those plans were now complicated by the Stamp Tax. William couldn't believe what the British would charge to record his deed.

"I can't afford to pay more. Sarah and I will need to buy a good wood stove and tools for our garden. We have so many supplies to buy, and I will need a horse and wagon if I am to continue working with father in the orchard. Now the government says I must pay for this official stamp before I can call this small parcel of land my own!" complained Will bitterly at dinner.

Joseph cautioned his younger brother to keep his annoyance with the Stamp Act to himself. He took some of his own savings and paid for his brother's stamp.

Joseph often nervously paced, unable to sit or rest and a deep grumpy-looking scowl warded off conversations with his family that only increased his unhappiness. Unlike his brother William who soon would marry and be settled, Joseph lacked a way to make his dream come true. He worked hard and dreamed hard, and he wanted acres of land. He had plans to build his farm into a business that would make him rich. He thought he had saved enough last year to buy land south of Albany, only to find his letter returned saying the price had gone up. He was so discouraged, and his discouragement had made him grumpy and tense. As he cut timber, he grumbled that he would never earn enough money to make his dreams come true.

Phebe could clearly see that Joseph was unhappy and watched, as Samuel did, the price of land escalate. In addition, their sons were not boys but young men, and they should earn their keep if they were to stay in the cabin. The three of them had taken over the dinner conversation that night, and Phebe thought they had ruined a good meal with their shouting. They had been quarrelling about the Stamp Tax when Phebe had heard enough. She sent them to fish and not to return without ample supply for the family. If they had to spend the night by the river, she would see them tomorrow or the next day. So, William and Joseph went fishing, and Matthew picked up his musket and headed out the door to hunt. He would not spend hours sitting by some trout stream.

Samuel called and walked to Matthew. Matthew turned to his father and Samuel embraced his son. "God be with you; be careful what you say, if you should meet someone. Not all Americans believe we should break our ties with England."

Matthew reassured his father that he would say little of politics to the deer in the woods.

Rue Family Tree

Samuel Rue *m* Phebe Martin
Joseph
William
Matthew
Patience
Susanna
Lucy

CHAPTER V

Big mistake?

Within minutes of settling by the stream, Joseph threw his fishing pole to the ground. Bored, he spied ripe peaches in the orchard on the other side of the creek. Thinking that no one would see him and not the slightest bit interested in spending the evening quarrelling with his brother, Joseph took off his shirt, rolled up his baggy leggings and waded into the creek. Once on the other side, he angrily ripped ripe peaches off a tree and stuffed them into his pant's pockets.

Alerted by his dog, the farmer came out of his cabin waving a stick. His daughter listened to her father's hoots and hollers while watching out the window the shirtless figure leap over their fence and into the creek. When Joseph slipped on the rocks and fell into the water, she imagined the sorry state of the mashed peaches in his pockets. As the soggy figure scurried up the opposite bank, her father quit waving his arms and just laughed.

Joseph was mortified. Stumbling up the bank, he was ashamed of stealing the peaches. He couldn't think why he had done it. He had never stolen anything before in his life. Looking back at the farmer, he felt his face redden. He turned and ran upstream. He had stolen peaches, and now the smashed fruit was ruined.

A week later, he dressed in his best shirt and pants and went back to the fishing stream. He took off his pants and shirt, carefully folding them, carried his clothes and stepped into the stream.

Dry and dressed, he walked past the orchard to the cabin. The man's dog raced first toward him, then back to the porch, and barked furiously. There were baskets of peaches lined up in the shade of the cabin. The farmer came to the door and immediately recognized him. With a stern gruff voice, he demanded his name.

36

Joseph heard the question and opened his mouth to speak, but forgot what he was going to say. Nervously, he looked into the cabin and saw a young boy dressed in bloomers. The farmer caught his glance and cleared his throat.

Joseph jerked his head back, swallowed hard, and stammered his rehearsed apology. "Sir, my name is Joseph Rue, and I have never stolen anything before in my life. Last week when I stole your peaches," nervously adding, "I wasn't even hungry, I was angry about something else, not thinking and foolish. My brother and I were fishing on the other side of the creek. I am truly ashamed and sorry."

"Well, well. It's the lad who visited the orchard last week and took an unexpected swim in our creek, Anne." Thomas gave a long pause, thinking of how this might be best resolved. "Joseph, maybe you might find time to come back again in late winter and help with the pruning of the higher branches in my orchard." Then with a relaxed voice, "I'm doing well trimming the lower limbs, but get a little shaky on the ladder pruning the tops of my trees. These old bones of mine would not favor a tumble."

Joseph felt relief, then remorse wash over him. How could he have stolen peaches from this kindly old man? "I will prune your trees as soon as the frost is out next spring...before buds form," he said, trying to impress the man with some knowledge. Then he looked at his bare feet, before stealing a glimpse of "Anne?" Opening his mouth to continue the conversation, nothing came out. But he did look into the darkened cabin again before fleeing off the porch and down the path. Thomas looked at Anne as he closed the door. She smiled back at her father, and then they both began to laugh.

Anne was the youngest of four daughters and lived with her father, Thomas Ducker. Her three older sisters were married and lived in Manhattan. On hot summer days, they came with their children to swim in the cool creek with their father and Anne. Thomas encouraged their visits both in summer and winter. His wife's quilting frame stood bare and ready against the back wall of his cabin. During the winter, his three daughters left their children with nannies and met on Wednesdays to quilt in their father's cabin away from the noise and sticky fingers of their children.

All but Anne were British citizens. Thomas brought his family to America after the collapse of his textile business. He once had been a successful clothier in London, but lost his business when his store burned to the ground. Unable to support his family, he sold their house and brought his family to America. His wife, Elizabeth, and their three daughters settled in Manhattan in a modest house, and Thomas's new shop had flourished in the colony.

Carly, named after her English grandfather Carlton, and Anne's other two sisters Hannah and Caroline, were married to Englishmen. They led quite different lives from Anne's. Their children went to English schools, and when old enough, they would travel to London. Her sisters' servants cleaned and cooked for the families.

Anne was born in America, and her mother died shortly after her birth. After Carly, Hannah, and Caroline wed, Thomas sold his house and business in Manhattan and moved with Anne to the countryside along the Hudson River Valley.

Anne walked to her school with the other children living nearby. She learned to read with simple books and learned to write with chalk on slates. She did not have the advantage of English schooling, but her sisters shared stories of their classes and travel and brought her their books to read. As a young girl, Anne read to herself and aloud to her father and dreamed of places she might visit someday.

With Thomas's urging, the four sisters embarked on a business of their own. They would quilt at their father's cabin. Their beautiful quilts had found favor and brought high prices from the English gentry in Manhattan. During the afternoons that Carly, Hannah, Caroline, and Anne spent at the quilting frame, Anne felt she had little to add to their stories and gossip from the city. But after today, Anne could not wait for the next quilting session. She had something to say.

Joseph, however, returned home after his apology in even deeper despair. The Stamp Tax, his poor wages, no land, and extra work to pay off his debt to Thomas Ducker now spoiled his disposition even more. He thought he might go crazy before his luck would change. In fact, he was desperate, and seeing William happily in love with Sarah made him all the more agitated. The quick glimpse of Thomas's daughter flashed again and again in his memory. It had been so quick. Was she short or tall? She was tanned and fair? She had been out picking peaches all day and her arms were tanned, he decided. A boy would be picking and he first thought she was a boy, but a boy would not wear bloomers. Yes, Thomas had said "Anne".

So, Joseph spent his winter nights in the timber camp dreaming and fretting over his obligation to prune Thomas's trees. He could hardly wait for the first robins to arrive, a sure sign of spring. He rushed home from the camp and at his first chance, made his way to Thomas's orchard.

Thomas met him at the door, and the two men spent the day pruning and clearing the limbs from the orchard into burn piles. Joseph could see that the orchard had not been pruned for a few years. It would take more visits. And when the orchard was finished, the garden needed a good ploughing.

At first, he barely spoke to Anne. She came out to the orchard with their lunch, said a few words, and then hurried back to the cabin. He had said but a few words to her. After the pruning and ploughing, Thomas gave him a tool needing repair. On his return with the tool, a dull saw needing sharpening, so Joseph never came home without a reason to return.

Anne noticed that his visits were shorter and shorter as she watched their exchanges from the cabin. She was her father's helper, and now she was in an awkward position. She longed to be out in the sun helping the men, but felt she must busy herself in the cabin while they worked.

When her sisters came to quilt, they listened to Anne explain her dilemma. With serious faces they talked about what she might do and questioned her more about Joseph. Anne could not answer their questions. She had hardly spoken with Joseph. So it was decided that Joseph should stay for dinner. Laughing as they plotted, they planned what Anne should cook, but more importantly, what questions she should ask to find out more about him. They shared with their sister their secrets on how to deal with suitors. Anne began to laugh and thought it a game, but promised to heed their advice. *Was Joseph a suitor?* she wondered.

Thomas did his part and invited Joseph to join them for dinner on his next work day. Anne was in a tizzy. First, the cabin must be cleaned from top to bottom. New curtains must be made for the front windows, and her menu was changing daily.

Thomas had watched his daughter prepare, but said nothing. As the men washed for dinner, he noticed that Joseph's hands were shaking. When all was ready, Anne called them in for dinner and set out the food. Joseph ate without stopping and barely looked up. Thomas was talking as usual and there was no need for a response from either Anne or Joseph. Anne's foot gently kicked her father's leg. He looked up and saw her tight-lipped expression. It wasn't long before Thomas was saying less and Anne more. It seemed Anne had no end to questions for the young man, and Thomas almost laughed out loud as he watched as his daughter very slowly cut the berry pie and even more slowly serve it to Joseph.

Anne reported on the progress of the friendship each week while the sisters quilted. The sisters laughed together at her stories and were quick to give her additional pointers with still more laughter as the four planned the menu and prepared the questions for the next dinner. Anne knew it was a game, and while part of her was enjoying the fun, part of her was unhappy. Joseph's talk and actions were still puzzling her. After the meal, he almost ran out the door. Anne could not tell if he was anxious to leave or just naturally nervous. She still didn't know who he was, and Joseph certainly did not know her. She longed to be herself and have more meaningful and private conversations and now was trapped in this polite format with her father at the table. She also wondered if he was still paying back her father and coming because he felt he owed Thomas favors. Did he already have a sweetheart? She had no confidence that her sisters' plan was working, or more importantly, if she wanted the plan to work.

Joseph, however, was smitten with Anne, and could barely conceal his feelings for her. He was afraid that she thought of him only as a country boy with no future or trade. He had serious doubts as to her affection for him. He must show her that he was a worthy suitor, but in trying harder, he only said stupid things that embarrassed him further. He must do more than fix the roof. He must have a plan to win this beautiful girl's heart.

Frantically, Joseph searched the Albany newspapers for affordable land. Land was available, but he had not earned enough this winter to buy a large acreage. He realized he was in love, hopelessly poor, and inwardly despaired he could never ask Thomas for Anne's hand in marriage. To Anne's distress, Joseph's visits became unpredictable. If he came at all, it was only for an hour or two before he would rush off.

Out of extreme frustration and a desperate longing for his dreams of owning a house on acres of land to come true, Joseph began cutting timbers for a house. When he closed his eyes he could see his house. A fireplace dominated half the downstairs. Beams hewn from local chestnut logs were buried behind lathe in the walls and exposed in the ceilings. Outdoor siding of pine lapboards wrapped the front and sides, and New Jersey white cedar wood shingles lapped down the back. Doors made of fine grained slabs of apple wood decorated the portals with their well oiled finished. He hoped his father would help him with the doors and trim as he knew his own skill with planes and jigs was no match for his father's. The dream of having land and a fine home would not let him rest. He had little time for visits with Anne or anything else. He worked and slept.

William and Sarah married. Joseph hardly recalled the day as he was so intent and preoccupied with building his house. The house would have a parlor with another great fireplace to heat that side of the house and a small room in the back. Upstairs, there would be bedrooms on either side of the open stairway with a hardwood rail and landing. The upstairs center hallway would be large enough for two sleeping cots for a large family. The saltbox would not have a full second story, but low tapered ceilings following the roof line. Inside window openings in the stairway would allow heat from the first floor to move into the bedrooms during the winter. And for summer ventilation, four little belly windows spanned across the front of the second floor free to be opened to let summer heat escape. Joseph had thought and rethought how his house would look and he imagined Anne in his house without even closing his eyes.

William, after listening to his brother's plans for several weeks, agreed to let his brother work on the house behind his cabin. Joseph hauled whole trees into the yard on borrowed wagons from the timber camp. As Joseph split the logs that would become the skeletal support for the walls, roof, and floors, he laid them flat on bare ground. He carefully measured their lengths and notched the ten-inch square beams until the joints fit perfectly.

Sarah watched Joseph, who now hardly talked, slept, or ate, as he labored on the beams. She worried that something had happened between Joseph and Anne. His long visits to her farm had grown short. She and William woke before dawn to the crack of Joseph's axe and fell asleep after sunset to thuds of heavy logs moving about behind their small cabin. William now could not resist helping his brother in the evenings. Together they cut shingles from huge cedar logs Joseph had hauled into the yard.

When finished with the framework for the front, back and two sides, Joseph carefully measured again, trimming and measuring until he was sure the four sides would fit together making a perfect rectangle. He bored holes for pegs at each of the joints. To satisfy himself that he could now store the beams and successfully reassemble the structure on his own land someday, he methodically scored each beam joint with matching Roman numerals. Only then did he remove the pegs from the joints and stack the beams in a neat pile on the edge of Will's land.

Matthew watched that summer as his two brothers worked on the house, but had little interest in their plans or projects. He had no thoughts of buying land, let alone building a house. He was content to stay with Samuel and Phebe and his sisters until he found a girl willing to marry him, then he would worry about a house. He loved to hunt and the girls he met were looking for good farmers and he didn't want to be a farmer. But his father put him to work each summer. There were stumps to dig out, fences to build, and firewood to chop, work that Samuel gladly watched his strong son do twice as fast as he could.

When Matthew finished, he walked over to Will's cabin to see how Joseph was coming along. Soon, Phebe and Samuel were walking over, too. The summer days were long and with Matthew along, they could enjoy the walk after dinner and their son's company at the same time. It wasn't long before Matthew was helping his brothers with their project. Patience and Susanna had little interest in walking with their parents or watching their brothers. They had friends to visit, and Lucy tagged after her sisters.

One evening William said, "Why don't we put the house together? You've marked the beams, when you find your 'acres of land', you can take the house down and move."

That was all the encouragement Joseph needed to work twice as fast finishing the rafters. William and Joseph laid out the house beams on the ground until the pile of beams now resembled the skeleton of four walls – front, back, and two sides. Joseph walked around the yard inspecting the Roman numerals, seeing that all the corners matched. Then Joseph stroked the square pins into the round holes, firming the walls into bents.

With Sarah's father and brothers helping and Samuel's oxen pulling, the structures were lifted side after side off the ground, lashed with rope, and then quickly pegged until the skeleton of the house stood on its own. Sarah and Phebe clapped their appreciation, and the men stood back in wonder at the size of the saltbox. It dwarfed William's small cabin.

The rest of the summer flew by. Joseph was either working on the house or briefly going to see Anne, who still knew nothing of the house. She only knew this man had come into her life and kept showing up at her door for dinner and long conversations with her father and often in a rush to leave.

But one evening as Anne and her father sat on the porch watching the sun set across the creek, Thomas spoke of Joseph. He had noticed big changes in the young man since that day with the peaches and said, "Anne, Joseph seems happy. Have you noticed?"

Joseph, always pleasant company at her Sunday dinners, was different. "Yes father, he has changed some, but he leaves so quickly." But on his next Sunday visit, Joseph arrived with a bouquet of flowers for Anne and the sharpened saw blade for Thomas. Anne noticed he slowed his chewing and seemed to enjoy her company more. Was he relaxing? Was he more self assured? He lingered after the meal talking sometimes and quiet sometimes while she now nervously chattered. She worried that her sisters might be wrong about how she was keeping this conversation going as between friends. But, she could not be mistaken; he wasn't in such a hurry to get home. He certainly smiled more and was not so serious. Her hands were shaking as she cleared the table, and her father offered to wash up the dishes.

After the table was cleared, Joseph asked if she would like to walk. Silently, they walked through the orchard and sat on the stones by the bank of the stream. Anne finally had a clue that this might be more than a friendship when Joseph reached for her hand as she slipped on a mossy wet rock and caught her from falling. He didn't let go of her hand.

They talked of farming at first, but quickly discovered other subjects. Anne relaxed, forgot what she was supposed to say and told Joseph she was interested in history and had read some of the classics that her sisters had brought to the cabin. Joseph was more interested in current events and the controversies he read about in the newspapers.

As his visits continued, they shared their thoughts and their lively discussions seemed to always end with the realization that they both shared their love of America. Joseph brought the Albany newspapers with him and together they read about new settlements to the north. Anne knew that she was not like her sisters. She held no desire to go to London, nor live in Manhattan. She loved being an American and living in the country. And she knew she was in love with this eager and driven man who had plans. Secretly, she knew she was longing for the day Joseph would ask her father for his permission to marry her.

Still, Anne wondered. Did he love her or was she just a friend? What had he been doing during his long absences? Her sisters, too, wondered. Carly, Hannah, and Caroline knew that their younger sister loved Joseph and prayed that her heart would not be broken by his mysterious lapses. They had never seen their sister look so pretty. She wore blouses and skirts and tied her hair back just like they did. Gone were Thomas's old pants and shirts that she used to wear. The good news they heard while quilting was that Joseph was coming in the mornings and splitting firewood for their father. Anne talked nervously all through their quilting sessions. There was no stopping their once quiet sister.

Meanwhile, Joseph and William were siding the outside of the saltbox with the lap boards. The wide floor boards and inside would soon would be rooms after the outside walls were closed in. As Phebe watched the progress on the house, she made little suggestions.

"Joseph, a woman would like a window about here," and "this closet really would be better if it were a little deeper." She walked around the unfinished house humming and stopped to measure with her sewing tape here and there.

"The little borning room behind the parlor must be snug but have a good window for sunshine and ventilation in the summer. When you take this house down and put it back up, make sure the borning room is on the southeast corner – warm and sunny is best for new mothers. They're always up before dawn! The sun should come to that room first."

The son's attention now focused on a "borning room" and he took note of his mother's suggestions.

CHAPTER VI

Decisions and promises

Matthew loved coming home from the timber camp each spring. His mother kept the cabin a bustle of activity. Her garden grew larger every year, and the roasted chicken and dumpling dinners were so much better than the meals served in the camp. But, this year he noticed something else, and said, "The traffic on your road has doubled, maybe tripled."

People passed by their cabin going somewhere every day. Some were families with push carts. Some sped by in carriages, and all day there were wagons filled with crops and goods to trade in Manhattan. He watched one day as his sisters sold peas and green beans on a small stand in front of their cabin. Patience and Susanna had a thriving business. Lucy was not old enough to count out money with strangers, but helped mind the stand and picked and sold the strawberries. Soon the cherries would be ripe, and then the peaches and apples. There would be work enough for all of them to do.

There was more news. The Continental Congress was looking into the rebellion in Boston. And the British were now charging the colonists to feed and pay the British troops who were protecting the colonies from Indian attacks on the frontier. England had repealed the Stamp Tax but added tax on tea and other British imports.

Matthew hated the foul tea his mother was now drinking. "Liberty Tea" she called it. A few home-grown leaves soaked in boiling water. "Give me ale or give me spit!" That would be his motto. No more "Liberty Tea."

The Boston newspapers told the bigger story. Ships continued to bring new families to the colonies. In fact, the ever increasing population was driving up the price of land. Some of these newcomers were not poor. They were rich English folk who saw America as a better place to live and had sold their homes in London

47

with intentions of starting new businesses and building fine homes in America. Matthew knew he had to find a way to support himself soon, and it wasn't going to be with all these rich English folks.

By late summer, the saltbox house was in the finishing stage. Samuel planed the long boards that would frame the two fireplace openings. His strong hands guided his plane until the boards were smooth. He worked with such intensity that he forgot how his hands ached and his back hurt. Each evening he added to the beauty of the interior. The double cross front door had taken him weeks to build in his workshop that winter. Now he was back at the house measuring for the paneling and trim. Because he knew Joseph would be moving the house to his own land someday, Samuel planned the trim assembly so the sections could be taken apart when the saltbox was moved. The house would have shutters, but greased fabric for windows. These windows were only temporary and would be replaced with real glass window panes someday. The kitchen fireplace was big enough for a crane and several kettles. It had a temporary chimney and there was no oven. The fireplace on the other end of the house would not be bricked at all and was boarded up. Phebe came with her husband tonight. She was sitting in a comfortable chair in front of the house watching him work. With the sun setting and the locusts singing their August songs, she put aside her sewing and could not contain her emotions another minute. Letting out a sigh, she wistfully said, "Oh, Samuel, this house will be beautiful!"

Anne and Thomas had dined at Samuel and Phebe's cabin, but this Sunday, Anne and her father had been invited to dinner at William and Sarah's cabin after church. Anne walked up the lane to William's cabin with Phebe and Lucy. Samuel and Thomas were behind them talking about their peach orchards. Joseph lagged behind. As Anne turned into the yard, she stopped.

"Joseph, your brother's house is beautiful! Is this what has given your hands blisters and calluses?"

"Yes. But it's not Will's house, Anne. It could be our house ... if all goes well." Joseph looked serious and nobody spoke.

Anne looked at Joseph, then at the house. "If all goes well?" She looked at her father. She looked at Phebe, who was now smiling and then to Lucy, who was pointing to the front door. Anne ran to the open door and peered inside. Then let out a little shriek.

By this time the whole family had gathered and watched as Anne's shape ran past the open windows from room to room. After walking through the parlor and back again to the kitchen, Anne ran to the hallway and climbed the stairs, stooping near the top of the landing, to inspect the two bedrooms. She raced back down the stairs. Standing in the doorway, she stared at Joseph's somber face. Then slowly, very slowly, she walked back to Joseph and her father.

Her face was just as somber. *Now*, she thought, *now, it is my turn to be serious. I must say the right words if this is to be my future.* She looked at Joseph, then, in a clear voice said, "I love you, Joseph."

There, she had spoken the truth of her friendship. Her heart was thumping in her chest and she could hardly breathe. She held her arms at her sides and summoned her courage once more. "Joseph, we are good friends, but I cannot go on without hearing those same words from you."

Joseph's face went pale and blank. He fought for words. Just as her sisters had months before predicted, Anne needed to hear the words. She needed to hear and feel his affection. She had to be herself, declare her love, and know if he loved the real Anne she had revealed to him. If this man's plans and dreams were to be hers, too, they needed to be bound with love, not just friendship.

Joseph reached for her and took her hands in his and looked down at their joining. Then he looked into her steady blue-green eyes and said, "Anne Ducker, I love you with my whole heart and wish you to be my wife." Then he took her in his arms and kissed her.

Everyone heard their conversation and saw the kiss. Cheers went up and Joseph blushed while his family laughed and clapped. Then Joseph turned to Thomas, "Sir, I came to you once with an apology. Today I am asking for permission to marry your daughter Anne. I know how much you depend on her. You are welcome to come and live with us."

Thomas was overcome with joy for his daughter and the wonderful offer from the young man he had gown to respect. Thomas was formal and seriously responded. "Joseph, you're a good man. I know that now. I give you my permission to marry Anne and my blessing. I will count on you to trim my peach orchard each spring and for you and Anne to help with the picking."

Joseph now could laugh about his peach raid; he took the old man's hand and shook it soundly. "Thank you. And I will prune and help with the picking."

Ducker Family Tree
Thomas Ducker   *m.*   Elizabeth Carlton
Carly
Hannah
Caroline
Anne

Plans for the wedding began in earnest. Reverend Barrett was contacted and the Sabbath afternoon service was arranged. Anne would be married in the Anglican Church, her family's church. The Morleys were invited along with their two sons, a daughter-in-law, and two little grandchildren. The Parish congregation and neighbors turned out for the wedding.

Just before the ceremony was to begin, Thomas spoke quietly to his daughter. "Anne," he said, "I want you to have your mother's locket. It meant so much to Elizabeth that you should have this token of her love. She knew she would not live to see this day, but wanted you to know that she would be with you in spirit today and always. She loved you and your sisters very much." And with that said, Thomas fastened the locket on Anne's bare neck. Thomas gave his daughter away with tears in his eyes. He was dressed in his best suit that he hadn't worn since Caroline's wedding years before. Anne wore her mother's wedding gown, just as all of her sisters had before her. Being last to wed, it would be hers to keep.

Joseph wore new breeches, shirt, and coat. He had dipped into his savings for the new clothes and a three cornered hat. His long hair was tied back with a black silk ribbon.

"You look like an American Patriot, brother," said William.

Joseph had never before worn such clothes and felt quite out of place until he saw Anne coming towards him. She was radiant in her mother's satin gown. Her chestnut brown hair was pulled back and little wisps escaped and encircled her face. She wore her sister Caroline's white satin buttoned boots and carried a bouquet of wildflowers Lucy had picked just hours before the ceremony. Anne and Lucy had spent hours together transplanting wildflowers from the woods to gardens around the saltbox in preparation for the wedding reception.

The ceremony was read straight from the Book of Common Prayer. Before Anne could catch her breath, it was over, and Joseph was holding her tenderly in his arms. Then, without embarrassment, kissed her hard. They ran down the aisle and out the door with the pipe organ still huffing and filling the sanctuary with glorious notes of wedding celebration.

The families recessed from the church and walked to their carriages and wagons for the hour-long ride to Joseph's house. Anne's sisters and families had come in carriages, and the Rues and their friends and neighbors had brought their wagons.

Father Barrett and his wife brought loaves of bread and freshly churned butter. Deborah and Jack Morley brought a spiced ham, glazed with brown sugar and dotted with cloves and ginger to add to the already laden table. Sarah's family and their neighbors brought baskets of fresh fruit and bowls of cooked vegetables. Many of the guests, seeing the saltbox for the first time, celebrated the completion of the house as much as the wedding. Sarah's father walked around the house twice, and was determined to build a saltbox with Joseph's help, as were other neighbors. It was no secret to them that Anne and Joseph would wed, so everyone was well prepared with their gifts. The families gave their presents to the bride and groom and the new house.

Anne's sisters made two colorful quilts, one filled with goose feathers for winter and one with cotton batting for summer. Carly, Hannah, and Caroline had set up a second quilting frame at Caroline's house. To make it a surprise, they had to quilt twice a week – once with Anne at their father's cabin and once without her at Caroline's.

Thomas had fashioned copper wall sconces for dipped candles. He now hung them where Anne pointed and watched her as she placed the candles in the small wall stands. Samuel gave them four chairs he had made during the winter. Phebe had embroidered a sampler with the house, bride and groom's names, and date of the wedding. Anne accepted the beautifully stitched sampler with tears of love for the mother of her husband. And Matthew had taken some wide boards and made a long crude table.

"It's just going to be jostled in the wagon all the way to some wilderness somewhere. I couldn't see spending a lot of time sanding!" Who could be angry with a young brother who brought and roasted two wild turkeys and tapped a keg of good ale for the wedding reception?

Patience gave the couple an embroidered linen tablecloth, and Susanna had made 30 matching napkins. "If that's not enough when we all get together, I'll make more!" Susanna laughed.

Lucy wove three slatted baskets with sturdy handles made from reeds gathered by the creek. "The small one is for berries," Joseph's youngest sister said as she just beamed with happiness. After all the Sunday dinners and gardening, she now loved Anne almost as much as her own two sisters.

The room with the fireplace was large enough for the long table so that the family could all sit together for meals on the Sabbath. Today the table was in the parlor covered with food, and the little Morley grandchildren were picking at the corners of the sweet wedding cake. As the families entered the room they could smell the candied orange and lemons in the Bride's Cake. The three-layered cake, which Anne's oldest sister Carly brought from Manhattan, stood in the center of the table. Dripping with white almond icing, the cake was surrounded by white paper chains with not a spot of the pencil that had copied the decorative eyelets and curls. Each detail had been carefully cut until the chains looked like fine lace. Some of the garlands reached across the table to touch the plates of sweets and nuts. The remainder of the table held platters of roast beef, cheese, and fruit and breads. Anne's sisters had brought furniture that had belonged to their mother. Now it was time for Anne to have it in her house.

Later, while the younger women were cleaning up, Deborah Morley sat by the fireplace in one of Samuel's comfortable chairs next to Phebe. She held one of her friend's favorite books, ready to turn the pages. Phebe, with William and Sarah's newborn son, Jack, in her arms, read the familiar story to Deborah's grandchildren. Deborah saw tears rolling down the cheeks of her dear friend and knew Phebe couldn't possibly be seeing well enough to read the book. But Phebe recited the tale without a pause as she knew the story by heart. Now and again, looking up at her good friend, Phebe would smile. She knew this was one of the happiest days of her life.

After all the good-byes and everyone had gone home, Phebe and Samuel walked back to their cabin. She recalled their adventure coming to America. They were so brave to leave home when they were so young. They had come with a few possessions and their dreams to a place they knew nothing about. She smiled to herself in the dark. As if he were thinking her thoughts, Samuel gently took her hand in his.

Now in their cabin, she sat at the small writing desk in their bedroom. Looking at her husband, she knew he loved her more than himself. She thanked God for his love that had brought her six healthy caring children, praying they would all have a good life in America. Before she slept, Phebe recorded her son's marriage in her Bible. Samuel came to her and watched. She looked up at him. Looking down he saw his beautiful bride of years ago.

Joseph Samuel Rue married Anne Elizabeth Ducker
June 16, 1767, New York Colony

At the saltbox, after everyone had gone home, Anne and Joseph climbed the stairs to the south bedroom. A cool summer breeze floated through the two windows, and moonbeams danced on their summer quilt.

One year later

Anne and Phebe were having their afternoon Liberty Tea sitting outside Phebe's cabin on the stoop. "The trees will be changing color, soon and the nights will have a chill. It's so nice living in the valley near the river. We shall not have to worry about frost for a couple more weeks," said Anne to her mother-in-law.

"Yes, but winter will soon be here, and Patience wants a new coat, and we have been arguing. She says she needs stylish new clothes if she is to catch a good husband!" Phebe continued. "The girls see the fashions that the traveling women wear and know homespun doesn't measure up to the finery they see. I'm knitting socks, scarves, and mittens for Christmas presents, and now with your baby on the way I have plenty to do in the evenings leaving no time to weave cloth for a new coat for Patience."

Anne was thinking. *Hannah had said, the last time they had quilted, there were American-made coats available at a good price in Manhattan. And shoes from a little town in Massachusetts called Hudson. And pretty textiles were coming from the southern colonies. How I would love a new dress after the baby is born.* Anne now responded to Phebe. "Maybe there will be time before winter to go shopping in Manhattan at some of the American shops. The British made clothes are much too expensive for country folk like us. I would love to visit my sisters in Manhattan; maybe we shall plan a shopping trip."

"I'm sure they would love your visit. You are blossoming! Make plans sooner rather than later. Why don't you, Sarah, Susanna, and Patience take the wagon and go into Manhattan. I will give you what money I have and the girls have been saving their fruit stand money all summer. Samuel, Lucy and I will watch the children."

"Won't Lucy want to go? What are we doing now?" asked Samuel as he walked up to the house and the women just laughed as they knew he had overheard their conversation. "Why not have Matthew drive the wagon and be home before dark."

Samuel had heard variations of this conversation from the men, too. The colonies were now producing goods that rivaled or even exceeded the quality of English goods. What bothered Samuel was the way the Americans tradesmen were being treated now by the Loyalists. There would be trouble.

William was still angry, and his pride was still suffering from having to borrow money from his brother to buy the stamp for his small parcel of land. He and other farmers were gathering at different homes, and thought the possibility of the colonies breaking away from England wasn't such a bad idea. Samuel, too, had heard similar views from the people who passed by their cabin on their way to and from Boston and Philadelphia. The women did not go shopping. The family decided it was not a good idea to go into Manhattan. Patience would wear her old coat again this winter.

Samuel Joseph Rue
Born March 12, 1769, New York Colony

By the time Anne was expecting their second child, Joseph and William were seriously looking for land. William's small farm was barely producing enough food for two growing families. Samuel's orchard, down the road, was producing enough fruit to give him income, but Will's orchard was still immature. Joseph, William, and Matthew continued cutting timber during the winter months to make enough money to buy seed and supplies.

Elizabeth Jane Rue
Born February 19, 1771, New York Colony

Joseph and Anne's second child was a daughter they called Lizzie, named after Anne's mother and grandmother. William and Sarah now had three children, Jack, Jonas, and Louisa. While the men were at the timber camp during the winter, Anne and Sarah took care of the children and the farm.

CHAPTER VII

Balls Town

"1771–October 12, Eliphalet Ball purchased 400 acres at Ballston Center, founded the Presbyterian Church there, served as its pastor, 1775-1783, and gave his name to the Township."

—Saratoga County Heritage

Stories of a new settlement in the New York Colony north of Schenectady reached the timber camp from the timber barge loaders. Newspapers from Albany reported land for sale. This so excited Joseph as he read the paper at dinner that he broke from camp and ran most of the way home to tell Anne the news.

Joseph read the paper to Anne, Sarah and his parents by candlelight. "A Reverend Ball, originally from Connecticut and said to be a Presbyterian, purchased land from the Kayaderosseras Patent."

The land was a five-square-mile parcel described by the newspaper as "composed of hard wood timber and at least three lakes. In addition, the beautiful Kayaderosseras Creek and other smaller creeks ran through the land."

"The plot had been sold to Reverend Ball to offset the cost of surveying the Patent," Joseph excitedly repeated. "They do this to cover costs. Five square miles is not a very big area when you divide it into farms."

The Albany paper told of several Connecticut families who had moved with Reverend Ball and already settled on the land. Joseph's voice faltered as his thoughts raced and he finished reading the article. He knew they must act. Without hesitation, he and Anne decided to send a letter to Reverend Ball and considered purchasing the land sight unseen. Their letter asked how much land their savings would buy. Joseph returned to the camp.

The letter was carried up the Hudson River to Albany by barge. From there it went west to Schenectady on horseback. After that, it waited for a Post carrier to Balls Town. The letter remained in Schenectady until Nicholas McDonald, in town buying supplies for his trading post, picked up the letter and delivered it to the Reverend.

Reverend Ball sent a letter back arriving two months later. Joseph tore open the envelope.

> *Dear Mr. Rue,*
>
> *Your money will buy you forty-five acres. To finalize the sale, I must have the money within a year, and you must further claim your land by clearing your fields of trees and occupying a cabin. Please sign and send the enclosed proper documents to the proper authorities in Albany.*
>
> *I cannot say that I can hold the land for you without payment, but I will promise to remember your letter. There are many families now arriving each week to buy land.*
>
> > *Your humble servant,*
> > *Reverend Ball*

Included in the letter were forms to fill out and English documents to sign. These all had to be sent to the English officials in Albany. When Joseph showed his father the letter, Samuel groaned. "This sounds like an empty promise to me. I know he is a man of God, but remember that even Queen Anne, who was of our faith, and later King George I, made statements and promises they could not honor or keep. The officials in Albany may be a problem, too. I wonder how much they will tax you for your purchase."

Joseph was undeterred. *Forty-five acres!* Forty-five acres kept running through his thoughts. *What I couldn't do with forty-five acres!*

The brothers talked about the opportunity and began to make plans. First, they would go to Balls Town and Joseph would pay Reverend Ball for forty-five acres. Second, they would begin clearing land and build a cabin. Matthew would spend the winter at the cabin. Third, Joseph and William would return home before winter, harvest the grain from the farm, and then work that winter cutting timber to make more money for their next trip.

After that, the next spring they would return to the land and take with them enough food and seed and equipment for a year. As soon as they arrived, they would begin clearing the trees, plant wheat and oats, and clear another field for hay for a horse.

Matthew said he would stay on the land again, "Not to worry about the cabin being vacant." He was ready for a wilderness experience.

Anne wanted to go with them this time. She would tend a garden, store the food, and prepare the cabin for the children. But the men were not listening. They continued: the following spring, they would take down the saltbox shingle by shingle and beam by beam, and bring it and the children to the cabin in Balls Town. That was now Joseph's plan.

But the plan didn't progress that way. It took Joseph over two years of letters to British officials in Albany to acquire the right to purchase their new land in Balls Town and then pay a tax. But with the slow King's Post, transactions by mail were hampered because Reverend Ball was afraid he might sell the same land twice. Other people had read the newspaper article, bringing their families with them to Balls Town and paying for their land. Most were more members of his congregation from the Connecticut Colony.

When the Rues received the next letter from Reverend Ball asking if they were still interested in the land, Joseph was frantic and said, "We must go at once. I fear we will lose this land to another settler." Joseph could hardly contain his emotions. "Anne, I must go. William, Matthew, and I will make the journey and see for ourselves. We can all swing an axe, and God knows I can build a cabin! I will come back for you and the children as soon as I can. William and I shouldn't be gone more than six months." Joseph then lowered his voice and added. "Families are leaving New York and looking for land west of Albany. The news of a Revolution has made everything more urgent. We must try."

The New York Colony was now overcrowded with newcomers. Ships were arriving from Europe with still more people. Families were looking for a place to live and in need of food and shelter before they starved. Beggars were on the roads and stealing from gardens at night. The orderly adoption by host farmers was over. People were desperate.

Anne was not going to be left behind. The two years she and Joseph had waited for Reverend Ball's letter and the British approval had been two years too long. Their saltbox was crowded with family – women and children all winter. And now Joseph's sisters wanted to move in. She said to herself, *when the men come home at Christmas, it will mean another pregnancy for Sarah and me.*

Anne knew she should visit Samuel and Phebe before saying anything to Joseph. They always gave her good honest advice, and certainly after their experience and survival coming to America, they were sure to listen to her concerns plus have her welfare and that of her children at heart. If they agreed that she could go, Joseph might agree too. And she must make sure that Sarah was willing to care for Sam and Lizzie this summer. She would talk to her father before leaving the quilting bee today.

Anne whispered a quick good-bye to Sarah and left the house. It was Wednesday. She would quilt with her sisters and visit with her father. She had muffins in her basket and was the last to arrive. Hannah had made English tea, and Thomas was already drinking his so he could leave the cabin and work in the garden. It was a beautiful cool day. He really couldn't cope with his four daughters' chatter spoken too fast and too loud. He ate one of Anne's muffins, and then excused himself.

They were working on a beautiful quilt. The appliquéd pattern of flowers and leaves was made from scraps of good muslin,

60

and the dyed colors were rich and vibrant. When bound and finished, the quilt would fetch a good price in Manhattan.

As they settled their bodies against the quilting frame, Carly started, "I can't wait to get back home today. There's a shop just past where we sell our quilts that I've heard good things about. They're selling felt hats that are all the rage in London. I must see them as I'm sure someone in New York is making them for half the price."

"You go alone. I don't need another hat," said Hannah, "but I must shop soon. I'm looking for buttons for a woolen jacket, and I promised little Kate a new coat for Christmas."

"We may be at war by Christmas," Caroline added. "Do you remember the Boston Tea Party? It's become much worse."

"Do I remember?" Hannah groaned, "That was the beginning of all this trouble and look what we got out of it, no more good English tea accept from our secret source. The Americans are making trouble, but I don't think we shall go to war. There are just a few troublemakers in Boston." Caroline looked up, and then glanced at Anne.

Her sister caught her glance. "Yes," agreed Carly in a soft voice, turning the conversation back to tea. "It was just luck that I heard about that little shop around the corner from the Court House. Remember, you must only ask the Frenchman with the beard, very quietly and off to the side, and he will sell you some English tea from his back room."

"How did a Frenchman acquire English tea?" asked Caroline.

"Maybe it is better we don't know," said Hannah.

Her sisters were now talking in whispers, and Anne stopped listening to their force conversation. She tried to put the Tea Party and a Revolution out of her thoughts and focused on her family. The forty-five acres could be theirs if they acted now. She was ready to go with the men.

"Anne, you're so quiet today. Is everything all right?" asked Caroline.

"Yes," she said. "I think I'll go out and talk to father. Can you do without me for a minute?" She got up and left without waiting for their answer.

As she walked out to the peach orchard, she remembered the fighting in Boston. The rebels had dressed as Indians and climbed aboard a British merchant ship anchored in Boston Harbor. That was years ago, but still the tale was told again and again. They dumped a full cargo of good tea into the bay. Her sisters half laughed and half cried when they heard the story. They had been born and raised on good English tea. She agreed; the tea she and Phebe were drinking was a poor substitute.

Anne found her father sitting by the stream near his favorite peach tree. "Do you remember the day Joseph stole our peaches?" he asked with a chuckle.

"Yes, and whenever he finds fault with my housekeeping, I remind him of his transgressions!" laughed Anne. Then she brought Thomas up to date on the latest news from Balls Town and the forty-five acres.

Thomas looked at the intensity in Anne's eyes as she spoke. In so many ways she was so much like her mother – a little headstrong and definitely not afraid of trying something new. He would worry for her safety on this trip, but knew he should encourage her to follow her dreams. He had much faith in his son-in-law and knew his daughter sought the trip as well as the acreage. She would never travel to London. Her life was not the life of his other daughters who had married Englishmen. He would pray and put her welfare in God's hands.

Thomas took his youngest daughter's chapped hands in his. They bowed their heads and Thomas prayed:

> *"Dear God, I love my daughter and want only her happiness. Protect Anne from the unknown perils of her journey. Give her strength and courage to meet whatever is in her path, surrounded by your protection and love. Amen."*

He let out a huge sigh. That was all a father his age could do.

Anne kissed her father's wrinkled cheek and whispered "I love you, father. I shall return and tell you of our adventure. Won't it be exciting to travel the road to Albany?"

Thomas bravely smiled at his daughter, but no sound came to his lips. How could he unwrap the words from his heart and tell Anne of his love for her? He had been blessed by this precious daughter with years of happiness; he must hold back his tears and let her go.

That night after the children were asleep, Anne walked the short distance to her in-laws cabin. They welcomed her with smiles, and she sat down to a cup of bark tea, Phebe's latest Liberty Tea. She asked them for their blessing as well, before confronting her husband. She hoped he could not say no.

Phebe and Samuel agreed to help Sarah take care of Sam and Lizzie. They would spend the summer with them in their cabin. Joseph's sister Lucy also agreed to help. When Anne returned and spoke with Sarah, she too agreed that Anne should go.

"Better that one of us go and keep the men working and not off hunting or fishing or exploring," she laughed with Anne. "Do be careful. I've heard stories of Indians in the woods."

"I promise to be careful. I'm not worried about Indians, but I will probably come home pregnant," said Anne still excitedly laughing. The women hugged. Anne's pregnancies after Lizzie's birth had not gone well. Sarah hope Anne was right.

Anne had little trouble convincing her husband that she should go too. By the time Anne retold all of her conversations with the family, he had stopped listening. His ears were not working, he could only think of one thing, buying the land. Plans were made in earnest for their departure. Sam and Lizzie only knew that they would be moving to a place called Balls Town if all went well. They agreed to live with their grandparents and their Aunt Lucy.

The small party traveled north up the muddy road next to the Hudson River. The road was still frozen in shaded places, but the sun was melting the ice into muddy puddles by noon each day. It was too rough to ride in the cart even if there had been room. Anne walked alongside with the men. The river was flowing swiftly to the south from the spring melt. Huge ice floes tore at the river's banks; there was no way to navigate by boat to the north until late spring. The brothers pushed and pulled the heavily laden cart loaded with blankets, food, seed, and tools.

Each night they stopped along the road and met other settlers traveling north. Men took their muskets into the woods to look for game, while women gathered firewood and fished along the banks of the Hudson River. It was important not to eat any of the food they had brought. They would need all of their stored food while building a cabin and clearing land.

Taking a short cut through the wooded land south of Albany, the Rues followed the Indian trail through Niskayuna to Schenectady. There, they ferried across the Mohawk River and then turned their small cart north on the narrow road to Balls Town. Joseph knew from his newspaper readings to give their route a wide birth around the British controlled Albany.

Reverend Ball was a tall, stern-looking man with bushy whiskers and a long black coat. He stared at the weary colonists. After a few moments, he cleared his throat and put on his spectacles. "Let me look in the book of deeds." While he slowly moved to the table where the book rested, he turned to them and asked again their names. "Oh, yes. It has been a while since I heard from you. I thought maybe you had found other land."

Joseph and Anne nervously glanced at each other, but said nothing.

Reverend Ball added, "I like to know a little about the people who will be my neighbors. Tell me again, where are you from?"

Anne now feared that Samuel had been right. Their letters had been forgotten. Joseph cleared his throat and stood as tall as he could. He took off his hat, something he should have done before entering the house. With a nudge from Anne, he began. He told the whole family history as far back as he knew. Anne nudged him to stop and gave him a look. It was obvious to her that Joseph was worried and telling too much personal history.

Reverend Ball caught the slight gesture and smiled. "Well, it seems you are a God-fearing family. Let's open this book and see where those forty-five acres are that you are looking to purchase."

"It does seem like the surveyors had quite a time measuring out this parcel. There is the Mourning Kill to ford and a pretty dense undergrowth and a swampy section and, oh yes, quite a hill, too. You will have neighbors to your south, but not much in the way of company. Looks like that hill will be an exciting ride in the cart on Sunday mornings. You'll be speeding down the lane to church! By the way, you will be responsible for maintaining your lane."

The Rues now relaxed a little. The land had not yet been purchased. Reverend Ball had decided to sell them the land. Joseph's hands shook as he passed the money to the Reverend. After carefully counting the money, he turned the book towards Joseph.

"Sign here. Remember, the agreement is binding on clearing land and settling in a cabin. You cannot leave or the land will be sold again."

Joseph agreed to the conditions and with a trembling hand signed. He turned and looked at his wife. Anne's face was serious, but her eyes were alive with happiness. He looked back at the Reverend and put out his hand. Joseph's hand was met with a firm grip of a strong and calloused hand and a hearty welcome. Joseph's face relaxed and Reverend Ball's smile was returned.

They could hear Mrs. Ball calling for dinner, and Reverend Ball returned her call with a request for Mrs. Ball to come into the office and meet the newcomers. A tidy woman with a bun of gray hair swept into the room. She smiled at Anne and welcomed her at once and hurriedly told her of other young women who would be neighbors. Then she just as quickly swept out of the room, calling over her shoulder, "Reverend, it's time for your dinner!"

Reverend Ball sighed, then drew them a map to their land and sent them on their way.

As the Rues turned west and pushed the cart on the bumpy road, Matthew was the first to speak. "What kind of land is this going to be? Steep hills and swamps?"

Joseph was still contemplating the Reverend wondering what his sermons would be like.

William didn't say anything until they had turned north and were halfway up the hill. "This cart has been hard to pull, but harder still to push. This hill may be the final test of my fortitude! Dear brother, you have bought yourself a small mountain!"

Anne had no trouble walking up the hill. In fact, at times she felt her legs were flying up the hill. Her mind was racing as she thought it was not yet planting time. They had made good speed. They had come early enough to get seed planted. She immediately noticed the stones half-hidden by the dead leaves of winter. This land didn't look like the rich, gently rolling river bottom of the Hudson River Valley. Anne walked east and looked down the hill toward the creek. She could hear the fast moving water rushing by their hill and glimpse the swollen creek. Wild grasses sprouted from the damp earth. The trees had not yet leafed, but wildflowers poked their heads above the leaves. Here and there scattered between the huge trees grew trillium and ladyslippers, and farther down the hill growing along the banks of the creek, she could see the bright green leaves of watercress. Anne spotted a walnut tree, and already bees were buzzing around the blooms of locust trees.

Joseph caught up with her. The fast flowing Mourning Kill rushed by with the spring melt and occasional frozen ice chunks. Across the creek he spied more of their land covered with tall white pines. *These will bring good money for sure. I can send the logs down the creek until they reach a mill. This is something I know I can do during the winter. Cutting down trees is what I do!* He smiled.

Then Joseph turned and stared at the hill behind them. "There's so much to do in just six months." He tried to hide his worried eyes from Anne, but she could hear it in his voice. They climbed back to the top of their hill.

"I will set out a celebratory dinner from our provisions," she said with conviction.

The brothers had returned from their scouting and sat around the basket of food with somber faces and few words. Anne heard something and looked behind her. As she ate bread and cheese, she glimpsed a startled turkey curiously peeking at them from behind a gigantic boulder. The hen stayed a while staring at the people, then slowly moved away behind a bush.

The men remained silent as they ate. They were all very hungry, but as they finished their meal, smiles and relief first from Matthew, then William, broke into hearty laughs. No one had said anything funny. The brothers just started laughing and punching each other and rolling on the ground. Joseph was thinking there was no going back on their agreement with the serious Reverend. These would be their acres. He could not laugh with his brothers. His money was spent! He was worried. Joseph got to his feet and started climbing a maple tree, partly to escape his brothers' laughter. From the second huge limb, Joseph could see far in three directions. To the north he could make out the gently rolling foothills of the Adirondacks, to the east he could see smoke from McDonald brothers' settlement at Long Lake, and to the south, back towards Schenectady, he saw smoke coming from the fires of the Scotch Bush settlement. To the west, their land flattened into deep a forest which he could not see over or through. This would be the swampy section. He now had to laugh, too, and his brothers heard his laughter and only laughed louder. He had bought a hill.

By the time he climbed down from the tree, his worries had been replaced by things he needed to do – the plan – fields to clear and plant, a cabin to build – a cabin big enough for a growing family. Hard work. But compared to wondering if he would ever have land, this was a much better feeling. He knew all about hard work, and this labor would be on his land. Samuel had told his sons years ago that they must do more than just survive. Now, thinking of his father again before he slept, a new plan began to form. Maybe, just maybe, this new plan might work.

Joseph and Anne awoke before sunrise. The eastern sky did not dull the stars. They had hardly slept on the cold ground. Not because they were cold, but because they were so excited. They slipped away from the snoring brothers and walked down the hill toward the creek. Anne tripped on a vine and clung to Joseph. With tears and a choke and tired legs from their long walk, Anne could not contain her innermost fears. Her lips trembled, Joseph held his wife thinking, *what might this be?* "Joseph, I might become pregnant before the hard work is finished."

Joseph laughed loudly over the roar of the creek. "The hard work will never be finished on this pile of stones!" As they released their embraced, the sun rose above the horizon, and sunlight bathed the top of their hill. "This land is beautiful! I think we will have a good life here. I promise to do my best for you and the children. And you just don't worry about having more children. Next to you, our children are the best part of my life. And as they get a little older they can help us. I have a plan."

They held hands and walked along the creek. The warm spring sun now reached the valley and welcomed them to their new land. Joseph shaded his eyes and looked across the creek at the tall white pines growing thick on the opposite hill. "Those are our trees," he shouted. "Those pines will make money for us at the mill."

They stopped by the walnut tree, and he told her of his father's idea. She agreed to help. As they were eating oatmeal porridge and drinking Phebe's tea, Joseph talked about Samuel's idea with his brothers. He walked to the cart and pulled out the sack of hop seed his father had given him for a cash crop.

"As we clear the land and dig up these big stones, well, maybe, we'll leave that big boulder over there right where it is, Anne will plant the hop seeds. The vines can grow among the stones that we build into fences along the edge of the fields. That will give the seed a year's head start. Hops might even grow on the steep back hill someday. We will try to sell some of our good barley and wheat seed to our neighbors with the best fields. Patriots must be brewing beer and we have good seed. And we will ask that the payment be made in wheat and cider and food for Matthew.

Matthew immediately understood his brother's idea. "We will brew ale, just like good ol' Sam Adams!" Joseph and William could only laugh and Anne reached over and gave the youngest brother a big hug.

"That was one of father's ideas," said Joseph. "He knows we'll have much to do, and the hops will give us something to sell. They grow quickly, and yes, we may brew ale some day. Americans drink ale, not English rum!" Now eager to begin, Joseph continued, "It will take us all summer to clear enough land for the cabin and two fields. We need to start on the cabin right away."

With that, Matthew renewed his agreement to stay the winter. "With some good hunting, I will have enough food. Let's get moving!" They didn't speak about a Revolution or Indians.

Anne had very definite ideas about the cabin location. "It must face south, Joseph, I know you like a window to the north, but the door and window must face to the south so the sun's warm rays heat the front of the cabin and greet me when I open the door in the winter."

Joseph agreed and added that the back side of the cabin would be exposed to the north wind, so locating the cabin lower than the top of the hill, would give it some shelter. Then they both thought about the summer southern breeze at night that would cool the cabin. He proposed an air vent on the north side with a sturdy shutter.

"One more thing," Anne added, "make the roof high enough so we can build a big sleeping loft for the children." Joseph blushed in front of his brothers and cleared his throat. "I will."

Joseph walked a short way off the peak of the hill. "This should be a good place," and he took his father's axe out of the cart and drove stakes into the ground where the four corners of the cabin would be. Samuel had given Joseph his axe before they left for Balls Town. It was the same axe Samuel's father had given to him so many years ago in Germany; the same axe that had built the shelter on the island. Joseph carefully sharpened the fine blade. He was ready to begin to clear land.

Anne interrupted his thoughts. "Where will the barn be? Not too close to the cabin and not too near the place where we bring the house. Joseph, where shall the house be? We must think about smells and flies and ...we shall have animals, and they shall need water from the well, and we shall need water from the well and...then there's a garden and maybe some fruit trees..."

Joseph leaned the axe against a tree. "You're right, we need to plan."

For the next hour, Joseph and Anne walked on their hill and considered the possible locations for the house and barn. They settled on the north corner of the hill as a good location for the barn. The barn would also have easy access to the lane in the winter and act as a wind break and protect the little field in front the house. The house would be rebuilt on the very crest of the hill facing west. The saltbox's long roof would face east taking the brunt of the northeast storms. Joseph was pleased with their plan and thought *that will put the borning room on the southeast corner. Mother will also be pleased.*

With locations decided, Joseph again picked up his axe and started to work. Joseph called to his brothers that they were ready. Matthew agreed to clear the limbs and relieved him when he was tired. William walked back toward where they would build the barn until his feet sunk in the soggy ground. There, he felt certain there was a spring. He went back for the shovel and began digging a well.

All day long for most of the summer, Anne heard the sound of the axe and the crashing of the trees. The smaller branches were thrown over the back hill to be used for kindling or heaped for burning. The bigger limbs were stacked to one side for firewood. The logs that were true and straight were notched for the cabin walls and roof. With three strong men working from dawn to dusk, the logs became a cabin and the 20-foot deep hole became a well.

Anne worked alongside the men, plugging wet sod in the gaps between the cabin logs, cooking their breakfasts and dinners. On sunny afternoons, she slipped away and walked down the back hill to bathe in the creek. The cool water soothed her sore muscles and soaked the dirt from between her toes. As she relaxed, she could feel the new life now growing in her body. Today, she rested on the soft ground and watched the ducks float by. She thought she might see the curious turkey, but she quickly fell asleep. The turkey watched her as she napped.

On a beautiful autumn day, a solitary rider approached the Rue hill. The rider was dressed in buckskin, and his pack horse was carrying a heavy load of supplies. The fur trader saw the beginnings of a foundation for a house, the piles of dirt and stones from the digging of the cellar, and the neat cabin backed into the hillside. He stopped to visit when he saw a man standing outside the cabin.

The Frenchman introduced himself. "I am called Francois, and I am a French fur trader who speaks a little of the British King's English!"

Now standing under the glowing canopy of fall leaves, Francois explained his livelihood. "I set out traps north of Balls Town. My trap line goes as far as Lake George on the north and the Sacandaga River on the west. In the spring I sell my pelts to the highest bidder. Last year it was to the British in Albany. But this year, I would prefer to trade with the French." What Francois didn't say was that sometimes he traded with the Indians in Canada, English goods for prime pelts.

Joseph's mind was racing. He knew so little about trapping and trading, but had read that the fur market in Albany was not as good as the fur trading market in New Jersey with the occasional French trading ships that flew any flag but French. *How might he help the trader and help himself? Could he come back to the hill early in the spring and take the Frenchman's furs to market?*

As they ate lunch together, Joseph told the trader of his plan to return to the lower Hudson valley before winter. "I might be able to deliver your furs to traders in the New Jersey Colony. We shall be making several trips to bring our children and our house to the hill."

The trader considered the offer. He felt he had been cheated by the British traders in Albany. "Monsieur Rue, I will think about your offer. The reason that your plan might just work is that the Canadians are mostly British now, and my French trader friends have been pushed further west to the land of the great lakes. But the trade is further complicated. French ships can no longer come up the St. Lawrence River to Quebec. So you see, I will not trade with the British and cannot reach the French. Yours may be my best offer. I will come in the early spring when the days are as long as the nights."

Indian summer ended in a flash. Overnight the weather changed from delightful to raw. The sky clouded over, and the wind blew from the north. Anne added more wood to the fire to keep a damp chill from the cabin. Joseph and Anne decided to stay at the cabin through the winter.

After the trader's visit, they had changed the plan. Joseph figured if he was to cut timbers all winter, he might just as well be cutting his own. Gordon's sawmill was one mile down the Mourning Kill. He and Matthew would skid the logs down on the ice before the thaw in the spring. With money from the white pines, he could buy a horse, wagon and provisions for his move back to Balls Town.

Another reason for staying was to protect their cabin from Indian raids. Two cabins west of Middle Line Road had been torched, and one farmer had lost his hay crop to fire. Rumors were flying that the Scotch Bush farmers who were loyal to King George had started the fires. Another reason to stay was they had agreed that Matthew could join the Balls Town militia. He now worked part of each week fortifying the meetinghouse with a high timber fence. The finished fort would be a shelter for the Patriot farmers and their families. If they went home, their cabin would be unprotected and vacant during the day. They could not risk losing their land to a new settler.

The decision to stay was much easier for Joseph than it was for Anne. She had promised her children she would be home before winter. *Why could she not leave and travel home with William? No.*

72

Did she think that something might happen to Joseph and he would need her? No. Did she crave the adventure, the challenge of a winter in the wilderness? Maybe. She knew she was not afraid, and when Joseph had asked her if she wanted to stay, she had answered "yes" almost immediately. But the promise. She had broken her promise.

CHAPTER VIII

First winter on the hill

Anne thought winter began too early. November days were cloudy and damp. Hard rains blew down the leaves until the ground was covered with the soggy foliage. As the temperatures dropped, the leaves turned brown and Anne gathered big armloads and packed them against the sides of the cabin.

Today, Joseph and Matthew were across their lane in the wood lot felling trees for a barn. But on days Matthew went hunting or worked at the fort, Joseph stayed close to the cabin and trimmed and fitted the cut trees into barn beams just like he had for the house. Only this time as he constructed the bents or hewn beam frames on the ground, he pounded each union into place permanently. The barn would not be moved as their saltbox in the Hudson Valley would. His father's axe was used for scoring the logs and Joseph's broad axe for hewing. The beams would lie flat and the wood allowed to season on the ground until spring.

Heavy snows began before Christmas, and travel was no longer an option. Anne tossed and turned in their bed and could not sleep knowing she was now separated from her children until spring. Soon it would be Christmas. Were Sam and Lizzie well? Were they warm enough? Did their clothes need mending? Who was helping Sam with his reading – who was brushing Lizzie's hair? She wished she had gone back home with William. Tears tumbled from her eyes and dripped onto her pillow. She could no longer hold back her sorrow and wept in Joseph's arms as he soundly slept.

Tension was replaced by loneliness. The wind howled down the make-shift chimney. Anne knew it was snowing. Exhausted with worry, but still unable to sleep, she remembered her wish for adventure and her father's prayer for her. Father. She rolled on her back and drew her hands together over her swollen belly and began praying. *Dear God, protect Sam and Lizzie and the new baby...........*Anne fell asleep.

By February, snow drifted in and almost covered their cabin. The Rues had little thought of Indian attacks during these cold months. Matthew went out each day to hunt, and when he shot and brought home his first deer, they knew they would survive the winter. Anne cooked the venison in pies and stews, hearty soups, and simmered hot broth to soak her hard biscuits to fill the men's stomachs. Matthew now worked alongside his brother cutting down the huge timbers of white pine, and together they rolled them down the hill to the frozen Mourning Kill. They would wait for the spring melt to push them into the creek and float the heavy logs to Gordon's sawmill.

In March, Anne ran out of sugar and was rationing salt; but her flour was holding out and the elderberries she dried last fall sweetened their hot porridge. While the men worked, she explored the hill. To her great surprise, she saw the turkey was hiding behind a bush, and it watched her as she walked by the boulder. It was a game and Anne, bored with being in the cabin, began to watch for and track the silly turkey. The day she found the hen's nest she laughed out loud and spoke to the invisible bird.

"I have found your nest, friend. I have plans for your eggs." Anne checked the nest each morning. When the twelve eggs hatched, she left dried seeds by the nest. When the chicks had the beginnings of feathers, she brought three young turkeys to a well protected pen by the cabin and raised them like chickens.

Anne also tended her window sill garden. Twenty saplings from wild apple trees were growing in a wooden tray filled with good bottom land dirt from the creek. As the March winds blew across the hill, her little trees were sheltered and warmed by the sun. The new growth gave her heart hope of spring. She had been watching the sun rise and set. She knew the days were about as long as the nights. It was spring. She would ask her husband if he agreed.

Joseph told her that night it was too muddy to push the cart and leave for home. Plus, he was still hoping Francois would take him up on his offer to sell the fur pelts to the French traders in New Jersey. When Francois came, they would leave for home. Anne was anxious to leave, and the trader was late.

Anne never heard his approach and was startled when the horses appeared by the cabin window. Joseph ran from the woodlot and couldn't believe his eyes as he looked at the Frenchman. Francois looked haggard. He didn't at all resemble the man who had stopped by their cabin last fall. Avoiding comments about his appearance, Joseph greeted him. "Welcome, we're mighty glad you have returned." Then as he turned and looked at the pack horse, "Francois, how did you trap all of these animals?"

"I didn't, I went far west to the great lakes to where I once lived with the Indians. I traded with them for the furs. The Indians are suffering; most are sick and many have died." Then with a loud voice covering his emotions, "There are more furs. I had to leave half of the furs by the Sacandaga River as my horses tired. The snow drifts are deep in the woods. I must go back for the rest of the cache."

"When might you be back? We are anxious to leave for home," Joseph asked.

"Two weeks, maybe more, maybe less." Francois answered.

"Well, good man, stay the night. Anne, set another place for dinner."

Anne replied she would make more biscuits and went into the cabin. Francois took his pack horse into the woods and made a hidden shelter for the furs. Joseph went into the cabin and tried to console Anne. "There is still too much snow on the roads for a push cart. Will you be all right for a few more weeks? Remember, you can ride in the wagon as far as the Hudson River with Matthew and me pushing the cart. Then we shall catch a ride on a logging barge and quickly float the rest of the way home. Francois has agreed to stay at the cabin while we are gone. He needs rest.

But Anne was not so sure they should wait. Francois had been late with his first delivery and might be late with his second. She knew they must not delay, as her time was nearing for the birth of their baby. She began to cry, but willed herself to stop and took long slow breaths, calming herself so not to disturb the sleeping infant in her womb. She closed her eyes and thought of happily hugging her children and then sleeping in her bed in the saltbox. When that didn't work, Anne remembered her words during her visit with her father, *"I want adventure, father, I'm not afraid."* Now she hoped her father's prayers would still protect her and bring her safely home in time for the baby's birth.

But Francois hurried and brought his second load of furs in two weeks, and the Frenchman helped Joseph spread the fur bundles in the cart. Anne told them to hide the pelts with straw and she would cover everything with her quilt to make it look like a soft bed.

Anne loaded the push cart with enough food to last until they reached home. Three plump young turkeys were hanging off the side of the cart in their woven cages. The turkeys would be presents for the family or food for them, if the hunting was poor. Finally, all was ready.

Francois again promised to stay on the hill until Matthew returned from Albany. He was tired, and his horses were tired. He would dig a sleeping den beneath the large locust tree. He was used to sleeping without a fire, and he could watch the cabin. But he would cook in the cabin and keep a little fire going. When Matthew returned from Albany, he promised to live at the cabin until Joseph, Anne and the children returned. Their land could not be claimed by another settler. Smoke would always be coming out of the chimney.

As she traveled in the bumpy cart, Anne could think of nothing but returning home and being with Sam and Lizzie, and prayed she would make it back to the house before the birth. When the men loaded the cart onto the timber barge, Anne distracted the captain, telling him of her turkeys. The captain, who had a jolly disposition and enjoyed ferrying up and down the Hudson River, had just eaten and drunk his fill before leaving Albany. Talking with

Anne was more than pleasant, and how could he refuse the turkey this pretty woman offered him as payment for their passage?

Anne cried with joy when Joseph turned up the lane and started laughing as she wept when she saw her house. The children spotted the cart and raced to meet them. She continued weeping again as her children greeted them, and the tears and hugs and smiles and laughter continued as Sam and Lizzie clung to her skirt. And when their father told them they were all going back to Balls Town together, the children raced around the yard, laughing and shouting to their cousins that they were going to their cabin on the hill! Joseph lowered the tongue of the cart and the turkey cages fell to the ground and broke open. The two remaining turkeys burst out of their grass cages. With shouts, the children ran around the yard trying to catch them!

William and Sarah were eager to hear about the Balls Town settlement and news of their journey. Joseph and Anne waited until the children had settled and gone to bed before they told the family of the threat of the raids in Balls Town and that Matthew had joined Balls Town militia. Reverend Ball's assembly house was now a fort complete with a lookout and cannon.

Joseph continued, "Our land was the Mohawk Indian hunting ground, and if you think the Indians are ignorant, you'd better think again. In their own civilization, they had a good, healthy life. There is much we can learn from them about farming this new land; in the spring, they burned the low limbs and shrubs around Balls Town. The burning forces new vegetation. Deer would come to eat the grass, and the hunting is still good. All of this I learned from the trader I'm going to tell you about. He has lived somewhere between Schenectady and Quebec, Canada all of his adult life. He knows the way of the Indians, and he thinks they are likely to fight us for our land."

Joseph sighed, "There is bad business. The British have given the Indians muskets and rum for their land and loyality. If there is a war, the Indians shall be feared worse than the British. Francois told us that there are Canadian Indians who will come for booty and take prisoners."

This was all too much for Phebe and Samuel. They said nothing. Sarah and William silently decided to stay where they were until the Indian problem was solved.

Joseph then told his family more about the fur trader. He opened the bundles and spread the beautiful thick glossy pelts on the floor. The trader's second delivery had been worth waiting for and would bring a good price. The trader had been thankful that Joseph had waited for him, and he looked forward to the additional profit the added furs would bring. Both men knew the risks Joseph would take in bringing the furs to market unseen from the eyes of the British trade officials. Joseph talked of new plans to buy a larger wagon with his profit from the sale, giving the family transportation to the safety of the fort.

Samuel interrupted. "Your best location to do business may be in the New Jersey Colony with the French merchants. Manhattan has become a stronghold for the English. I think Jack Morley might go along with this, but it's been a while since we've seen him and Deborah."

Joseph nodded, hoping his father would help with the sale, but also knowing the danger. He changed the subject and talked of how Anne had secretly planted Samuel's hop seed on the back hill and down the hedgerows of the hay fields. "You were right, father. As General Washington went from town to town recruiting men for the Continental Army, he encouraged Americans to boycott English rum and drink ale."

But Joseph explained this had become a problem because their 45 acres was west of Middle Line Road. Farmers west of Middle Line Road were loyal to the Crown, while those farmers east of the road favored independence. If it were known that Anne had planted hops, and they had plans for a brewery, their cabin, fields, and lives would be in danger. So they had kept the hops a secret.

Samuel listened and worried. *Matthew had joined a militia. The Revolution and Indians were threatening Joseph's plans. The move for independence was happening far to the north. Could he help his son sell the furs?*

Now, it was Samuel's turn to tell about the Revolution. The British Army put down the rebellion in Lexington and Concord. The response of the militias had been a standoff on Breed's Hill. But General Washington bottled up General Gage and the Redcoats in Boston after a fierce battle on Bunker Hill. Gage was forced to load his troop ships and abandon Boston, taking with him hundreds of British citizens. They sailed to the British settlement of Halifax, Nova Scotia.

William spoke up. "Rumors are the British General Howe is waiting for reinforcements before sailing to New York and striking a blow at the Continental Army. There is talk that Hessian soldiers have been paid to join forces with Howe's Army. If that happens, the lower Hudson Valley and all of New York will soon be in great danger."

Samuel concluded, "The family will be in danger here and in Balls Town. We must keep our plans to ourselves and be careful what we say to our neighbors. There is danger in talking too much. Phebe saved a pile of newspapers for you to read, Joseph. You might also want to read the pamphlets written by a fellow named Thomas Payne. If you weren't a Patriot before reading what this fellow has to say, you would be after reading them. He's got people stirred up into revolting against the King."

Samuel and Phebe rose to leave for their cabin. "Joseph, I will bring my horse and wagon and we will leave for Morley's at dawn."

Anne handed her supply list to Joseph as he and her father-in-law loaded Samuel's wagon with the furs and left for New Jersey to trade and buy supplies. They needed sugar, coffee, flour, and salt in larger quantities than the first trip. Anne needed cloth to make clothes for the children. They would all need heavy warm woolen clothing for the coming winter. And everyone needed heavy high shoes.

She would bring sewing needles, pins, and thread to trade with the women she had met at church. They were thinking of setting up a quilting frame at the fort to quilt during the summer. She asked Joseph to go to shops for these items. He made no promises, but would do his best.

When the men had left, Anne told Sarah and Joseph's sisters of their first winter in the cabin: her loneliness and the worry of Indian attack, their quiet Christmas without Lizzie, Sam, and the family. Tears came to her eyes, and Sarah hugged her.

Anne told how she tended the smoky fire to keep the cabin warm and prepared food for Joseph and Matthew with the barest of supplies. She had been unprepared to spend the winter in the cabin. Without the wild turkeys, deer, and rabbits to eat, they would have starved. Having few cooking utensils, they ate roasted meat off sticks. "Sometimes I felt like an Indian!" Once the snow had drifted across their lane, they were cut off from the fort and civilization. "I had no thread or needles. I thought I would go crazy on those winter days by myself in the cabin with nothing to do."

Then smiling, she described the plentiful elderberry bushes. She had gathered walnuts and sliced wild crab apples very thin and hung them about the cabin using thread from the seams of her skirt. "Joseph made me needles from pieces of bone. I wove baskets from pine needles and grass."

Sarah agreed, "You would have made a fine Indian squaw. I am so proud of you Anne. You had your adventure and then some."

Word had been sent to Anne's sisters that she was home. Carly, Hannah, and Caroline arrived in a coach driven by Carly's husband that night. They hugged their sister, but remained in the background listening to Anne's telling. She was so eager to talk and share news that sometimes they would have to ask her to talk more slowly. Anne felt such a rush of love and relief that she was home, that she often openly wept. She had been so lonely for her children's hugs and kisses. The first winter on the hill had seemed so long and the dangers so great that she had to pinch herself that she was really among family again.

Then her sisters drew her aside and told her their sad news. Her joy at being home was turned to grief. Their father, Thomas, had died peacefully in his sleep that winter. Her sisters had found him in his bed with his dog curled up at his side. They had come to quilt.

During the night, surrounded by her sisters and Sarah in the tiny borning room of the saltbox, Anne gave birth to a son. She would ask Joseph on his return if they could name him after her father. Her sisters held Anne close and let her cry.

Thomas Ducker Rue, Born April 14, 1776, New York Colony

When Joseph returned, the preacher came to the house. He baptized little Thomas and gave the family God's blessing, and they sang hymns of thanksgiving and hymns of remembrance. Anne would be in deep mourning for a year.

Rue Family Tree

Samuel Rue   *m*.   Phebe *Martin*

Joseph   *m*   *Anne Ducker*

Sam

Lizzie

Thomas

William   *m*   *Sarah*

Jack

Jonas

Louisa

Abby

Matthew

Patience

Susanna

Lucy

CHAPTER IX

Farewell

As soon as Anne was able to leave for Balls Town, the women prepared a dinner of thanksgiving, sparing the turkeys. The cousins named the turkeys George and Martha Washington, and the turkeys were free to roam with the chickens in the open pen.

The day before they left, Anne went into the attic through a trap door in the ceiling of the upstairs bedroom. She searched in the dim attic light for her belongings and found and opened her trunk. She gathered her wedding dress in her arms. It would be a long time before she could wear a dress as fine as this in Balls Town, but someday maybe Lizzie would wed and wear her gown. She wanted her belongings with her now. This might be her last trip to see her family until the Revolution was over. She knew she would stay in Balls Town with their children when Joseph returned for the house.

Nestled below her dresses were small gifts from her English grandmother, Jane. She would keep them safe. She put her Mother's English Bible to her chest and sighed. She found her doll and wrapped in a handkerchief was the locket, her mother's locket that Thomas had given her mother on the day of their engagement. She knew her mother only through her father's and sisters' memories. Sadness flowed over her as Anne put the necklace with its thin gold chain around her neck and tucked the locket under her blouse.

She called to Joseph that she was ready to come down from the attic and that she wanted to take her trunk back to Balls Town. She handed it down then feet first lowered her dangling shape through the trap door. As he caught her in his arms, she whispered that she was sad to be leaving their house behind. Joseph agreed and said her trunk would fit just fine under the seat of the wagon and that he knew of a dry corner of the cabin cellar where it would be hidden and safe.

Joseph's youngest sister, Lucy, was going with them to the hill. Lucy had begged her mother to let her go with her brother and Anne. She longed to have an adventure and could help Anne with the children. Phebe had been reluctant to let her go, but Samuel gently told her that she had only been a few years older than Lucy, when she had left home, boarded a ship, and sailed to America. With tears, Phebe now understood only too well the heartache her own parents must have felt when she had married Samuel and left for the New World.

Joseph's newly purchased wagon was loaded with supplies, equipment, and food: food for his family now numbering six and food for the horse. He knew from the last trip there was little firewood for cooking or grass for grazing along the road north. Whole families were leaving Manhattan in anticipation of the conflict over independence. He was lucky to have found a sturdy wagon and strong horse. Only the English citizens now called Loyalists were remaining in Manhattan, safe in the knowledge that their lives, homes, and shops would be spared.

The wagon was also loaded with bags of seed and farm tools, plus all the goods he had bought for Anne. There were rolled up bolts of woolen fabric for clothes and muslin for the bedding and shirts she would sew. Joseph had hidden a special package for her that would be a Christmas surprise. He had bought everyone new shoes for church and leather boots for winter.

William added vegetable seeds and potatoes from the garden. Under these were Joseph's two crates with food: flour, sugar, coffee, molasses, salt, and spices. There had been plenty of goods for sale in Philadelphia. Gunpowder and arms were coming from France on ships from the West Indies that docked near the colonial capital.

Next to the crates were an iron kettle and Dutch oven, cooking forks, a crane for the fireplace, flat stones for baking bread over the coals, plus spoons, knives, forks and plates that Phebe had brought over from her cabin. Samuel had made two more chairs.

On the left side of the wagon was a makeshift bed for the children with their feather quilts and pillows. Then there were the things that meant the most to Anne, the spool crib that had been her father's that would now be little Thomas's bed and her trunk from the attic.

Hidden beneath all of the goods in a sack filled with more hop seed was the trader's money. Joseph still could not believe his good fortune in dealing with Jack Morley and the French fur merchants. Samuel had not known what kind of reception they might receive from his old friend or even if they still were in New Jersey living in the same house.

But, Jack had welcomed them and at once offered to help with the trading. Jack explained that he and Deborah would support the Revolution. They knew they had much to lose if the British won, but they, too, saw how unfair England's taxes were on the colonies. Jack was a respected man in his town and carefully traded with the English and the French. The sale of Francois's fine furs had been favorable for all the men.

Now, looking at Anne, Joseph appreciated her careful avoidance of a British search before they boarded the timber barge south of Albany. Distracting the captain with her turkeys had done the trick. Joseph could scarcely believe his good fortune: a smart wife and a wonderful family. Now it was his job to make sure his family was safely settled in their cabin and the trader's profit safely delivered to Francois.

At the last moment before leaving, Joseph's sisters, Patience and Susanna, burst out of the house with a candle stand and little three-legged stool that had been among Joseph's and Anne's wedding presents. They had already packed Anne's sewing table with all of its drawers full of new needles, pins, and thread and even knitting needles should she be able to trade for some wool. Anne's sisters, Carly, Hannah, and Caroline, had brought over more supplies with their gifts for the children and the quilting frame from Thomas's cabin. It looked like a stack of lumber, but Anne knew it was a fine frame and would someday be in the parlor of her house. There had been so many good-bye tears that it was a relief to have this loud and happy farewell.

Then the cousins ran into the house and brought out a broom, the candlesticks off the table, and even dragged the braided rug Joseph's sisters had made last winter from scraps of old coats.

"Jack and Jonas, that rug's better left at the house, we have a damp floor in the cabin." said their Uncle Joseph.

So the cousins dragged it back to the porch and dropped it. If they all couldn't go to Balls Town, at least some of their things would make the trip, they figured. Sam had packed his fishing pole that grandfather Samuel had made, and Lizzie had her doll. The big wagon was stuffed.

Impatient to get started, Joseph called to load up. Thomas would ride in a sling tied around Anne's shoulder. She and Lucy sat on the bench seat of the wagon. The baby would feel every bump in the road, but the bumps would be softened, and little Thomas would be soothed by the closeness of his mother's heartbeat. Sam and Lizzie rode on top of the feed sacks or on their quilts, and Joseph walked beside the horse leading the mare around the deepest ruts in the road.

Joseph gently drew his father aside and said, "Your cabin is on the Post Road and only a short distance from the road north to Albany. If the British troops move up the Hudson River, you will be in their path."

As he reminded his father of the dangers, he told him to make ready to abandon their cabin and hide in the woods if they heard cannon fire. Samuel understood his son's concern, but he had just planted his garden and there was much to do. Plus the fruit trees were in full bloom.

"We will stay near the cabin and be careful." Samuel promised. "Some of our American neighbors have British flags hanging on their houses. They think they will be spared."

But Samuel knew this was wrong. He and Phebe were now Americans. Their children and grandchildren were Americans, and as Americans they would now fight for their freedoms with General George Washington as their leader.

"There will be no British flag on our cabin door," Phebe agreed. She knew that Samuel would fight for independence. They had worked too long and hard to abandon their land and country now.

Phebe had tucked a small sapling along with her books in the wagon. Only Sam knew about the small tree. He had promised his grandmother that he would water the tree on their journey and plant it on the hill. They had agreed that it would be the family's Liberty Tree.

Sam and Lizzie were big enough to jump about the wagon, and sometimes Sam ran alongside as they steadily moved north. Sam thought this was a great adventure and explored the campsites each evening and fished. He was especially happy when he could hand his slippery fish to his Aunt Lucy for their supper.

If they camped for the night next to the forest, he and his father went hunting. They quietly crept through the woods so as not to not surprise the game birds. Joseph took aim with his musket, and if the shot was true, they roasted the skinny bird over the fire.

Lucy did most of the cooking and didn't complain. She was happy just to be traveling. Everything was new to her: the couriers who rode for the Continental Army, the Loyalist carriages transporting ladies in fine gowns and officers in red coats, and the endless timber barges floating swiftly down the river.

Lizzie helped her mother with Thomas when she could and clung to Anne's long skirt as they sometimes walked alongside their wagon as it bounced and jiggled up the road. Lizzie was unsure of just where their hill cabin was, but looked forward to her new home and cheerfully carried Anne's doll about as Anne carried Thomas.

The road north to Albany followed the bank of the Hudson River. There was great excitement on the seventh day of their trip. Joseph pulled off the road and stopped the wagon. Lucy followed Sam to the gathering by the river. Sam wiggled his way through the crowd to see a kindly old gentleman sitting on a stump. He had a common brown coat, a furry beaver cap, and spectacles perched on the end of his nose. The boat that had brought him to shore was securely tied to a tree. The sloop was waiting for a strong wind from the south to fill its sails so it could run north with the wind against the Hudson's southerly current. The ship's captain had decided to wait out the weather and give his passengers an opportunity to come ashore and stretch their legs.

Sam was curious. The old man had a wide merry smile that he flashed easily to the crowd. He was telling a story at the moment, and the crowd hung on his every word. The old man was reading from a small book and, because Sam loved to read, the six year old tried to get close enough to look at the pages of the book. The reading stopped when Sam bumped the book as he squeezed his small body onto the stump.

"Well, hello there. What's this, can't you see I'm reading?" Sam was mortified. He told the man this was where he always sat when his grandmother read to him. He only wanted to see if he could read the book as he loved good stories.

"Well, young man, let's have a try. Why don't you read *Poor Richard's Almanack* to these good citizens?"

Sam looked at the page, then looked up and saw his father with Lizzie perched on his shoulders. He could tell his father was upset that he had pushed his way into the crowd. Sam looked down at the page and read to himself. He did not understand what he was reading. It was a riddle. But the kindly old man insisted he read:

> *"For want of a Nail the Shoe is lost;*
> *For want of a Shoe, the Horse is lost;*
> *For want of a Horse the Rider is lost."*

Sam turned his head to the man and said, "Do you have nails in your shoes?" The crowd laughed, and Sam's face turned red.

"No, no, young man. This is about a man who doesn't take care of his horse. Let's try another sentence," said the old man.

Sam read:

> *"Great Estates may venture more;*
> *Little Boats must keep near Shore."*

Sam knew what this meant and said, "That's why you came ashore!"

Hearing that, the crowd cheered, and Joseph called to Sam to get back to the wagon. Sam understood the second reading and knew why the people had cheered. He also understood his father's meaning, he was in trouble, and quickly ran towards their wagon.

Turning just south of Albany, the family traveled west along the Niskayuna Road to Schenectady. They passed through a roadblock. The British soldiers did not stop them to search their wagon. Joseph looked straight ahead when passing and Sam did the same.

The family would spend the night at a tavern on the main drag. The tavern was a roadhouse with a huge barn around back. Anne was tired and needed to rest. The road through Niskayuna had been through deep sand, and the horse had labored with the heavy load and needed a rest, too. This was fine with Joseph as he wanted to read the latest newspaper and post a letter home to his father.

As they drove into Schenectady, Sam watched men taking down timbers from a fence and building cabins with the logs. Sam thought the timber fence looked very old. Joseph told Sam the stockade had been built to protect the people of Schenectady from Indian attacks.

Joseph drove the wagon around to the back of the roadhouse. He unhitched the horse and told Sam and Lucy to see that the mare was fed and bedded. Joseph helped Anne from the wagon and led her, carrying little Thomas, and Lizzie around to the entrance and paid for a room for the night. The women would all sleep together in one room while Joseph and Sam would bed down in the barn near the wagon. Joseph would not leave the wagon unattended at night.

He went into the roadhouse and asked the innkeeper about the new cabins he had seen. Before the innkeeper would answer Joseph's questions, he wanted to know who he was and where he was going. When he was satisfied that Joseph wasn't a Tory spy, he answered that the cabins would be barracks for the new American army. He passed him the latest copy of the *Schenectady newspaper*.

Joseph read the Schenectady newspaper. General Washington was counting on the men of Schenectady to defend the western frontier from a possible British and Indian attack from the west. It wasn't too late to sign up. The recruitment tent was located by the house of John Glen, the quartermaster of the local militia. This was where Washington had stayed the previous year and had again lodged this year. The newspaper also reported that new recruits would be paid in the newly printed New England paper dollars. Joseph further read, the Continental Congress in Philadelphia had authorized Washington to raise companies of minutemen, men who had their own muskets and powder who could fight in a minute's notice to stop the British from taking Albany. In response to Washington's request, the men of Schenectady had formed a militia. Further down, Joseph read there had been no reports of Indian attacks on the Balls Town settlement.

While his mother was resting and his father was reading, Sam explored the barn. He and his father would sleep in the wagon. This would be the first night they would have a roof over their heads since they had left home. The barn had fresh well water for their horse, and his father had promised that the family would drink cider. Later, Joseph returned with warm cornbread, chicken, and cool apple cider. The family gave thanks for their safe journey to Schenectady and ate beside the barn. Dinner was good.

Later, lying on fresh straw with a full stomach, Sam closed his eyes and thought about someday having his own inn and barn filled with sweet smelling hay; a place for people to board their horses and drink cool cider and eat warm chicken. Schenectady was the first city Sam had ever seen, and he liked what he saw.

After the children were asleep, Joseph told Anne of his conversations with the men. He had no plans to join the army, but the militia was a possibility. He would protect his cabin and land from the British soldiers and Indians. They would leave Schenectady before dawn.

90

As they turned the corner and headed up the hill toward the Rue cabin, they saw blackened fields. Anne cried out, and Joseph hurried the horse up the hill. There had been a fire very near their cabin. As they pulled off the lane at the top of the hill, Matthew ran to meet them.

"They burned our fields," he shouted. "The Indians burned our fields last night. They started a fire near the cabin and the wind quickly carried the sparks across the field and down the hill to the creek. I was sleeping in Francois's den and woke to the crackling of the fire."

The side of the cabin was damaged, and Anne's saplings were burnt, but Matthew had managed to save the cabin.

"I fired my musket, and I think it scared them off. They left strange footprints, Brother."

Sam and Lizzie stared at the blacken fields and cabin. It did not look as big as their grandfather's cabin. Lizzie began to cry, and that set off Thomas. Lizzie wailed, "I want to go back to the house."

Sam just stood in the wagon not knowing what to say. His Uncle Matt picked him off the wagon and twirled him over his shoulder. That put a smile on his face and he began to laugh. Then Sam blurted out, "Guess what, Uncle Matt? Little Boats must keep near shore." The family spent the night at the Balls Town fort.

At sundown Joseph took his musket and slipped out of the fort. There was only a crescent moon, but that didn't matter. Joseph knew the way to their cabin by heart. He crossed the Mourning Kill and silently climbed the hill toward the cabin. It was a short mile. He joined Matthew, and they hid behind the stone wall and waited. They didn't speak or move.

Matthew noticed the men first, and then they saw the torch flame up. They cocked and fired their muskets at the Indians. The two dark shapes sure looked like Indians, but jumped into the air and their howls sounded like farmers. When the brothers ran to the cabin, the two imposters were trying to hide behind the trees. One had been wounded in the leg, the other clipped in the arm.

Joseph picked up the torch and held it in front of the men. They were from Scotch Bush, clearly Tories up to no good.

Matthew wanted to take them back to the fort and lock them in the jail. Joseph held up his hand in protest. Moving the torch closer, he asked them, "Why are you siding with the British when your freedoms are at stake?"

The men said they hadn't thought about it much. They only knew there was going to be a war, and they wanted to be on the winning side. They knew the Indians would do the same.

The man with the bleeding arm said, "The Americans don't have a chance against the Redcoats. They outnumber us. And they have more cannons, plus all those wretched Indians. They'll take your scalp so fast, you won't even know it."

The other man said, "You live west of Middle Line Road. Join us and your family and cabin will be safe."

The brothers looked at the two men with disgust. "I think you burned our fields just because you are afraid to stand up and fight for your rights to be free Americans." Joseph took their muskets and knives and put out the torch.

On the way down the hill, the men again tried to persuade the Rues to join them and fight with the British. Joseph argued, "Do you want to be ruled by a King in England? Haven't you heard the words of Thomas Payne? 'A government of our own is our natural right.'"

Matthew followed shouting, "and sometimes you have to fight for your rights."

Lucy woke up with a fit of sneezes. Not a good sign. The family was bedded down in a corner of the fort with blankets thrown over last year's hay. Lucy shuddered, "Something dead must be buried in this hay." She hoped it was not a rat.

She could hear voices nearby and quietly got up and went to the outhouse. There was a basin of water for washing, and a tiny piece of tin for a looking glass. She looked a fright; her eyes were red and puffy and her hair matted from her sweat. She could hear her brother Matthew telling Major Gordon about the second raid on their cabin last night. She listened and was relieved that the "Indians" were not Indians after all.

Matthew was anxious to be off. Major Gordon was sending him to Schenectady. He saw Lucy was awake and introduced her to Major Gordon and two of his men. She tried to fluff up her hair, but realized a freshly scrubbed face was the best she could hope for at the moment. She said a quick hello and excused herself. She went over to the cooking fire, sat down, ate a bowl of oatmeal and drank warm cider from a mug.

Joseph was quietly talking to Anne, trying hard not to wake the children. All of the other farmers and their families had left the fort before dawn. The fort was almost empty.

As soon as the rest of the family was awake, Matthew kissed them all good-bye. Then, he was out the gate and quickly walking toward Major Gordon's house. He would ride one of the major's horses to Schenectady. Sam loved his Uncle Matt and ran out of the fort and yelled, "Better not travel in a small boat. But if you have to, stay close to shore."

Matthew turned, waved good-bye, and was gone from view.

It took a few days, but the burned timbers on the cabin were replaced and the wagon was unloaded. Anne, nursing Thomas in the chair by the open door, watched Joseph ploughing the blackened south field. The horse did not like to pull and was jerking the plough from side to side. Joseph's shoulders would ache tonight, but the field was almost ready, and she would help plant the bright Timothy grass and oats in a few days.

The horse was going to need feed when the snow covered the fields next winter, and the oats they had brought were almost gone. For now, it was Lucy's job to feed and brush the horse, whom she had promptly named Yankee after listening to the conversations at the fort. Best of all, her brother had arranged for her to ride Yankee to the McKnight's for milk.

The vegetable garden could not be planted quite yet. They were still waking up to frost. But in another week Anne, Lucy, Sam, and Lizzie would plant the bean, carrot, turnip, and onion seeds near the cabin. They would carefully cut the potatoes grown in Sarah's garden into chunks making sure each piece of potato had an eye that would send up a shoot and send down a root. With the fruit tree seedlings lost in the fire, Anne reserved the space for growing herbs.

She spoke to Thomas, "The rabbits and deer like the herbs and vegetable plants as much as we do, little fellow. It will be a battle to keep animals from eating everything in the garden. I wish you could help, but you're just too little." Thomas looked up at his mother's face, his lower lip quivered, then began sucking again.

They were still eating the food from the wagon, and Anne rationed out the supplies as if their lives depended on it. She reminded herself to ask Joseph to hunt this week. There was no meat for the potato and onion broth today.

Sitting there in the doorway, Anne thought of her house and Sarah and the cousins. She missed her chicken coup and wondered how her turkeys were doing. She hadn't seen the hen since their return. *Too many people around for wild turkeys,* she thought to herself. *Oh, how I would love a plate of eggs with my potatoes for lunch. Nursing a baby was hungry work.*

CHAPTER X

Sam's trap

Sam stopped by the big boulder to check on the Liberty Tree. The little tree was putting out new needles so he knew the roots were growing. He ran back to the cabin for a pail and down to the creek for water. He thought of his grandmother Phebe as he poured the water around the base of the tree. He wished he could tell her the old man's jokes. He really missed his grandfather, too, and wanted to tell Samuel how good a fisherman he was. Now that the ice was out of the creek, he had actually caught a fish. His father cleaned the small fish and they all ate a small bite.

The back hillside was a bright green pasture clear down to the creek. The grass roots survived the fire. As soon as Joseph finished ploughing the new field, he would hobbled the horse and let her graze over the once blackened hill. She ate grass, weeds, and even nibbled the hops that sprouted up along the walls. The hops were still a secret, and with so many wildflowers growing in the pasture and stone walls, they remained well hidden. Joseph would spend the rest of his day clearing the ploughed field of stones and stumps. He had hit a stone every few feet and the blade would need sharpening before he could plough again.

Sam and Lizzie explored their hill. Lizzie picked wild flowers for the table, and Sam dug tender dandelion greens for his mother to boil for their lunch. They both would soon help weed the garden. Lucy was helping her brother in the field, picking up the smaller stones the plough turned up and carrying them to the edge of the field. The stone walls were higher than her knees. She heard Anne call to Lizzie and watched her little niece run to the cabin. Lizzie was no longer asking to go back to their house. Lizzie played with her doll and watched Anne care for Thomas. But mostly, she played little made-up games around the cabin. She missed her cousins and would ask her mother what they might be doing at the house today. Anne could only guess, and told Lizzie she thought they were doing the same things that she was doing. On rainy days, Anne had the children sit at the table and write their letters on slate boards. After lunch she always brought out the books and read to Lizzie before her nap, then read longer to Sam.

Francois had come for his money soon after they arrived at the cabin. Sam had never seen a fur trader before. The trader was shorter than his father and had long dark hair that hung loose under his hat. He was dressed in buckskin; even his boots were made of hide. He spoke French better than English. His horse, Lulu, was a gentle mare but his pack horse, Bess, was a bit temperamental. Everyone knew to stay away from her back end because she would buck at the flies. Her front end was just about as dangerous as she would stretch out her neck and nip you if you got too close. Sam just figured that a pack horse led a terrible life.

While Francois stayed with the family he slept in his den. He had dug a hole that was big enough for two men to sleep in under the roots of their locust tree. He told Sam he was used to sleeping outdoors and preferred being away from the cabin. He never put food in his den, because he didn't want to wake up and find a bear eating beside him. Sam hadn't thought of that before.

Francois gave Sam one of his small traps before he left. It was good for squirrels and rabbits. Sam was strong enough to pry the sharp jaws open and set the trap baited with a potato skin. A bigger animal could snatch the bait and pull free. They probably got a bloodied nose, but escaped. Sam had tied the trap to a tree, and it had been two days since he had checked it. Lately he had found the trap sprung, but the animal missing.

Today he would check his trap. His father had taught him to walk quietly through the woods. It meant he couldn't whistle, cough, or clear his throat. He avoided stepping on any twigs or dry leaves that might snap or crunch. This afternoon, as before, he had the feeling he was being watched. He had figured it was probably a small animal or maybe a hawk that was silently circling above the trees. But today the feeling was so strong that he felt danger and slowed and listened and looked up into the forest canopy, then down to the ground. He was now close enough to see his trap. His heart gave a leap; there was a good-size rabbit caught in the iron jaws of the trap.

Just as he was about to step towards his trap, there...there was a growling noise. Was he imagining or did it sound like a rumble from his stomach, but it wasn't his stomach. His body froze, now he was afraid. Someone was watching him. *Why don't my legs run?* He thought. Then he caught a movement to the side and saw a human shape crouched behind a bush. Sam's breathing now came in short gasps. *What to do? The person hasn't moved and is naked!*

Sam tried to think calmly, but that was impossible. Next he thought of just pretending he didn't see the movement, grab the rabbit and trap and run home. But just as he was about to lunge for his trap...there...the noise...the stomach growling noise again.

Sam straightened. Not even knowing what he was doing, he said, "Hello," while holding his hands stiffly by his side. The shape moved, and Sam could now see it was a face, a brown face with black hair peering at him from behind the bush. Again, Sam stood up straight and said even louder, "Hello."

A boy stood up. He was naked except for an apron of deerskin draped from his waist. The boy was thin, very thin. Sam knew his guess had been right. The rumble that he had heard was from an empty stomach. His fear now was under control; his head was thinking again. Sam walked slowly toward the trap. The boy turned, as if to run away.

Sam stopped and said, "Hey, don't go." The boy did not have red skin. Sam had heard Indians were called "Redskins." But this boy who now stood taller than Sam did not have red skin. *Could he still be an Indian?*

The boy now spoke. "Yoo-hoo!" It startled Sam. But thinking again, Sam repeated his hello. The boy repeated yoo-hoo. Sam began to relax. They just stood staring at each other for a long moment, neither boy moving or speaking.

Then Sam pointed to the rabbit and said, "Rabbit." The boy responded, "Che-mum-es." Sam repeated, "Che-mum-es." The boy was an Indian; Sam was certain now.

Sam dropped down on one knee, opened the trap, lifted out the dead rabbit, and stood. The Indian boy looked at the rabbit. Sam said, "Che-mum-es," and without hesitation, held the rabbit out in front of him, offering the rabbit to the Indian. The boy's eyes grew big with surprise, then, he reached out, snatched the rabbit and fled into the woods.

Sam stood there a long time looking at his trap. Then he reset the trap with scraps of potato skins from his pocket, brushed some dry leaves over the trap to hide the jaws and headed back to the cabin. It seemed more like a dream. *What will I tell mother?* He knew they needed meat. Only then did he realize what he had done.

"Joseph, plan on staying at the fort tomorrow," said Matthew. "There'll be a muster. Bring your musket. I think they are setting up targets. And be forewarned, Major Gordon doesn't take kindly to a dirty musket barrel. And oh, wear your boots; rumor has it we'll be marching."

Joseph groaned. The weather was perfect for planting the field and no telling how long it might stay that way. If he weren't planting, he'd be busy working on the foundation for the saltbox. He and William had dug the cellar for the house last fall before the ground had frozen. He would now finish stacking the small boulders for the foundation of the two fireplaces at either end of the cellar. The rest of the stones would be used for the foundation walls.

This fall, with Matthew's help, he would roof it over with pine boards. Before the first frost, the cellar would need a temporary roof of elm bark. Joseph had convinced himself that he didn't have time to muster.

Matthew quickly changed his brother's mind. "You must muster. If you don't have a good excuse, you'll be tossed in the jail or worse."

Joseph passed along the news to Anne, and they all would stay at the fort with him and watch. For everyone but Joseph and Matthew, it would be an unexpected day off and promised to be a social outing for the women. Anne would pack a basket dinner as well as the usual breakfast.

Before they left for the fort, Anne gave Joseph a haircut. Then Joseph got out his sweet oil and tools. He ran the scourer down the barrel with an old flannel rag wrapped around it. After a few runs, he put the rag to his nose.

Sam asked, "Why are you smelling the rag?"

"Rust," said Joseph. "Rust in the barrel."

Sam looked at the musket. "Maybe we should go hunting this fall. I would sure like to see you shoot a pheasant for dinner like you did when we were on our way to Balls Town."

Joseph didn't answer. He had little time or energy to do anything. There was the cellar to finish, and a shed to build for the horse. He was a farmer now, not a hunter. But he needed to remind Matthew, that they needed meat.

After Joseph had put the musket in the wagon, he greased his boots. "Let's see, I'll need my hatchet."

Anne said, "I unpacked your best hunting shirt."

"What I wear is not going to make a bit of difference. I've just got to show up with a clean musket, four flints, balls, and a pound of powder," fumed Joseph. "Load up everyone."

Anne closed up the cabin and prayed that her garden would still be there when she returned. There was no telling how many rabbits would dine on her vegetables tonight. The carrots and turnips were up. The fence that Joseph had built around the cabin and garden kept some of the deer out, but most knew how to jump the fence and help themselves. The fence was no barrier to a hungry rabbit. As they loaded into the wagon, Anne mentioned this to Sam. Here was a perfect place for his trap!

"Mother, I have set up my trap in the garden. Father thought it was a good idea, too. But I forgot to tell you." replied Sam.

"Yes, I should hate to spring it on my bare foot, Sam and Joseph! You might have trapped me!" Anne then asked where the trap was.

"In the row of carrots," answered Sam.

There was a bonfire that night at the fort. Marie McDonald was telling ghost stories to the children, and afterward it took awhile for Lizzie to get to sleep. She was afraid of ghosts and a little afraid of the storyteller. Marie was Nicholas McDonald's half Indian-half French wife.

Anne, Lucy, and the other women stayed up after the children went to bed, visiting and sharing their news. They could talk faster than a quilting needle through muslin!

Major Gordon asked Joseph how his cold cellar was coming along. "Was the planking long enough?" He still had more of Joseph's logs ready to be cut. "Just let Matthew know when you think you'll need them."

Matthew had helped him move the logs down the Mourning Kill to Gordon's sawmill. Gordon had been so impressed with Matthew's quick actions with the huge logs, that he hired him on the spot. Now Matthew had also become the Balls Town militia's junior officer. He was the best marksman.

The men gathered around the cider keg and compared farming tales of woe. They needed rain, but not right now. Everyone's hay would soon be ready for the first cutting, but like Joseph, few had a barn to store their hay and oats, that is, if they got any. Mention was made of a barn-raising. By the end of the evening, the men had actually more than just grunted to each other.

The next morning Major Gordon ordered the fort bell rung for the muster. He had come from Schenectady the day before and brought with him the latest news about the Continental Army and General Washington.

"Quiet down! I say quiet down. You men need to know what's going on," shouted Gordon.

"We know what's going on," said one of the men from Scotch Bush. "Rebels are making noises about splitting with the King. What's the good in that?"

"I repeat, let me speak." Gordon began again, "In March General Washington's Army forced the British soldiers out of Boston with cannons brought over from Fort Ticonderoga. Not only the British soldiers and Major General Sir Thomas Gage, mind you, but Americans loyal to King George are gone from Boston! The New England Army lost some good men at the Battle of Bunker Hill. Breed's Hill is what made the difference. The cannons relocated from Fort Ticonderoga spoke loud and clear."

This was good news or bad news depending on who you were. Some of the people started to cheer, but then thought better of it when Major Gordon paused and raised his arm.

"The next bit of news is a little closer to home. The Continental Congress sent Benjamin Franklin up the Hudson, down Lake George and Lake Champlain, clear all the way to Montreal. They set off north in such a rush that they had to wait for the ice to clear out of Lake George. Franklin was sent to persuade the Provincial settlers to become a fourteenth colony. If anyone could talk those folks into kicking the British out of North America, it would be Franklin. Franklin's pushing seventy years. He went all that way only to find the British Army and English Loyalists crawling all over Montreal."

Gordon continued like he couldn't believe it himself. "Americans loyal to King George have abandoned their farms and taken refuge in Montreal." This was news to the local farmers loyal to the King, but they hid their shock as Gordon continued. Then, they lightened up and laughed as he described Ben Franklin's journey.

"Old Ben entertained people all along his trip with stories from *Poor Richard's Almanack*. He answered questions about his inventions and the parties with French King Louis. The French loved his stories and gave splendid parties in his honor."

While the people were laughing, Joseph looked toward his family, and Sam blinked back. That was the man he had interrupted.

After a huge sigh, Gordon continued. "I've got some bad news. The Continental Congress had hoped that the British might be forced out of Canada, but the Continental Army sent to Quebec last winter to fight for control of the St. Lawrence River failed. The British Army to our north is armed with cannons and well provisioned. We lost a good man in that miserable winter battle; General Montgomery has died of his wounds. But that's not all. Half the Continental Army got smallpox. The survivors are now at Fort Ticonderoga."

When Major Gordon had finished, the Balls Town farmers were speechless. They could meet the same fate. If the British were to the north, Balls Town would be in their path as the army advanced south to Albany and then on to Manhattan. The war could be fought near their farms.

Major Gordon called his men to attention. "Line up for roll call!" he barked. The Balls Town militia stood and faced their commander. This was their first muster, and they didn't know what to do. Their officer was dressed in a clean white shirt and buckskin trousers. He had brushed the dust from his hat and tied his hair neatly behind his head with a black ribbon.

When they finally formed a line, Gordon read each man's name off the list of Balls Town settlers. If there was no answer, there would have to be a good excuse, or else there would be time in the jail. That meant if a farmer was a Tory Loyalist and failed to muster, he could be put in jail.

When Joseph Rue's name was called, he answered with a firm, "Here." Then Matthew Rue's name was called and he responded, "Here."

Next the muskets were inspected. Those who had dirty barrels were sent to clean them and bring them back in good working order while the rest of the militia waited. Then Gordon had them form into two lines, and march within the fort grounds. There was no drum and the farmers looked a bit sloppy. Gordon shouted for his men to stand up straight. Joseph could only think of William and Samuel as he marched. He wished they were here or he was there.

By noon, the final inspections and drilling were over, and the women brought out their baskets. Joseph joined his family already seated on the grass. Anne passed out small pieces of cheese, bread, and berries. Matthew brought over a pitcher of cider to share. Anne thought of her burnt apple tree saplings. She would have no cider from her little trees.

Matthew told Sam and Lizzie to go over to Sally McDonald who was standing at the gate and buy a cake. He gave them each a penny. They rushed over with the other children. They could smell the hot gingerbread. Sally made the children line up to buy one of her sweet cakes. Sam had to buy Lizzie's, as she wouldn't get near Sally because the ghost storyteller, Marie McDonald, was passing out the gingerbread.

The beautiful cakes were toasted on the sides and gooey in the center. Sam's mouth watered before he'd even had a bite. The cake was delicious, and he ran back to his mother to give her half of his cake. Lizzie shared hers with Lucy. Joseph took a small bite. He would remember to bring pennies to the next muster. There was much running around playing tag, and Sam and Lizzie laughed with their new friends. Joseph and Anne lay back on the grass and rested. In no time, they were napping with Thomas.

Lucy was having a good time. One of the men began playing a fiddle, and two young men were trying to dance with her. She would swing off the arm of one, onto the arm of the other. Her petticoat twirled about her legs. Lucy was happy to laugh and dance. The morning had been so serious. She had begun to wonder if she had done the right thing by leaving the house, her sisters, and her parents. This was wild country, and she rarely had even seen another person her age until today and never danced before. The muster had changed all that.

The family loaded up in the wagon the next morning. Two nights at the fort had been long enough for Joseph, but not nearly long enough for Anne, Lucy, and the children. Before saying good-bye, the women had already planned the menu for the July muster and decided to take the children swimming in Long Lake. You could see the blue water of the lake from the fort look-out. By July, the water would be warm enough for even the little children to swim. It couldn't be colder than the creek.

As they turned to go up the hill to their cabin, Anne was the first to spot the single column of smoke. Joseph couldn't believe what he was seeing. He snapped the reins, and Yankee took off at a trot.

When they broke through the trees, Anne saw the cabin was still standing. The fire was just over the crest of the hill. Joseph reached for his musket and told everyone to stay low in the wagon. Sam peeked between his father's legs, and saw two horses – Francois's two horses!

"Father!" he yelled. "It's the fur trader!"

Francois's head appeared over the hill. He was dressed in the same clothes and as grubby as he had been the last time they saw him.

"Bonjour, Rues!" he bellowed out. "I have come back to ask to stay with you awhile!"

Then they could smell the wonderful aroma of roasting meat. Everyone jumped out of the wagon and raced to the cooking fire. Sure enough, roasting on the spit was a hind quarter of venison. Joseph laughed and smiled for the first time in weeks. The stress melted away from his face. He stood straight and held out his hand to Francois.

But there were more surprises, Sam ran to his rabbit trap now in the garden. He didn't know how he could possibly put bait in his trap that would be preferred over the tiny carrot tops now showing. He had buried the trap beneath the dirt hoping a careless rabbit would step on the trigger. It had worked. Now they would have rabbit for lunch and venison for dinner.

Francois laughed, "Sam, you are pretty smart garcon, one jump ahead of a rabbit, at least!" Sam blushed and then a heavy blanket of guilt fell over him. He remembered the day he gave away the rabbit.

Francois asked to stay on the hill with the Rues until winter. He explained to Joseph that it was too dangerous to be traveling through the woods right now. There were Indian campfires and fresh Indian tracks on the trails. He feared for his horses' lives as much as his own. This was no time to be collecting pelts anyway. Rather than go north to Canada for the summer, if it was all right with Joseph and Anne, he would stay on the hill and go back north in December. He would not sleep in the cabin. After the fine meal of venison, Joseph and Anne had no trouble saying yes.

The Frenchman slept in the dug-out den under the tree. Matthew was glad he spent his nights at the fort. Francois had a disgusting odor. Uncle Matt told Sam it was because of his smell that Francois was not bothered by the mosquitoes.

Joseph was happy to have another man on the hill. Even though Francois was a small man, he was strong. He was a good shot, and he never left his musket far from where he was working. Anne was glad that Francois decided to stay too. It meant they would have meat for dinner every day.

Anne's garden was growing; her herbs were growing in the side garden and hop vines were all over the stone walls. She thought to herself, *this hill may have stones, but the soil is good.* Her garden was looking better. The crows, rabbits, and deer had taken their share, but there were plenty young plants left.

Anne felt good. Thomas was sleeping through the night. What a difference an uninterrupted night of sleep made. And now they ate meat and fresh vegetables every day. For the first time since they brought the children to the hill, she and Joseph had walked down to the creek after lunch holding hands. Tomorrow morning Sam and Lizzie could pick strawberries.

That afternoon Anne was sitting by the door mending Joseph's torn shirt. Lizzie was taking her nap in the loft, and little Thomas was cooing in the crib by Anne's chair. Sam came over and sat by his mother. He talked in whispers. He told her about the Indian boy and the rabbit he had given away. Anne sat quietly for awhile.

Then she told Sam to go into the cabin and read. They would talk in the morning.

Anne's heart was thumping in her chest. Her hands shook as the thread and needle fell to her lap. Her happiness vanished and a deep fear took its place. She had just heard about the Indians from Major Gordon, then again from Francois. This was not adventure any more, nor was it exciting. She dropped her head to her chest, closed her eyes and prayed.

"Sam, last night after you went to sleep, your father and I talked about the Indian boy and the rabbit. You put yourself in danger and might have come to great harm. The Indians are all mixed up. Some are our friends, but most are our enemies. You've even heard Francois say he was afraid to be in the woods right now. You have to promise us not to leave the hill. I want to be able to see you and Lizzie from the cabin, always. That means you and your sister can not go down to the creek without your father. Do you understand?

Sam looked up at his mother and said he understood and he promised.

Then Anne went on. "About the rabbit, you knew we were in need of meat. You knew your family was depending on you to bring home the animals that you caught in your trap. You used poor judgment in giving the rabbit to the Indian boy. At the same time, we know that the sight of the starving boy must have shocked you. Your father and I think you did what your heart told you was the right thing to do. It is passed."

CHAPTER XI

Revolution

Describing George Washington:
"his uniform, house, horses, bearing of his staff –
appearances were of great importance: a leader must
look and act the part."

> *–1776, David McCullough*

The drill to go to the fort was the same as last month, only this time Francois was staying at the cabin, and Joseph was much relieved. He hitched up Yankee and the family loaded up. Their lane was barely a road. The horse picked her way around the biggest ruts and slowed the wagon's descent down the steepest part of the hill. It was later than usual, but sunsets were later now that it was summer. Joseph waved to someone at the corner and turned to the fort.

As the wagon rolled through the gate, Lucy spotted Reuben, one of the young men from the militia she had danced with last

107

month, leaning against the one of the horse stalls and searched for Jacobus. She kept her gaze low and spoke to Sam about the dust. "Does my hair look okay?"

Sam said, "It looks okay. It always looks okay."

Lucy said, "I mean, does it look especially nice?"

"What are you talking about? You washed it last night in the creek longer than it took me to wash and get a haircut."

Joseph pulled up the reins and jumped off the wagon. Then he helped Lizzie, reached for Thomas, and helped Anne down from the wagon. Lucy jumped off the back and waited for her brother to unhitch Yankee from the wagon. Then she led her over to the end stall, speaking kind words in the horse's ear.

Yankee brushed her head against Lucy with a little snort. Lucy figured that Yankee was thinking the same thing she was, a day off tomorrow.

Reuben walked toward her and said hello. "I gotta new shirt on today!"

Lucy looked at Reuben's shirt.

"Thought it would be nice to dance with a new shirt, don't you think?" Lucy shook her head yes.

She could hardly believe what she was hearing. Reuben had cleaned up so he could dance with her.

"Ol' Jacobus's going to be here soon. He'll probably want to dance with you, too"

Lucy looked toward the gate.

"I've been doing a little target practice so I can beat Jacobus during muster practice tomorrow. I bet he's been too busy working for his father at the mill to even look at his ol' musket," Rueben crowed.

Lucy didn't know what to say back to Reuben, so she excused herself and said she had to help with Lizzie and walked toward the women.

The single cannon outside the fort fired at dawn. People jumped from their mats. Then someone played a trumpet, rather badly. Major Gordon was standing on the lookout tower.

"We have declared our Independence from the wretched English," he yelled above the noise of the crowd. "A document has been signed. We are at war with England!"

He signaled his men to fire the cannon again.

The cannon rolled back as the flame shot out of the barrel. Then the shock of the blast was felt again by everyone. The horses screamed anew, and the boom rattled the camp kettles. The children covered their ears and watched the men load the cannon for still another blast.

Gordon yelled, "Fire!"

That was enough excitement for everyone. Gordon signaled his men to stop.

"Muster at 10:00 sharp!" He ordered.

The shaken families stumbled back to their cots and made normal motions to dress and cook their breakfast, but the shock of war and a Revolution could not be good news for the men or women.

At 10:00 o'clock, Gordon had the fort bell rung. The men lined up with their muskets. There were men missing. Gordon had the roll call taken, and marks were made by the names of the men who were missing.

Lucy searched the militia for Jacobus. Yes, he was there, standing by Reuben. He was passing his musket for inspection. Jacobus was standing tall, and even in his old clothes, Lucy could see how handsome he was even with his hair squashed under his hat. She hoped the fiddlers would come again.

No musket was dirty. The men marched around the outside of the fort to the thump of two logs hitting on each other. At least this time they had a beat. When Major Gordon was satisfied with their marching, he had them drill in loading their muskets, aiming at a target and shooting. It was now plain to see that farmers weren't much with a musket. They would practice again while the women and children went swimming. The children were afraid of the loud bangs, and the babies were crying.

That night Major Gordon hosted the men and their families to a fish fry. The fiddlers were there and so were the gingerbread cakes. Lizzie had made sure her father had brought pennies. She intended to eat a whole cake herself. Sam stood in line again and bought her cake. This time everyone had their own cake, except Lucy. She said she was much too full and would rather dance. But, Jacobus left after the musket practice. Lucy danced with Reuben.

The families left the fort at dawn.

With Francois and Matthew's help, the cellar was roofed with wide pine planks, then covered with large curls of elm bark, and weighted down with saplings and stones. The cellar foundation was plugged with small stones and sod inside and out. Joseph made a heavy wooden plank door for the cellar opening on the south side of the hill. The heavy iron door hinges and latch were purchased with money from the sale of the pelts. As the family inspected the cold cellar, Joseph shook the fur trader's hand in thanks again. Without Francois there would have been no money for such fine hardware.

Anne watched the men shake hands. They now had a secured room to hang meat and store their food, and Yankee would have a storage bin for her oats. Having the cellar closed in was a huge relief. Anne could now concentrate on harvesting her garden and storing the food and stop worrying about hungry Indians stealing her vegetables. In fact, none of her friends from the fort had mentioned Indians. She was beginning to think that her son had just seen a very hungry boy who had been stealing from Sam's trap.

The cabin was warm in late August. They had the small window in the loft open; the door let in a good breeze at night, but it was stuffy during the day. Anne asked Joseph to move the cooking fire further from the cabin, maybe under the shade of the maple tree. She had much work to do. Anne slept well that night. She dreamed of storing apples and carrots and sweet maple syrup. She even dreamed of chickens and fresh eggs and a tidy cabin.

The next morning Anne awoke with her dreams fully intact. The cabin still had crates of supplies pushed against the walls. "Joseph, I know it's hot and you have much to do, but now that the cellar is finished, can we clean up the cabin? We are going to need every inch of space when we're cooped up this winter."

As they went through the crates, they found books that Phebe had stuffed into the bolts of muslin. They also found the candlesticks that the cousins had dumped into the wagon at the last minute. Anne just sighed in disbelief and thought to herself, *how could I have been in this cabin for four months and never gone through all our possessions? Not even once!* "Joseph, what have I been doing?"

"You've been too busy to think about the crates," said her husband. "Plus, what's the use if you don't have a better place to put it!" Joseph took another load, of what could be stored in the damp cellar, out the door.

Anne sat down. They had done so much, yet there was so much more to do. She touched the locket at her neck and thought of her mother and how sad it must have been for her family when her mother had died. Then she thought of her father and how together they had laughed watching Joseph fall in the creek with a peach in his mouth. She wished her father was here now to see her children, especially little Thomas. Anne closed her eyes and fanned herself with her apron. She and Joseph had accomplished much. Someday, the saltbox would be sitting on the foundation. Someday, she would have a proper kitchen and a summer kitchen for hot days. Someday, she and Joseph would sleep with the cool evening breeze flowing over their bed, listening to the crickets.

"A package, Sam, Lizzie! A package!" Matthew was half running, half leaping up the back hill. His leggings were wet from crossing the Mourning Kill. His sweaty, tanned face was handsome in the afternoon sun. He called to his brother to hurry. "A package from home!"

Sam could not believe the words he heard from his Uncle Matt. Anne rushed out of the cabin, and Lucy stopped picking beans. Sam eagerly took the wrapped parcel from his uncle with *Sam and*

Lizzie Rue printed in big letters. "Let's wait for father," said Lizzie, but the twine was undone and the heavy brown paper fell away. Sam was looking at *Poor Richard's Almanack*. Tears of happiness rolled down his cheeks. He looked at his mother, couldn't say a word, his hands shook. His grandparents had sent him a book, the book read by the old man sitting on the stump, Benjamin Franklin. Sam just sat there and gently ran his fingers over the cover. He opened to the front page and there, hooked on a piece of muslin, were two beautifully tied flies on tiny fish hooks. They were just the right size for catching fish in the creek. Sam wiped his eyes with the sleeve of his shirt. He had so much to tell his grandfather.

Anne called again to Joseph to hurry. Out of breath, Joseph first asked to look at the flies and then saw the cover of the book. He smiled at his son and thought of his parents so far away. He wished they could see the happiness in their grandson's eyes.

But there was more! Tucked under the *Almanack* was another package with Lizzie's name written in big letters. Wrapped in red muslin was a doll's dress, pantaloons, and little leather boots. Lizzie screamed with joy.

"Grammie Phebe remembered me!" She ran into the cabin for her doll. And as the red cloth fell away, a letter dropped to the ground. Joseph picked up the letter and read:

> *July 4, 1776*
> *Dearest Family,*
>
> *We hope this letter finds you well this summer. You have no idea how many times a day we think of you. Samuel thinks of you ploughing your fields and building your cold cellar. He knows your vegetable garden is planted. He hopes the back hill has recovered from the burn. If we close our eyes we can see you riding in the wagon to the fort and sleeping safely under the watch of Matthew. We are very proud of him. We think of you splashing in the creek, maybe picking strawberries on the side of your*

hill and laughing with little Thomas. We miss you. Thank you, Anne and Lucy, for your letters. Lucy, dear daughter, we miss you and your strawberry patch is keeping me very busy.

There is much news from home – some very good, some unsettling. The good news is that we are well and William's family is well. Patience has a beau and Susanna thinks she has a beau – but he doesn't know it yet! Your new cousin Abby is always into mischief and Sarah is pregnant again and says she is feeling well. Your house and our cabin are just as you left them.

The crops are planted, and our garden is already producing peas, beans, and carrots. We have had enough rain to germinate the field seed, and William is expecting a good harvest of wheat and oats. He also put in some buckwheat, so we can look forward to pancakes for breakfast next winter. We hope you get lots of maple syrup from your big maple trees next spring. Samuel thinks our late spring frosts might mean a smaller crop of peaches and cherries, but it's too soon to tell.

There is extraordinary news from Philadelphia. On July 2 a document was signed by our new government officials declaring our independence from England. This should make the King of England very angry, but Loyalists have bragged to us that it will only humor him. Two days after the signing it was already printed. Samuel saw the Declaration of Independence tacked on the town hall tavern door this morning.

Word has gone out from our new government that farmers must be prepared to feed General Washington's Army. Samuel says we will be paid by the Congress for the food we sell them, but at this

*time we are not worried about being paid so much as
how can we feed an army of hundreds of men?*

*We have decided that the best thing to do is
wait for the fruit to ripen and then pick what we can
and move to the safety of your house. We shall stay
with William and Sarah until it is safe to come home.
The soldiers will probably take over our orchard and
garden, and we are prepared to let it happen. They
will need food if they are to fight a war. They will
surely be risking their lives for our freedoms. William
will come for us in his wagon when we're ready. We
shall take as much from the cabin as we can with us.*

We send our love and miss you all very much.

Samuel and Phebe

Joseph finished the letter and carefully folded the sheets of
brown paper. He gave it to Anne and asked her to put it safely in her
trunk under the floor boards. He told Sam to save the wrapping paper
and write a thank you note from him and Lizzie. They would mail it
from the trading post at the next muster. He headed back to the cellar
with another load.

Anne's vegetable harvest was large and beyond her
expectations. Now the hard work began. Sam handed his mother the
big carrots and watched as she carefully loaded them into barrels. His
father had traded extra pine logs for Major Gordon's extra barrels. By
burying the carrots in dry sand in the barrels, the carrots would last
the winter and not rot in the cold cellar. His mother hadn't dug the
potatoes yet, but Francois had already offered to help with the
digging.

He didn't tell his father, but Sam kind of guessed Francois
was sweet on his mother. He hauled water for her and helped with the
firewood. He loved her muffins and liked being around a good-
looking woman. He was a Frenchman, after all. Sam was learning
facts like that from the *Almanack*.

Most of the onion tops had been bent over and the ones still standing would be harvested for the seed pods on top; the same story with the beans. Anne let the beans from the strongest plants keep right on growing. Before frost Lizzie opened the dry bean shells and put the hard beans in a sack. Some would be seed for next year's garden, but most would be soaked and cooked in soups. The cellar was filling up.

In the back of the field, almost at the same height as the hay and oats, were corn plants, dozens of corn plants in tidy hills. No one could explain the mysterious appearance of the plants. By the second hay cutting in September, the corn stalks were as tall as Joseph. The family and Francois now stood in the field looking at the tasseled ears of corn fat with seed. Lizzie thought this was a miracle, and Sam was guessing who might have planted the corn. Joseph let them guess and then helped Lizzie explain the mystery by saying, "The Indian corn will keep in the cellar."

Lizzie gasped and said, "Papa, maybe Indians planted the corn."

Anne and Joseph looked at each other, and then asked Sam to tell his story about the trap and the rabbit and the hungry Indian boy.

When he had finished, Francois simply said, "There are good Indians and bad Indians, just like there are good Frenchies and bad Frenchies. One thing about the Indians is that they are smart, and they will fight on the side of the army they think will win."

No one spoke. Sam looked at his mother. He wished she knew the Indian boy. She wouldn't be so afraid.

CHAPTER XII

No muster planned

There was no muster in September. Gordon's militia was too busy harvesting and preparing their farms for winter. Lizzie had her own surprise to announce after the first frost. As she went looking for flowers in the weedy stone fence, she found the dried up vines now attached to orange, yellow and green gourds.

Lizzie ran up the hill to the cabin shouting the news, "I found big growing things, big orange fruits."

Joseph could not help smiling. He had sent Sam and Lizzie to discover the gourds. "Papa, did the Indians plant these fruits, too?" asked Lizzie.

"Maybe. Yes, I think they did Lizzie, and they are called squash and the big orange squash are called pumpkins," said Joseph.

"Sam, can you carry those heavy pumpkins?" asked his mother.

"How about if we roll them?" teased Sam, winking at his father as he picked up a pumpkin and followed his mother back up the hill.

Joseph looked at Lizzie and said, "I think we owe our Indian boy a thank you, don't you?"

"Oh yes, Papa, but where is he?"

"Hiding in the woods, I suspect. Maybe the best thank you would be to share some of the corn and pumpkins with him this winter," said Joseph.

Anne walked into the cold cellar. She would ask her husband to build shelves for the squash. They might rot on the cold, bare dirt. Better that they were up off the ground and not touching. As she looked around the cellar, she knew that her family would not starve. Francois and Sam had made jerky from the smaller pieces of venison and smoked pheasants were hanging from the cellar beams. Francois had declined to help with the haying as it made him sneeze, but hunting he could do. The deerskin was racked and drying, and Sam again was at Francois's elbow as he scraped the beautiful hide. Anne had watched the Frenchman and her son as they worked together and knew that each was filling a space of a dear family member and it was good. Anne knew that Sam was very fond of Francois. He had told her he wanted to hunt with Francois one day, to travel north and west and see the America Francois knew.

Francois hadn't talked about leaving. *I feel his affection,* she thought, *maybe it is my dark coffee and hot biscuits.* She laughed. But she felt it was more than that. Their long talks in the mornings as they worked side by side in the garden were comfortable times for both. Francois had not spoken of a family. Again she thought to herself, *I feel sure he has been married, and there were children.* She knew the Frenchman had grown accustomed to the warmth of a fire.

Anne focused again on her larder. "What are missing are apples." She stepped outside the cold cellar to ask Joseph about apples. Standing in the sun, she watched as a small parade came toward her from the far stone wall, first Lizzie holding two squash, then Sam with a second armload of squash, then Joseph with two big pumpkins.

"There's more to come!" yelled Lizzie.

"And there's more after that to come, Mother!" said Sam.

"Joseph, I will need shelves. And what about apples? We sure could use a bushel or two of apples. Maybe we should think about planting a few trees before the ground freezes."

"Starting an orchard now? That's a whole other story. It's almost winter and I have yet to build a shed for the horse and a barn for the hay that is piled and waiting in the field ready to be turned. That hay will rot if it's not undercover before winter. That comes before an apple orchard. And I thought you wanted a chicken coop first." Joseph looked exhausted.

But, Anne countered, "We should plant fruit trees and get them growing now. It takes years for trees to bear fruit. Father would plant new trees in the fall so they would be ready to grow in the spring. Don't you remember Father's peaches?" she said with a smile.

"Anne, I will do my best, but not this year. The orchard must wait."

The children were listening and could almost taste one of Grandfather Rue's juicy apples.

"The wood lot to the west would be a good place for fruit trees. It would drain well," said Anne, not yet ready to give up. "I have been looking forward to making apple cobbler and drying apples with the children." She knew Lizzie would love to thread the apple rings and hang them about the cabin. "Then there are little Christmas decorations we could make with dried apples, maybe a crèche of apple head dolls for Mary and Joseph and Baby Jesus."

Joseph threw up his hands. "I will ask Lydia's husband if he has apples for sale!" He knew they had a good crop, but he had planned on buying only cider not apples, too. "We will plant an orchard next year."

The children were happy. Apples, cider. This was the first time Lizzie had really watched as food was stored for winter. Last winter she and Sam were with Aunt Sarah and Uncle William at the house. Their cold cellar wasn't near as big as this one. Lizzie loved her new cabin, even if it wasn't a house.

"BOOM!"

"That's the call to the fort. I'll be back as soon as I can."

Joseph grabbed his musket and supplies and ran down the back hill.

"I'm sorry to call you from your work." Major Gordon got right down to business when most of the men had arrived. "I know you have much to do before winter, but you must know what is happening. Manhattan has been taken by English General Sir William Howe. Ships unloaded hundreds of soldiers, and Long Island has been completely overrun. The farms have been stripped of food. British losses were minor. The Continental Army, on the other hand, retreated and fled Long Island." Major Gordon paused, and then continued. "General Washington managed to bring his soldiers safely to the New York shore in fishing boats brought down from Massachusetts by John Glover's men. Then, his army, or what was left of it, marched north to Kingsbridge. They have made camp up the Hudson River."

Joseph knew that Washington's Army was close to his father's cabin. He hoped William had come for them and taken them to the house.

"The Continentals are low on powder. They are melting down lead from window sashes to make bullets. Men, Washington's Army is in bad shape. He has little hope of winning even a small skirmish. If General Howe had followed them, we might not even have an army," said Gordon. "The Continental Congress has moved its operations to Baltimore. Our government documents, including the Declaration of Independence, must be preserved at all cost. The men who signed the Declaration will be hung as traitors if the document falls into British hands."

The crowd of men was silent. Major Gordon went on. "Washington needed information about what Howe would do next and sent his spies into Manhattan. Word came back that half of the city's shops and homes had mysteriously burned to the ground one night. Washington's spies also heard some drunken British soldiers boasting about the plan to win the war. The plan was to divide the thirteen colonies in half. They joked, saying:

> "'The New England colonies will be easy to recover once they lack support from the New York colony. Most of New England's citizens are King's Men anyway. That rebellious Massachusetts militia and their little Tea Party in Boston Harbor involved but a few men. Paul Revere and Samuel Adams can easily be captured.'"

"How do you like that?" asked the Major. Some men muttered in anger to each other, but some only nodded their heads in disbelief or was it agreement?

"The Redcoat kept bragging," said Gordon. "*We control the seas. Without ships, there will be no rum for the poor Americans!*' The British soldiers had laughed and slapped themselves on the back."

But as Gordon continued, the one big reason the British knew they would win the war was because the King had bought fierce soldiers from his cousin, Wilhelm, to fight alongside his men. The German men from Hesse were highly trained and fearless soldiers. The Hessians had taken no prisoners when they chased the American Army off Manhattan Island the night of the Continentals escape by boat.

Again, at Gordon's pause, the crowd was silent. Their 25 militia men would be no match for these soldiers. Joseph looked at his brother. Major Gordon said the threat was real. General Howe was planning a three-way attack against the Americans. One force would strike from the west coming across the Mohawk Valley. A second army would sail up the Hudson, and the third and most powerful strike would be down the Champlain Valley from Canada. The battleground would be in the New York colony. This Northern Army of English Redcoats, German Hessians, and the fierce Canadian Indians would converge on Albany and defeat the Americans once and for all. The new American government would surrender.

The militia trained and practiced with their muskets away from the fort. Some of the men still hadn't improved. Their wild shots were just wasting good powder. Major Gordon decided to split the militia in two. Half of his men would shoot, and the other half would load. This way the better marksman would always have a loaded musket.

None of their muskets had bayonets. The Balls Town militia would carry hatchets to defend them in hand-to-hand combat. The knowledge that they might be fighting German soldiers with body armor was sobering. They would have to be cunning and skillful, Gordon had told them.

"You must hide behind the trees and only shoot when you have a clear target. You must watch out for each other and not let the enemy surround you and attack from behind. There will be New York militias and militias from as far away as Boston, Connecticut, and Rhode Island. Rogers Rangers have been alerted, and Ethan Allen's Green Mountain Boys have promised to fight."

Taking in a long breath, "You all must be ready to fight at a minute's notice. The militias will swell our numbers. If you hear the fort cannon, pack food for a week, and meet here. Be sure to tell your families to be on guard. If they are afraid to stay alone, bring them with you, and as much food as you can carry to the fort. General Washington says the Indians will take advantage of the war and may rob your farms. You need to think about what food you can spare to give to the Continentals." With that, Major Gordon turned and mounted his horse. He waved to his men and left for his house.

The men did not tell their wives all the details of the training, but the woman had their own way of finding out these things, and word passed quickly among them.

Joseph said nothing about the muster, only that he needed to build a shed for the horse before winter.

Before Francois left, he and Joseph harnessed the three horses and dragged two trees to the mill. They brought only some of the boards back in the wagon. Gordon would mill the remaining trees in the spring when the Mourning Kill was flowing faster. Yankee now had a shed and stall of sorts. It was closed on three sides and the roof hung over the opening at least a foot. The shed was just a short distance from the cabin.

Joseph, with Lucy's help, had loaded most of the piled hay into the wagon and stacked it out of the wind by the door to the cold cellar. It wasn't under cover, but it had large pieces of bark weighted down with stones. This would have to do.

The tied oat bundles were still in the field ripening. Joseph would take these to Mill Town where Jacobus's father had a thrasher. It would be a race to the end to save the oats from the bad weather.

The six bushels of apples and two barrels of cider were bought and stored. Joseph said he would finish up the oats this week and then rest a couple of days before chopping firewood.

The fort was cold and barren. With a gray sky and a good stiff north breeze, the men were in a hurry to get the practice over and head for home. The families had come as always, but there was no social. Everyone realized winter was near. The trees had lost all of their plumage. The dullness of frosted, dead hay and blowing dirt kicked up by the horses had left the women in bad spirits.

They had come for news, not to muster. Not knowing when the first heavy snow would fall, Major Gordon decided this would be a short meeting and the next muster would be in the new year when the roads were clear of snow and ice. The last thing that he wanted was a fort full of snowed-in farmers with hungry families. After the lunch, Gordon gathered the militia and their families together in the corner of the fort, out of the wind.

"Major Arnold has stopped the British advance at Fort Ticonderoga," began Gordon. "The Redcoats under Sir Guy Carleton have turned back to Canada. Benedict Arnold and a small flotilla of boats quickly built on site by men from Schenectady delayed them. The weather even turned against Carleton's fleet pushing them back north. It seems Carleton's spies were passed some bad information that Fort Ti was heavily fortified." Gordon winked.

"Carlton has been outsmarted by the Army, the militia, and the weather. Seems he hadn't even brought enough food. They turned their bateaux around and returned to Canada hungry." Gordon smiled, "General Washington has put General Gates's men in charge of Fort Ticonderoga, and the small company of Continentals will spend the winter at the Fort." The crowd cheered. An American victory, no matter how small, was good news. "Patriots of Balls Town, we are at war!" shouted their leader. The men cheered again, but it was not a happy cheer like the first. "Reverend Ball, will you lead us in prayer?"

The Americans stood and took off their hats, bowed their heads in prayer as the Reverend stood before them.

"Good people of Balls Town, our newly formed government declared us an independent nation. We humbly pray that in achieving these new freedoms and forming this union with our neighboring colonies, we will be a country like no other. We hold dear the individual freedoms that God has seen fit to give us as men, women, and children. Bless the men of the Balls Town militia that they may fight with courage and honor in the days ahead. Bless the families who send these brave men to battle, that they may survive what ever should befall them. Amen."

With that, he turned to Major Gordon. The Major turned, saluted his men, and walked to his horse. The fort would be closed until spring.

By mid-December the rain had turned to snow. The little cabin was crowded and when Thomas started to fuss, it got even smaller. The days were so short and the nights so long, that they were burning candles in the cabin by five o'clock. Anne made some firm rules for the children. Unless it was raining, Sam and Lizzie had to go outside and play a couple of hours each day. This was important to keep them hardened to the cold and to keep their bodies exercised. This worked until it got really cold. Then only Sam could go out and make a quick dash to the cellar for a squash for his mother. But most days, if the sun was shining, the children played off the south side of the hill and out of the wind. On cold days Francois went hunting, often gone for weeks.

After a snowfall, Sam went looking for animal tracks. Francois had drawn animal tracks on Sam's school book cover. He told him that during the night, the animals walked around the cabin, and it was true. Sam took his book and tried to match the tracks in the snow with Francois's drawings. Sam was already keeping a diary in the book with Francois's tracks. Anne had told him it was all right to write in his school book. He wrote the date and then some of the things he did each day. He called it *Poor Sam's Almanack*.

He had identified deer, rabbit, martin, and porcupine tracks. Before the creek froze, he could see where the ducks had spent the night, too. His father had knocked apart the beaver dam because it backed up the creek and made a pond. After that, a fast-flowing creek carried their timber to the mill. As much as Sam looked, he didn't find any beaver tracks. But he did find turkey tracks, and it must have been a good-size turkey as its landing had dumped the turkey deep in the drift.

They all missed Francois when he was off in the woods. He had such a merry sense of humor and kept them laughing at themselves. Plus, he always had a tale to tell about one of his Canadian adventures. Francois's stories were so real that Sam sometimes felt as though he were riding Lulu and exploring some undiscovered river in far-off Canada where the fish were so big that you had to tug your pole with all your might to keep from falling into the river. When Lucy would ask him how he could trap a beautiful red fox, Francois would say, "C'est la vie, Mademoiselle Lucy."

Lucy had plenty of chores, so she was in and out and riding to the McKnights often enough to keep Yankee exercised. Sometimes Lizzie went along riding in front of her aunt on the horse. Lizzie liked visiting the McKnights. Mrs. McKnight always gave her a little treat, and Lizzie loved playing with their cat. The McKnight's daughters were a little older than Lizzie and made a fuss over her while Lucy was out in the barn. Their little sister had died from pneumonia last winter.

Joseph spent a part of each day splitting logs for firewood. Sam would stack the wood inside the horse shed. He and Lucy had raked the damp maple leaves and packed them against the north side of the cabin. The corn stalks held everything in place. They would soon freeze and be covered by snow. The barrier would insulate the cabin against the wind. Joseph had woven a blanket of tree limbs to cover the well, and he hoped that it would help to keep the well water from freezing.

Anne worried about Thomas. Children at the fort were sneezing and coughing at the muster, and now Thomas had a bad cold. She and Lucy took turns feeding him broth and holding him at night so he could breathe. The smoky fire didn't help.

To keep the children occupied during the day, Anne organized projects. On afternoons they took the dried herbs and made bouquets to hang about the cabin, or Anne sliced apples and they strung them around the fireplace to dry. One day when the snow turned to rain beating on the cabin roof, she made apple head dolls. Anne got out little scraps of her quilting materials and Anne, Lucy, and Lizzie made skirts and trousers for the little stuffed bodies with wrinkled apple heads.

Sam didn't care about making dolls and would check his trap or go to the field where his father was working and pile the loose cut limbs into big burning piles. He couldn't stay as warm as Joseph who was actually sweating as he felled the tall trees. It was hard work. Sam wished he had a friend.

Sometimes Matthew would stop to visit if he had been to Schenectady for Major Gordon. But there was no news from home. They all prayed for word from the families before the snows closed the roads and Balls Town would be isolated from all news from the colonies.

A week before Christmas, it began to snow. Sam and Lizzie made little presents for everyone. Lizzie worked on the table in front of the fire, but Sam worked in secret in the loft. Joseph spent each evening carving by the fire. Nobody was allowed to peek. Last year they had all opened the presents that Joseph had bought with his profit from the furs. He had given Anne a looking glass and Sam a spy glass. He had carved a cradle for Lizzie's doll and made a small chair for Thomas to use when he was old enough to sit at the table. This Christmas would be a quiet Christmas.

Anne and Joseph put on their coats and stepped outside the cabin. It was Christmas Eve. The stars were so bright that you could see your way through the dark. They walked over to Yankee and gave her some extra oats. Joseph had put a wreath on the horse stall just as he hoped his father was doing tonight. Joseph thought of home. "This is where Jesus was born, Father would say, in a lowly stable with stars shining overhead." Tears rushed down Anne's cheeks as she remembered her father.

On December 26, the Continental Army was crossing the icy Delaware River in overloaded boats filled with troops and cannons. General Washington would lead one more attempt to defeat General Howe's Army before December 31.

CHAPTER XIII

Nor'easter

"A stitch in time saves nine! BF" announced Sam as he wrote the words in his *Almanack.* "That's what Ben would tell you," he teased.

"If I hear one more quote from Benjamin Franklin, I'll...oh...!" said Lucy.

Anne was helping Lucy with a new skirt, and Lucy's sewing wasn't going well. She was forever forgetting what she was doing and had to rip out her stitches, rethread her needle, and start the seam again. Lucy missed seeing her friends at the fort and often asked Joseph if she could ride Yankee to the fort someday. But Joseph always said no. Sam was recording the wet January weather in his *Almanack:*

> *South breeze all week. Big melt during the day and slushy, but frozen and slippery at night. Straw showing, the snow is almost gone. The path to Yankee is gross. Lucy is very unhappy. I slipped twice, my boots are drying by the fire. SR*

The soft-packed snow melted during the day and froze into smooth hard-packed ice at night. Footprints in the snow would now freeze at night and be wet during the day. Everywhere they walked, the paths were treacherous. Joseph threw fireplace ash by the door and on the path to the outhouse. The small cinders kept everyone from slipping but were terrible when tracked into the cabin.

Anne complained. "Why doesn't it snow again?" After a week of mild winter weather, bare ground was beginning to show, and by Saturday the lane down the hill was free of snow.

Inside the dark damp cabin, Thomas was fussing; he still wasn't over his cold. Lately, he was pulling on his ears, and Anne was worried. Lizzie had a slight cough, and Sam was cranky. This was a bad time of the year to get sick. With the gray sky and a cooped-up family, Anne was at her wit's end. Try as she did this past week to keep her children occupied with songs and stories, they picked on each other and slept fitfully.

Sam was up with Joseph at dawn. Anne was saving the candles for evenings, so Joseph poked the banked fire and added logs to warm the cabin and provide some light. He whispered to Sam to be quiet. Anne had been up most of the night with Thomas. Joseph went to the well for water, while Sam made his morning inspection of their hill.

He first checked for new animal tracks. The dirt around the cabin was still frozen. Whatever animals had been by in the night had not left tracks. Then he headed out to the boulder to check on the Liberty Tree. It was okay. He repacked the dried weeds and leaves around the base of the tree, just as his grandfather would do. Then he half-walked and half-slid down the hill to the creek. Being very quiet and trying hard not to fall, he slowly approached the Mourning Kill. There was ice along the edge, but in the middle, the water was freely flowing. It would have to get much colder for the creek's surface to freeze solid again.

Just as he was turning to climb back up the hill, out of the corner of his eye he thought he saw something move. He stood very still. The sun was just beginning to brighten the sky, but it was still hard to see. He stood for what seemed a long time before the animal made a break for the back hill. It looked like a small wolf or a fox. Sam was not afraid. He heard his mother calling to him for breakfast.

Entering the cabin, he could see that Lucy was in a bad mood. She and Anne were having a terrible fight. Lucy wanted to ride Yankee somewhere. She said she could not stay another day in the cabin with children sniffling and coughing all around her. She wanted to wash her hair and was tired of her clothes, and bored with her sewing and on and on. Joseph ate his oatmeal and apple slices without comment. Now, looking up, he could see from Anne's expression that he had better say something to his sister, and it had better be quick.

"Lucy, I've changed my mind," interrupted her brother. "Yankee needs a long walk. She's kicking the back of the shed so badly that I will have to replace a couple boards before the month is through. How would you like to go to the trading post today and mail my letter home?"

Lucy almost choked on her oatmeal. "I would love to go."

"Then that's settled," said Joseph. "Sam, do you think you can find your thank-you note to your grandparents? Let's get that in the Post." Sam climbed into the loft and jumped down with the note he had forgotten to send to Phebe and Samuel.

"Good," said his father, "Why don't you and Lucy make the trip?"

Lucy let out a groan. "Why can't I go by myself?"

"Well, Sam needs to mail his own letter, and I thought maybe Mrs. McDonald might have paper for sale, being the King's Post. *Poor Sam's Almanack* is making a pretty good mess of the school book. Plus, I think both of you deserve a break from your chores. I have written a letter to Uncle William. Maybe you could stop by the mill and check with Matthew if he has a letter to post."

Lucy agreed. She would not provoke her brother's anger this morning. A trip to McDonald's Trading Post was definitely in the right direction. Joseph gave her money for the Post carrier and paper for Sam and some extra for treats.

Lizzie was disappointed and crying. "I want to go!"

Anne was a bit put out, too. "Why don't we hitch up the wagon and all of us take a break?" Then Thomas started to cough, and Anne realized she could not go with a sick child. Joseph kissed Anne, patted Thomas's sweaty head, picked up his axe and sharpening stone, and headed out the door.

Lucy was all in a tizzy. First she had to fetch a pail of water from the well. The water would be so cold that she would have to heat it in the kettle over the fire. She must wash her hair! Her pantaloons were clean, but her coat had mud on the front that she hadn't washed off. Sam, however, was ready.

Lucy told him to find something to do and quit nagging her to hurry. He took his book and went back down to the creek. This time he found some tracks in the mud that were fresh, and it looked like a fox had made them. He found a second set just a little smaller farther down the creek. He would come back tomorrow later in the morning.

By the time Lucy was ready Sam had filled the wood box, brought more water for his mother, and swept the cinders out of the cabin. Anne had fed Thomas his oatmeal and nursed him. He had gulped and choked on Anne's milk because his nose was so stuffed. Now he was crying, and Anne was trying to get him to take a morning nap. While everyone was out, she and Lizzie would have a little quiet time and peel vegetables and make soup for dinner.

"Sam, fetch onions, potatoes, a small squash, some carrots and a good piece of venison. This family needs a hearty meal in this horrid damp weather. Here, take the basket and bring four apples, too. I'll make a cobbler," said Anne.

Lizzie was happy with anything that sounded like a treat, and cobbler was close to the top of her list. She and her mother would cook and bake while the others were out.

Sam took the basket and went to the cold cellar. He lifted the latch, opened the door wide and waited for his eyes to adjust to the dark. But before his eyes could really see in the dark cellar, he walked straight into a cobweb.

"Ugh!" He wiped the spider's web off of his face and out of his hair with the tail of his shirt, then walked into the back of the cellar, reached down and got a big onion and five potatoes. When his hand reached up above his head to the squash shelf, it felt nothing. There wasn't a squash. He had been keeping track of the vegetables and was working his way down the shelf. His hand reached again to the place where the next squash should be and felt instead a small rock.

He took the rock back to the door and in the light saw that it wasn't a rock at all, but a kernel of Indian corn. Sam put it in his pocket, went back for the carrots, apples, and meat and shut up the cold cellar quickly. He raced back to the cabin to tell his mother.

But Lucy was finally ready, and she had the horse bridled. She and Anne were arguing about her hair. It was still wet and she wouldn't take the time to dry it by the fire.

Anne insisted, "I don't want another sick person in this cabin."

Lucy calmly replied, "I'll be warm on the horse, don't worry." She climbed up on Yankee's back and with a little kick, headed down the hill.

Sam handed his mother the basket, ran into the cabin and grabbed his cap and light coat, said good-bye to Lizzie and ran after Yankee. He jumped on the horse's back almost pulling Lucy off as he grabbed her waist. Anne went back into the cabin and shut the door.

Sam was riding close behind Lucy on the horse's back. Yankee had started out at a walk, but as she limbered up, was now at a fast trot. Sam had Lucy's blowing wet hair in his face and was tightly hanging on to Lucy's waist on the boney, bumpy ride down the hill. Lucy, on the other hand, was first humming and now happily talking to him, "Do you believe my brother is letting me go to the trading post by myself?"

He loved his Aunt Lucy. Actually she wasn't all by herself, but he didn't say anything. She was the big sister he would never have had if she hadn't begged to come to Balls Town. Lucy was a good rider and knew Yankee's ways. Sam knew Yankee would do anything for Lucy.

Their first stop was at the sawmill where Matthew gave them a big welcome, and Major Gordon asked about Anne and Joseph. Matthew hadn't had any time at all to write letters, but scribbled a hello on the back of the letter to his parents. Then they were off again. Lucy took a couple of short cuts through the woods that just happened to go by the fort. But Joseph had been right, the gate was closed and there was no sign of anyone.

By this time, both Sam and Lucy were cold. Even though it was just above freezing, without sun and riding against the damp east wind, the air felt extra cold. Sliding off Yankee's back at the McDonald Brothers Trading Post, Yankee was all warmed up, but Lucy and Sam were chilled down. They burst into the trading post with rosy cheeks and cold hands.

Sally McDonald welcomed them with one of her big smiles. She invited them to sit by the fire while she warmed up mugs of apple cider. Here was a woman who loved to see children and knew just what to do. She just happened to have a couple of gingerbread cakes left. Since she had made them three days ago, she wouldn't take any money for the hard cakes.

"I haven't seen the Post carrier since before Christmas," she said. "Word from Manhattan just isn't getting through. Mr. McDonald made a quick trip to Schenectady, but there were no letters for people in Balls Town." She didn't think it had anything to do with the weather, as the river was not frozen and the ground was bare clear to Albany. She took the letters from Sam. "I'll hold your letters for the carrier."

Lucy asked, "Mrs. McDonald, do you sell writing paper?" Sally said no, but she had some blank sheets of her own that they might have. Sam started talking about *Poor Sam's Almanack* and how he kept records until Mrs. McDonald excused herself to get the paper.

Lucy was wandering around the store wiggling her cold toes. She could hear Mrs. McDonald talking to her sister-in-law, Marie. Then Lucy heard nothing. Marie's mother was a Mohawk Indian and Marie had grown up at Sir William Johnson's fine home and schooled with his children.

Suddenly, Marie was beside Sam and startled him. "Sam, I haven't seen you in a while. You're growing tall and looking well." She asked him about his parents, Lizzie, and Thomas.

Sam blabbed just about everything that had happened since the last muster. Marie now knew his family's history to date. Lucy came over and gave him a poke in the back, and he quieted down. When he turned back, Marie had disappeared. Lucy paid Mrs. McDonald for the postage, smiled and put her last bite of the dry gingerbread cake in her mouth.

At that very instant, Jacobus Rogers yanked open the door and walked into the store. When Jacobus said hello, Lucy couldn't speak but blushed scarlet. She tried to swallow, but the dry cake didn't move. He smiled and turned to Sam, "Hello, Sam."

Sam had no trouble saying hello back, and they were soon talking about traps and animal tracks. Jacobus thought that Sam probably did see a fox. "They are in their winter fur colors right now and will blend in so well with the snow that you'll never see them unless they move. If there is a pair, like you think, you might find a den of kits in the spring. Keep tracking!"

Sam listened to Jacobus's every word. When conversation is limited, every word is worth remembering! By this time, Mrs. McDonald was back with a small package of paper. "How's Lizzie?" she asked, and Sam said, "Good."

"Here's a gingerbread cake for Lizzie. And here's a little sack of herbs from Marie that your mother can boil and give the syrup to little Thomas. It will help him breathe easier at night." Sam thanked her and stuffed the cake and sack inside his shirt.

Jacobus was talking to Lucy now. He warned they better be heading home. "We're due for a change in the weather. When that wind comes blowing out of the northeast like it is today, you might find yourself in a snowstorm in a couple of hours."

Lucy and Sam said good-bye, got back on Yankee, and headed home. They were just past the fort when the first snowflakes swirled around them. The storm was coming from the east; in no time Sam's jacket was white. Lucy nudged Yankee to go a little faster.

As they had reached Gordon's mill, the snow was piling up on the road and blowing into shallow drifts. "Should we stop?" shouted Sam.

Lucy turned her head, "We're almost home. Let's keep going, Joseph will be worried." Lucy knew the turnoff to their lane should be coming soon, but the storm had become a whiteout and Lucy couldn't see the lane or their hill. She bent over Yankee's neck and shouted over the wind, "Take us home, Yankee girl, help us find our way home!"

The mare lowered her head, continued walking, and after what seemed a long time to Sam, started up a hill. The snow was making little drifts across their trail, and Yankee stepped through them, not changing direction, but always climbing up the hill. As the wind blew harder and the distance from the safety of the mill increased, Yankee raised her head, then, snorted. Sam thought he heard a whistle. He wasn't really sure what he heard, but there it was again. Yankee heard it too and moved quicker, now to the left in the direction of the whistle.

Sam looked over his shoulder and saw their tracks being covered by the blowing snow. The temperature had dropped. He felt Lucy shiver. They were both getting cold, and Yankee was walking even slower now, breaking trail. Sam thought they might be heading up the steepest part of the hill and gripped with his knees so not to pull them both off the horse's back. Lucy was careful not to hurry the horse. She let Yankee walk at her own pace. She knew there were potholes covered with snow if they were on the lane.

The storm had brought winter back to Balls Town. Sam wished he'd worn his mittens and his heavy coat. Then he heard a familiar voice and saw a dark shape in their path. It sounded like his father. They heard the voice again, and called back. He called again, now closer, and they called back. Joseph was now in sight. He had his musket and a blanket thrown over his back. He had come half way down the hill searching for them. As soon as they saw him, they shouted their relief.

Yankee brought them home; she found the way. Joseph told Lucy to follow him, and when they reached the cabin, Sam jumped off and hugged his father. Joseph led the horse into the shed while Lucy followed. She buried her head in the horse's thick mane hugged Yankee's head, and then kissed her wet nose.

"You saved our lives. We would have been lost in the storm," she tearfully whispered into the horse's ear. The horse let Lucy hold her head close.

"Sam, fetch more oats from the cellar," ordered his father. "I'll dry her off. Then you both better get in by the fire."

When Sam returned with the oats, he was shaking. "Did Yankee really save our lives?"

"I would say she did. I was only a short distance down the hill. I would not have seen your tracks in the blowing snow," said his father as he continued to dry the horse's shaggy winter coat.

Sam tried to hug the big horse, and the horse lowered her head and nibbled at Sam's wet hair, then Sam ran after Lucy to the cabin.

Lucy and Sam stumbled into the cabin. Their hands and feet were very cold. Anne gave them more big hugs and told them to sit by the fire. As she shook snow from their coats, it hissed on the hot stones around the hearth.

Joseph came in and said how he had been wrong to let them go out today. He should have read the sunrise better. "Nor'easters are nothing to take lightly. I'm afraid this storm will close the trails again for a week or more."

"Father, will Yankee be warm enough in the shed tonight?" asked Sam.

"Yankee will be safe now that she is dry and fed. Her thick coat will keep her plenty warm as long as she is dry and out of the wind."

After the family had eaten the rich venison stew and apple cobbler that Lizzie proudly reminded everyone she had helped to make, Sam remembered the kernel of Indian corn. He told his parents what he had found on the shelf.

Joseph looked up at the children. "I think we all must understand what's happening. I think the mystery of the corn and squash growing in the garden has been solved. Lizzie, you made a good guess, the pumpkins may have been planted by Indians, too, just like the corn. I will watch for tracks in the snow. I want you all to be very careful and if you see the Indian boy, come to me at once. It doesn't seem like he will harm us, but there are other Indians in the woods who would rob us. Remember, there are good Indians and bad Indians, just like there good settlers and bad settlers. And now we know there are hungry Indians."

Anne finished boiling down the roots that Marie had tied in a bundle and Sally had passed to Sam. Anne spooned the thick syrup into little Thomas's mouth. He didn't like the taste and turned to the side. She put a little sugar on the tip of the spoon and tried again to feed the baby. This time Thomas's chapped lips sucked the sweetened syrup.

Before bed, Joseph retold the old story of his parent's trip across the cold Atlantic Ocean to America. The children listened to their father as he explained it was the friendly Delaware Indians that brought fish and clams to the island where Phebe and Samuel were recovering from their long voyage. After Joseph finished his story, they all said their prayers. Thomas could breathe a little better and was able to nurse without gasping. He smiled when Lizzie kissed his blond head and said good night.

The baby slept while the storm raged outside the small cabin. During the night, Joseph added logs to the fire. Lucy awoke when she heard her brother. She lay under her warm quilt and softly her tears spilled across her cheeks and onto her pillow. She knew she and Sam could have been trapped in the storm.

CHAPTER XIV

Excellency of hogs

The Nor'easter left drifts behind the cabin and shed. All of the dirt was again covered with a white blanket, and only the taller stumps and a few stray cornstalks were showing. Sam would put on all of his winter clothes before he ventured out. Anne had been sewing extra shirts and pants from the woolen bolts of cloth. Joseph unpacked the boots he had bought with the fur trader's money. Sam's were too big for him, but they would be just right next year. Phebe's knitted woolen socks, mittens, and caps for the family lay on the table. Sam thought of his grandmother and missed her happy smiles as he put on the warm cap. He would love to laugh with her reading *Poor Richard's Almanack.*

Lizzie, who was bundled with so much oversized gear that she could hardly turn her head, waddled towards the open door. The sun was shining and the rays warmed her round face. She thought the day after a big storm was magical. Anne spooned bread crumbs on to her outstretched hands as she stood in the doorway of the cabin. Fluffy little black and white Chickadees flew past, then back again, and perched on her mittens eating the crumbs. Francois had given her the mittens for Christmas. They were sewn from the soft hide of a rabbit's belly and lined with the pale fur. Francois had given everyone clothing made from his cache of pelts. Joseph had a fine buckskin shirt that he wore almost every day. Sam, Lucy, and Lizzie had been given fur jackets.

Francois gave Anne a supple fox fur vest that she wore about the cabin. And when Anne or Joseph took a walk, Thomas was snuggled in a fur-lined carrier that Joseph strapped on his back. Francois explained that he had learned to sew while living with the Indians in Canada. Joseph thought to himself, as he had done many times, how thankful they were to have met the Frenchman.

137

Lucy came out of the cabin, rubbing her cheek on the soft fur collar, wearing her matching hat, scarf, and mittens knitted by her mother. She had a mischievous gleam about her. "I've got a great idea. Let's take some of those big pieces of leftover bark and slide down the back hill."

Sam and Lizzie ran for the shed, laughing and falling into the fluffy snow when they tripped. The back hill was steep and covered with stumps, but the snow deepened into firm drifts as the wind swirled it over the crest of the hill and dumped it on the slope covering stumps and stones. It was now perfect for sledding. Sam was first down the hill. He grabbed the leading edge of the bark and easily gained speed. With a shout he barreled down the hill and dumped at the bottom. Lizzie was next. She couldn't hold the front edge of her bark, so after a few feet, she rolled into the snow and slid half way down the hill in Sam's track. Lucy had the best slab of bark and with a jump, fell onto the sled and ploughed down the hill as her nephew and niece yelled her name in their excitement. Laughing and shouting, the three had fun climbing up the hill and sledding down again.

Lucy spotted him first. She saw Jacobus at the top of the hill watching them and laughing at their sport. He skidded down their trail and joined them. By now Lucy's cheeks were red, and her eyes sparkled in the bright sun. She gave Jacobus a big smile.

"Father came to see Major Gordon, and I tagged along. My mother sent your mother a ham," said Jacobus. "Father butchered three pigs last fall."

"Ham will sure taste good. Thanks." said Sam. Then he remembered, *"The excellency of hogs is fatness, of men virtue."* Sam now had *Poor Richard's Almanack* written by Ben Franklin, embedded in his memory. Often, something he heard or saw would trigger these phrases. Then he would puzzle the thoughts, and in the end feel like he knew what it meant. His brain was whirling around the words hogs and virtue right now. *Was bringing a fat ham a sign of a virtuous man? Was his Aunt Lucy being courted?*

138

Meanwhile, Lucy had asked Jacobus if he would like to try sledding. He said he hadn't ever gone sledding on a piece of bark before, but he'd give it a try. The laughs and smiles made the new snow even more exciting.

Anne, excited as she prepared dinner that night, spoke her thoughts. "A ham! That means sliced ham with our oatmeal for breakfast, ham and baked beans, ham and pea soup, ham cooked with potatoes and onions, ham and eggs? No eggs yet, but maybe this summer. Oh, an egg. Wouldn't that taste wonderful, Lizzie?"

Lizzie laughed at her mother, who returned a grin. Then they both looked at the fat ham on the table and could hardly wait to taste its salty meat. As Anne cut a slice from the butt end, they both gave a little sigh. Anne carefully cut the slice into small pieces and added it to the beans already cooking in the kettle hanging from the crane over the fire. She sighed again and rubbed her hands on her apron. "We need a pig or two, Lizzie."

"Yes, Mama," replied Lizzie, "Two pigs would be nice, but I should miss them when they become hams."

Sam was watching from the loft. He was writing about the day in his *Almanack*. February was much better than January, he decided. The sun was still low in the sky, but somehow the snow had made being outdoors much more fun, and Sam noted as he wrote in his *Almanack:*

"When you are having fun, you're warmer." SR

Lucy, too, listened as she threaded her sewing needle again. She was humming a little ditty that had no beginning or end. With Anne's help she had cut, pinned, and tried on her new bodice before sewing the seams. This time her needle sewed a straight line.

Anne was also sewing in the afternoons. Earlier Sam had stood on the bench while Anne measured him for his new pair of pants. He was thankful that sewing was women's work. He spent his inside time recording the weather, his observations on the hill, and new animal tracks in the snow in his now bigger *Almanack*. Sam had cut two squares of deer skin from the hide Francois had given his father and made a book with the paper Mrs. McDonald had given him. He tied a narrow strip of hide through holes to bind his book. Now his *Poor Sam's Almanack* looked like a real book. It took him a long time to copy his previous writings and carefully draw the animal tracks as Francois had drawn in his school book. But he had lots of time. He wondered where Francois was camped tonight.

Every morning after breakfast Sam followed his father to the wood lot that would become their orchard. Sam worked right alongside Joseph piling the tree limbs into big burn piles. The tree trunks would go to the sawmill before the spring thaw and be cut into boards for their barn. What was extra would be sold to the mill. In early spring they would burn the dead branches, and the field would be ploughed and made ready to plant.

Sam was not very interested in farming. He knew the family had to eat and that meant farming, but Sam had plenty of time to think about Schenectady and the inn where they had stayed last spring. He would love to read the newspapers and hear about George Washington. He knew he was missing news, books, and school.

Anne made sure that every afternoon Sam and Lizzie "went to school." She drilled them on their addition and subtraction, and they read from all of Phebe's books. They even read from Anne's English Bible, but some of those words were too hard and took some practice to say. Anne had to explain their meanings. Most days Sam read from Ben Franklin's *Poor Richard's Almanack*. He would read a sentence aloud and his mother would laugh at the funniest things. He had no idea why some of what he read was so funny. But Anne said he would know soon enough.

Then there was the Indian boy. Sam had wished over and over that the boy would come to their cabin so they could be friends. When Sam thought of that, he missed his cousins. He decided he was ready to get on Ol' Yankee and go somewhere. Anne just smiled at her son. "You have cabin fever. Go out and play in the snow!"

Another string of long, cloudy days with each day like the last settled over Balls Town. Everyone sniffled with colds again, even the adults. It was still snowing, but the deep snows that were good for sledding were over. When the weather changed now, it happened fast.

The strong winds sucked your breath away when you talked. Daylight hours were now about as long as the night hours, and the sun was slowly climbing higher in the sky. There were more birds arriving, and Lizzie's little chickadees followed her about. There were hawks too, and that meant Sam's trap might work. When there were hawks overhead, there were rabbits on the ground.

One good thing about winter was that the outhouse didn't smell. The freezing temperatures kept the fumes frozen in the pit. Now that the sun was warming up the ground, the smell was back. Joseph put ashes down the hole. The snow was dirty with twigs and cinders, and the ground around the cabin was muddy during the day again. Sam and Lizzie picked up twigs and piled them for kindling. They raked the soggy leaves from behind the cabin and threw them down the sledding hill. Anne didn't like the moldy smell. In fact, their mother had lost her temper more than once, and when that happened, everyone had to find something to do and be quiet.

Unexpectedly, on a sunny morning Anne boldly announced that she was leaving the cabin. Everyone stopped eating their oatmeal. "Lucy, you watch Thomas for me. If he gets hungry, just spoon him some warm cereal." Lucy wasn't too sure about this. Ever since his bad cold, Thomas wanted to be fed only by his mother.

"Sam and Lizzie, you do your chores just like you always do and Joseph, please stay near the cabin today. I'm taking Yankee for a little ride. I'll be home before dark." With that she put on her fox vest and left them sitting at the table eating breakfast.

"Your mother is tired of winter. She needs to talk to another woman," explained Joseph. "That's why she's been so cranky. She's probably just going down to visit the neighbors. We'll be all right for the day." And then Joseph added a whole bunch of chores to the list. "Clean the ashes from the fire hearth, Sam."

Joseph rose and put his empty bowl by the washing pail. "Lucy, get all these blankets and quilts out on the fence. They can sure use an airing." Joseph looked at Lizzie and Thomas who had not yet finished their breakfast. "And Lizzie, you can play dolls with

141

Thomas so we can all get our work done. Sam, collect any rotten food in the cold cellar and bury it in the field, then clean out Yankee's shed. Get rid of everything that smells bad and spread it over the field, too. Lizzie, you just help Lucy clean up the cabin. I'm going to chop firewood until your mother comes home."

When Anne finally did come home, the cabin was clean and smelled fresh. Joseph had cooked a fine stew, and Lucy and Lizzie had made a cobbler. It was just getting dark when they heard her coming up the hill. She had pails hanging around her waist that clanged as Yankee walked up their hill. Anne's cheeks were red from the wind, and her eyes sought out each upturned face. Her smile lifted everyone's spirits!

"I've been to McKnight's and Palmer's. They all say hello. McKnights are letting us use their maple syrup pails this year. They don't have time to boil with all the new lambs. We will trade syrup for lamb chops! And Palmer's cow is freshened, and Lucy can come for milk in the morning. And Lydia and I had just the best ever talk. She has started a new quilt, and I have a new recipe for venison. But best of all, we are going to meet every other Wednesday and quilt together. And...I have eggs!"

Sam's Almanack:
March took on new meaning after Mother's outing and visit. We had neighbors and news again, and it was back to church on Sundays. SR

The next day, Joseph hitched up the wagon and picked up the rest of the sap pails and the boiling pan at McKnight's. He took Sam and Lizzie along for the ride, and they had a good talk about everything Sam could think of. Sam felt it was so special to have his father to talk with all by himself. In fact, Lizzie was so quiet that he'd forgotten that his sister was sitting next to him on the bench seat.

142

Soon, the dozen maple syrup spikes, pails, and lids went into action. Joseph tapped the big sugar maple trees, and Sam and Lizzie hung the pails, put on the lids, and waited for the drips. Joseph explained, "The nights need to be cold and the days must be warm; when that happens, sap will flow into the pails."

The sap started flowing as the sun warmed the air, and by noon the spouts were dripping pretty steadily. Joseph rigged a fire pit beneath the maple trees. Everyone helped with the sugaring. It was so much fun to collect the pails and pour the watery sap into the pan. When the big pan was a third to half full, Joseph started the fire. The fire burned day and night. Even during a late March snowfall, the heat from the fire boiled away the water leaving the thin sticky liquid. A sweet smell was in the air and on their skin and jackets. When there was just an inch of sap in the pan, Anne brought the "almost syrup" inside and boiled it off until it was a thick amber liquid. The cabin smelled of the heavenly syrup, and it made the breakfast oatmeal delicious.

As they washed out the pails and were raking up the fire pit, Joseph heard his brother shouting as he came running up the hill. "News from home, at last," shouted Matthew, catching his breath. "Major Gordon brought it from Schenectady today. I wanted to open it, but thought we should all be together. This letter was written last November."

Joseph's hands shook as he tore open the envelope. He recognized his brother's handwriting.

November 30, 1776
Dear brother,

I'm mailing this letter not knowing if it will ever reach you. The mail carrier is said to be a Patriot, but there are rumors that some "Patriots" are really spies; no one is to be trusted anymore. In any case, I will not name him for fear if this should be discovered by the enemy; he would be in mortal danger. As you can see I have mailed it to the tavern in Schenectady as you said he was a Patriot. I hope it finds you after that.

General Washington has set up his headquarters across the Delaware River. His men are still slowly marching by the house from their Long Island battles. They are a miserable lot. They are hungry and tired, ill-clothed, and totally unarmed, without bullets and powder. Some do not even have their muskets anymore. Half of the men have rags tied around their feet for boots. Their enlistment time will end on December 31, and they can return to their farms.

In the meantime, we have joined with our neighbors in setting up food and shelter for them so they can rest and eat on their way to Pennsylvania. Patience and Susanna have cooked oatmeal and baked pones every day for a week. We have given away much of our cider and roasted two pigs for the men. Other farmers are doing the same. We have 16 wounded soldiers staying in the barn tonight.

Father and Mother are here. I brought them and a few of their possessions as soon as we heard of the retreats. I threw their quilts and some food in the wagon. Father has but his musket, tools, and fishing pole; Mother grabbed her butter bowl, blankets, and Bible. I have never been so afraid. I whipped the horse into a gallop and sped away from the cabin. War and hunger does crazy things to men. I don't expect there will be much left in the cabin.

Mother and Sarah are tending to the wounded, and Father and I handle the rations. Yesterday, I loaded the wagon with men who were too weak to walk and took them directly to the bank of the Delaware where boats ferried the men across to General Washington's new camp. The children are upset but begged to help, so they pass out the corncakes to our soldiers as they march past the house. Some of our neighbors have thrown rocks at the house at night. They don't want this Revolution.

We are doing all that we can, I worry about Sarah as the baby will be here soon. She is so tired, but insists on tending to the soldiers' wounds long into the night.

One of General Washington's officers stopped yesterday to thank us. He went to the barn to see about the men. I fear they are anticipating that Howe's army of Redcoats and Hessians will come through here. Father and I will fight, and the women and children will hide on the hill behind the orchard. Brother, we may lose everything.

God be with us all,
Your brother, William

The children were frightened. Joseph's hands were shaking and Matthew made a fist now hitting his other hand. Lucy and Anne had tears running down their cheeks. Sam looked at his father and then ran to him. Nobody spoke.

Across the field, Yankee let out a whinny in alarm. The men were so shaken; they now felt fear towards the approaching rider. Joseph reached for his musket. But the family let out sighs of relief when they saw who it was.

"Francois!" Sam ran to the fur trader coming towards them up the hill.

Francois saw the family gathered around Joseph and greeted the Rues with a big smile. Looking down, he saw the letter in Joseph's hand, a letter with bad news. Francois looked weary but well, and his pack horse was loaded down with pelts. Sam ran up to Lulu and stroked her neck. "I've missed you, girl." Francois's pack horse, Bess, just stomped and was impatient to be unloaded.

After the children had finally gone to sleep, the adults sat by the fire and talked. William's letter was discussed thoroughly. The fact that he had written and sent it four months ago was of great concern. What was happening now? Anne was visibly worried. She rubbed her hands on her lap and then rubbed her arms. The cabin was warm, but she had felt a chill. Sarah's baby would have been born by now. Had the British troops followed Washington's Army past their house? Was everyone safe? Joseph would write a letter tonight, and Matthew would take it to the trading post in the morning.

Francois had not interrupted but sat on the floor, leaning back against a couple of logs next to the fire. He always insisted heat felt good and was accustomed to sitting on the ground, not in chairs. He thanked Anne again for the stew and dumplings, then pulled out his pipe and lit it; the rich smoke drifted up to the loft where Sam was listening.

Now Francois spoke of even more disturbing events. He carefully chose his words so not to alarm Anne further. But the truth needed to be said. First, the Adirondack Mountains, north of Balls Town, were crawling with Indians, Canadian Indians in war paint. He had stayed as far from Lake Champlain and Lake George as he could after a close encounter at Crown Point.

He had stopped at Crown Point to visit an old friend. But after seeing smoke where the cabin would be, and warriors paddling their canoes along the east shore of the lake, he went back into the woods. He feared for his friend and hoped he had escaped harm. This had meant a longer trip, but he had safely made it to Balls Town and didn't think he had been followed. He had used all of his tricks to cover his tracks and had spent many nights without a fire.

His news from St. John's, just north of Lake Champlain, was all about the English fleeing to Canada. Loyalists from the New York Colony were crowding the small provincial town. Whole families of Loyalists were staying with the Canadians. Many had spent the winter in Canada, and food was running short. They were dependent on ships traveling up the St. Lawrence River to bring food from England. The few British troop and supply ships that had made it up the river before winter had left. It was still snowing when he left, and thick ice covered the St. Lawrence River. People were hungry and sick.

Francois took another long draw on his pipe, blowing the smoke into the fire, and began with a sigh. "Your letter from William mentioned the Hessians. Word in Canada is that King George has hired more of these soldiers, and they will be part of Burgoyne's army." Anne lowered her head and let out a little cry.

Francois continued. "If there is any good news, it is that the Indians hiding in the woods near the Kayaderosseras appear to be still on the fence. They are mostly from the Oneida tribe. The trappers by Lake George think they haven't decided yet who they would fight or if they will fight, and some of the warriors are thought to be scouts for the Americans."

Francois confirmed some of what Major Gordon had told the militia. Seeing Anne and Lucy so distressed, Joseph quickly changed the conversation to their winter in the cabin.

The only adult who slept soundly that night was Francois. He took his bed roll and went out to his sleeping den beneath the locust tree. He was used to the cold, and no one would complain about his snoring. His snoring wouldn't have mattered to the adults as they tossed and turned in their beds. Only the smaller children got a restful sleep in the cabin. Sam was scared.

CHAPTER XV

Spies

There was no new information, and no one talked of the impending war. Joseph had posted his letter to William, but had not yet received a reply. Major Gordon didn't call a muster, even though the trails were clear and the muddy roads passable. He knew it was a busy time for the men in his militia; his soldiers would be ploughing their fields.

Anne was true to her promise and met with her neighbor Lydia every other Wednesday. Francois took over the cooking on those days, and Sam watched the Frenchmen's knifeblade slice up roots and plants from the woods for the stew.

Lucy took care of Thomas, now a happy child with rosy cheeks and a dimpled smile. Francois and Sam had made a little cart for Thomas. Francois had ridden Lulu to Schenectady and brought back newspapers, coffee, chocolate, and wheels! Sam had been hoping to go along, but Francois said he would spend a night at the tavern, and that was no place for a young boy.

The whole family took turns reading the Schenectady newspaper. Even Lizzie could now read some of the words, and Anne helped her with the hard ones. Their children would know how to read and write when they went to school, and Anne dreamed of the day she could watch her children run safely home from a real schoolhouse. For now, Francois was teaching important lessons about surviving in the woods, and Anne would continue with the school lessons in the cabin. That was fine with Sam. Francois taught him more about tracks and tracking. He gave Sam a small knife and showed him how to make a trap from a green sapling and how to weave a cord from long strands of green vine. Now Lizzie was helping him dig weeds and roots that he stewed up for their dinner on Wednesdays.

Francois and Sam fished, and Lizzie would tag along and listen to Francois's long stories. Lizzie's memories of her grandfather Samuel were blended now with Francois. She would curl up on Francois's lap and listen to his stories. This was hard for Joseph to watch, but he didn't say anything.

Lucy's feeling for Francois was another story. She thought that Francois didn't bathe enough. One warm night she showed her temper and insisted that he eat by the door. Francois just laughed and moved to a stool by the door. That night there was a south breeze. Francois might have well been sitting at the table next to Lucy.

Sam thought he understood his aunt. Ben Franklin had been clear about how to court a woman. Lucy's fears were all about an unexpected visit from Jacobus. Lucy's hair was always clean and brushed. The ribbons and combs that Joseph had bought, now adorned his sister's hair everyday. When Jacobus rode up the hill to their cabin, Lucy would pinch her cheeks and rub her lips hard. Sam thought that was a complete waste of effort, because as soon as Jacobus smiled at Lucy, she blushed red.

Jacobus would visit with the family first. Anne always invited him to stay for lunch, and Joseph heard about the mill run by Jacobus's father and the people who came to the mill. Winter was a quiet time, and Jacobus's father was earning hard money by helping people assemble their barns. Joseph listened, but he knew that his money was running short, and he would never have enough to pay someone to help him with their barn. The timbers were curing, but the assembly would have to wait until he had more family to help. After lunch, Lucy and Jacobus walked down to the Mourning Kill.

Sam remembered *Poor Richard's Almanack. "A man without a woman is only half a man."* Sam now knew what that was all about, and Anne told him not to say anything. Lucy was almost sixteen and soon would be marrying. Sam thought Jacobus was a good fellow, and maybe he might run his father's gristmill someday. His aunt, however, had so many good ideas. Sam knew she would make a good wife. She could do anything!

May sunshine had warmed up the ground enough on the back hill so the family ate the tender watercress that grew along the banks of the Mourning Kill. Lizzie picked bouquets of wildflowers for the table and was on the look out for strawberries. Sam was trapping rabbits near the ploughed garden, and the few robins had multiplied into flocks of song birds. It would be still weeks before the leaves came out, maybe longer, on the maples, but the freedom to go without boots and heavy clothes was felt by all, and spirits were good.

"BOOM!"

"What was that?" said Lizzie.

"Joseph, oh Joseph," cried Anne. Joseph grabbed his musket and bullet bag. He pulled on his boots and hat. Anne packed him a slab of jerky and biscuits. He kissed Anne hard and raced down the hill.

"BOOM!"

Major Gordon was waiting and pacing back and forth in front of the fort when Joseph ran up breathless. Gordon's horse was still lathered after his fast ride from Schenectady, but it had taken about an hour for the militia to assemble. Some men had forgotten food or their boots. Some of the men were so upset that they couldn't stop talking. But most were like Joseph, silent and serious.

"I was about to blast this cannon again! You men need to get here quicker next time. This war waits for no man!" he verbally blasted out to the stragglers. Major Gordon took a deep breath to calm him, and began again, "The British have stirred up the Hurons. Those savages have been sighted as far south as Crown Point. There were reports of canoes and maybe 80 to 100 warriors coming up Lake Champlain toward Fort Ticonderoga. St. Clair's scouts spotted them with their bodies painted for war. This is old news. No telling what's happened since then."

Joseph thought out loud to Matthew, "This confirms what Francois told us. The Indians are scouting south from Canada ahead of the British forces."

Major Gordon continued. "As expected, the British have promised the Indians rum and weapons, and they've joined General Burgoyne's army. Those naked cut-throat warriors have come clear across Canada from the Great Lakes; they left their squaws and came to fight. If they join up with our local Mohawks, we're in for it! General Schuyler has issued orders for our northern militias to reinforce the troops under General St. Clair at Fort Ticonderoga. We have not been called."

Gordon puffed up his chest. "As soon as the ice was out of the St. Lawrence River, the British supply ships sailed up to Montreal. Our Canadian 'friends' have been busy building bateaux all winter. Canadian shipwrights have constructed 50 bateaux to carry troops and supplies up Lake Champlain to Fort Ticonderoga, and one sloop, named the "Betsy" is to be for the British officers. That's not all; they were commissioned to build two galleys, each with twelve six-pounders! Those are big cannons. The British plan on blowing Fort Ticonderoga right off the map!"

While Gordon was catching his breath, the men talked among themselves. Few had ever been to Fort Ticonderoga, but they all knew the massive fort was to the north and their farms would be in harm's way if the British were to make it to Albany.

"Our spies have done a good job. They have even given us a glimpse of British army life. Some of the supplies are tents, beds, tables and chairs, table cloths and napkins, tons of bread, meat, and rum. The Hessian and British troops will be well fed."

Gordon continued with a sigh, "You've got to agree our spies have really outdone themselves this time. The officers' meals will be prepared by special cooks, and they will be served champagne with their dinners. General "Gentleman Johnnie" Burgoyne has brought women to cook for his Army, and some of the soldier's wives and children will follow behind the army as it marches to Albany."

The men started to talk among themselves again. Matthew whispered to Joseph. "Our spies are making me hungry. Gordon didn't say our spies were Indians."

Gordon went on reading the official Army document from General Schuyler. "The English and Hessian troops arrived in Montreal on 78 ships! Think of that, men. We will be seeing quite a few Redcoats, and the Hessians are said to be well trained fighters with well made weapons. Our spies think the army will be starting south this month."

Gordon stopped. There was little point in saying much more. The British were preparing to defeat the Americans so soundly that the war would end within the next two months. The rebellion would be crushed. The new Americans would once again be British subjects. The men listened and thought about becoming British again. Those weren't happy thoughts, but the thought of going to war against such a huge army wasn't a happy thought either.

Major Gordon summed it up. "We'll have our hands full, men. We'll be fighting the British and feeding the American Army. And we can't count out being attacked by our own Tory neighbors who would be happy to see the British troops take over our land. We've set up a jail in Slade's barn on Middle Line Road and will begin arresting Tories who have refused to join the militia. So, be careful whom you trust with this information, protect your families, and come when you hear the cannon again. We'll have a quick muster, and you can go home."

When Joseph returned to the cabin, he was silent about the muster. Again, as before, after the children were asleep, the adults talked. Sam was prepared; he had purposely stayed awake as long as he could and was now still wide awake. Joseph told the news. Francois said he believed every word. Anne and Lucy did not cry this time.

Finally Francois said, "One thing you need to know about Canadians – they are not a healthy lot. Last winter they lost many civilians and soldiers to smallpox. Somehow it got passed to the

Americans that were trying to take Quebec. Indians came down with smallpox too and took it home to their tribes. I wouldn't be surprised if they weren't still carrying the disease with them as they traveled south."

Anne knew about smallpox. The little blisters made you sick with fever and vomit. Some people survived with just a few marks on their faces and bodies from the itchy pox, but some, especially the little babies, died.

Warmer weather and abundant sun made the grass on the back hill a brilliant green, and the trees were fully leafed. Lizzie had her basket in hand every morning and followed Sam around the hill searching for strawberries. The tasty red berries were small but sweet.

Joseph's musket was still hanging over the door, and his bullet bag, powder horn, a light jacket, hat, boots, and canteen were ready in the corner. Muster was scheduled for July 4th. Until then, the Balls Town farmers worked from daybreak until sunset clearing stones and stumps from their fields and planting seed. Women and children planted the vegetable gardens. This was no easy task for the Rue family as their garden was twice as big as last year.

Anne tucked hop seed under stones along the edge of the garden. Lizzie followed her mother and planted squash and pumpkin seeds in the stone walls. She announced she would share her pumpkins with the Indian boy, and this year she would watch the little pumpkins grow. The plan was to buy young fruit trees from the Lydia's husband, and Joseph and Anne would plant the orchard together when everything else was planted.

Everyone worked hard. The quilting bee was cancelled this month. The women were too tired at the end of the day and too unsettled to sit together pretending nothing was going to happen. The goal was to get everything done before the July muster. Anne prayed that the cannon would not fire before then.

Matthew spoke with Major Gordon early one morning before the other men came to the mill. He told the Major that he wanted to enlist in the Continental Army. He knew the militia needed him, but with the British heading up the Champlain Valley, he wanted to fight with the Continentals. He also explained, "I don't have any land of my own." He had been too young to earn enough money to purchase farmland from Reverend Ball, and try as he might, working at the mill would never earn him enough money to buy land. He had stopped at the recruiting tent in Schenectady and knew the Continental Congress would pay him for his service with 100 acres of land at the end of the war.

"I have bought a good musket with a bayonet with the money I earned working at the mill. Next I will buy a knapsack, and I have an old blanket." He listed off the provision the Army would provide. "The Army will issue me two shirts and two overalls, a long-sleeved woolen coat, breeches, hat, and two pair of stockings and shoes."

Major Gordon sighed. "I hear what you are saying, and you will make a good soldier." He paused and then looked Matthew in the eye, "I am asking you to stay with the militia until Balls Town is safe, and then I will write a letter recommending you for the Continental Army that you can take to Schenectady."

Matthew agreed.

Joseph drove the wagon to the cabin and called to his wife; he had been to Palmer's. Anne could hardly contain her excitement. Lydia had set aside twelve cuttings from her best producing trees. Anne had eaten apples from all the Palmer's trees and chosen the three varieties she liked the best.

The beautiful Baldwin apple could be harvested in October, long after the first frost, and when Anne would be done with the garden. This was good timing for her and good timing for the firm, thick-skinned, good-storing apples.

The second variety she chose was a Rhode Island Greening. She had to explain to Joseph that this would not be a green apple, but had gotten its name from a man named Mr. Green who had the first and only tree.

Anne nervously continued as Joseph dug the holes, "Apples are a funny sort. If you planted a seed from an apple you really like, chances are the tree would produce an entirely different apple! Mr. Green found an apple tree growing by his tavern and let it be. The apples from his tree are now famous all over New England. People come for cuttings from his tree and then score the small stems hoping roots will sprout from the slash."

Anne paused a minute and caught her breath. "This is how Lydia has grown the cuttings from a Rhode Island Greening that was her mother's." Anne was so proud of her friend and hoped that she would grow cuttings and fill their orchard with the best trees.

The third variety was Northern Spies. "Spies for Pies," said Anne seriously looking at the little tree she now held in her hand. "...tart and good-keeping apple that will blend well for cider, too. We could plant this tree by the house and I could run out with my basket ..."

Joseph started to laugh and dropped the shovel. Anne looked at her husband. Was he laughing at her or was it her plan? They both knew it would be years before they had their first apples, but buying the right trees was very important. He was still laughing, and she pushed him and turned her face away. This was important, and she had done her research well. But when she looked back, she could see his eyes were merry and his smile genuine; and he was gently teasing her, and she soon began to laugh, too.

Joseph took Anne in his arms and kissed her tenderly. It was a beautiful warm, sunny day. It had been so long since they had had time together. He pulled her down onto the warm grass and held her close. The worry of war and fear for their families had all been jumbled into a tense dialogue that had worn them down emotionally. They had worked hard for so long getting everything planted, that they had forgotten to look at each other. Today, Anne's eyes were full of life, and Joseph couldn't let her go.

Later, after Anne and Joseph had planted each little tree with care above ground level, Anne mulched and then protected the trees from rabbits and deer with woven cages she and Lucy had made. Actually, Lucy was such a fast weaver that Anne had only made three cages in the same time Lucy had woven nine. Then Anne staked the cages to the ground. Each little tree now sat on its own hill where the rain water would not puddle and rot the roots. Each skinny sapling tree was protected by a sturdy cage that looked like an overturned basket.

"Maybe we could get a few more rabbit traps, Joseph."

Joseph didn't answer. The money for the trees had dipped into their savings. Joseph was thinking all the time about this. Everyone was a farmer, but the successful men he knew all had a trade or business to earn "hard" money." But, Joseph thought again, this time, thinking of all the good things: his wife was happy, his children healthy, and the orchard and fields and garden were planted.

The warm sun made them both sleepy, and they slept on the warm grass field while Yankee grazed on the grass and weeds along the stone walls, pulling the empty wagon behind her.

"BOOM!"

The cannon at the fort blasted again, but the families knew that this was not a drill but a celebration for the United States of America. Major Gordon had sent out the word that there would be a repeat of the fish fry, and everyone was to bring additional food. The fiddlers would provide music, and the trading post would be open at Long Lake. It was the Fourth of July!

Major Gordon had also passed on information to his militia that General Schuyler's spies had warned of Indian raids, and that Americans were now fleeing from their farms ahead of General Burgoyne's advancing troops. The men of his militia were required to bring their provisions and be prepared to stay at the fort in case of trouble. Families could return home or stay at the fort with the militia after the celebration.

The morning of the Fourth dawned clear and hot. Francois would stay at the cabin. The children knew their mother had been preparing extra food for a wonderful celebration, and the wagon was well provisioned for an overnight. Joseph had not told the children about the Indian raids.

The militia assembled at 10:00 a.m. They had inspection, target practice, and this time drilled to a real drum. The drummer was from the Malta militia and a friend of one of the men who worked for Gordon. The sound of the drum sent shivers down Anne's back.

After the muster, Major Gordon called to the women and children to join the meeting. He told his men to hold off on the cannon. "Save your powder," he ordered. Major Gordon had an additional announcement. "On June 14th the Continental Congress approved a new American flag of Grand Union. It will have seven red stripes and six white stripes; this has been the flag of our small navy, a stripe for each of the thirteen colonies. As I understand it," he continued, "there will be a field of blue, the same color blue of our Continental Army uniforms, in the upper left hand corner filled with thirteen white stars, one star for each state."

Anne could feel the excitement building in her. She would make a flag for the fort. She stood and raised her arm, "Major Gordon," she shouted, "How many points do the stars have? I should like to make a flag for the fort."

Major Gordon responded, "Splendid, I shall give you the notification that was delivered to me in Schenectady."

Anne could hardly contain her excitement. Most women could easily sew straight seams but quilting the white stars on a blue cloth would be a challenge to some. She would have to teach these women some of the stitches she knew. She nodded to the other women. Finally there was something other than cooking that they could do for America!

Gordon encouraged his men to spend the day with their families. The sun was high and hot. Men gathered their families and walked to Long Lake to swim, even Joseph. Anne insisted.

"Joseph, it is so important that you spend this day with the children and me. You have been so busy with the farm that we hardly see you. Sam spends much of his time with Francois, and Lizzie needs to be with you, too. She could use a swimming lesson." Anne put her hands on her hips, "I don't know of a better person than you, who is not afraid to jump into fast moving streams with his clothes on, to give her a lesson. And little Thomas has yet to say your name! Maybe you could work on that a bit today."

Joseph knew when Anne got going on one of these discussions that he better listen. All that she said was true. He had been looking forward to a nap; he and his sister had spent the last week in the hay field making the first cutting. His shoulders and arms ached, but he would go to the lake and swim with his family.

The afternoon proved to be fun for everyone in the family. Sam and Lizzie laughed as their father threw them into the air only to splash in the warm lake. Lizzie practiced her swimming kick while Joseph held her steady in the shallow water. Little Thomas didn't know what to think when his father drew him up and settled him on his shoulders for a ride as the family walked back to the fort. He hung onto his father's long hair and smiled down on his mother.

Anne knew she had been right. On her way back to the fort, she stopped at the trading post to talk with Marie McDonald. She wanted to know where to find the herbs that had helped Thomas with his cold last winter. She watched her family go up the road to the fort. She memorized the image. Forcing her body to move, she quickly turned and went into the trading post.

Lucy didn't go swimming, but stayed at the fort with the fiddlers. She danced with Jacobus, then Rueben cut in, then Jacobus offered her cold cider and they sat in the shade of the tree. Then Rueben brought her hot gingerbread. By the time she had nibbled the crusty edge off the cake, the fiddlers started playing, and Jacobus grabbed her hand before Rueben had time to finish his gingerbread and stand up. Lucy felt alive with the music, and her skirt swirled around her legs, the dancers didn't mind the heat. Raking and gathering the hay crop was forgotten.

CHAPTER XVI

British, Hessians, & Indians

As the British Army under General Burgoyne moved south through the Champlain Valley, the Continental Army was ill prepared to defend Fort Ticonderoga. American General Philip Schuyler ordered the abandonment of the fort after he inspected the incomplete repairs to the stone fortifications. Another reason to call an immediate retreat was the placement of the British cannons now overlooking Fort Ti. British troops had chopped down trees and hauled their cannons to the top of Mount Defiance, and the Americans could see the fires of the enemy camps overlooking the fort. Outmaneuvered and severely outnumbered, the Continental Army had little choice. They would fight another day.

Fort Ticonderoga fell to the British on June 2, and the Northern Continental Army fled south. General Washington did not hear of the defeat until July 10. The loss of the great stone fort was a severe blow to the Americans.

On securing the fort, the British Army abandoned their bateaux and built wagons to continue to Albany. So sure was General Burgoyne of victory, he sent his supplies up Lake George, a longer route by water, and took a direct route overland with his Army.

American General St. Clair's retreating Army slowed Burgoyne's overland travel by cutting down trees and burning bridges all along their route. Clearing the fallen trees and pulling bogged down cannons and wagons with tired and hungry horses delayed the British. Moving heavy loads in the swampy valley between Lake George and the Hudson River was sweaty hard work. It took Burgoyne's men sometimes a day to cover a mile. Despite counsel from his generals, Burgoyne did not turn back and take the Lake George route.

The Redcoats were dressed in heavy wool uniforms. The biting No-see-ums and black flies that had crawled beneath their sweaty collars and cuffs in June were now replaced by biting mosquitoes and horse flies. The still air and humid heat made their days and nights miserable. The German soldiers, however, looked about them and saw the beauty of America. During the passage up Lake Champlain, the Hessians could hardly help but notice the plentiful fish and game their Indian scouts were eating. The troops could not hide their growing appreciation of the deep forests and clear water from their German officers.

The Hessians had signed-up for combat, but most were young men seeking opportunities in America that were unavailable in their home villages. The troops from Hesse spoke no English and could neither communicate with the British nor the Indians. They proudly wore tall helmets, body armor, knee-high leather boots, and beautiful blue coats. They had great pride and confidence in their uniforms as well as their weapons, which they knew were superior to British weapons. England's King George had paid the German Elector dearly for the service of his soldiers.

There was now panic among the New York settlers. Tories were abandoning their farms and fleeing south to Albany as the retreating American Army approached from the north. The Continentals were under orders to burn farms and scatter the cattle to keep food unavailable to the advancing enemy. So rebel families, too, fled ahead of the advancing armies seeking shelter with farmers to the east and west of the route. Terrified, and taking what they could load into their wagons, they looked back only to see their cattle killed and cabins and fields in flames.

Newspapers in New York, Massachusetts, Maryland, and Virginia all contained stories of random attacks on isolated New York and Vermont farms as Burgoyne's Army of troops and Indians moved south. The soldiers were not always a part of the brutality. In fact, British officers found the Indian attacks on the American farms appalling. Headlines inflamed the American settlers with their news of brutality. The colonial newspapers focused on the Indian attacks including the death of Jane McCrea.

British General Burgoyne Cannot Protect His Own

Jane McCrea is murdered and scalped. Jane, sister of John McCrea, who lives east of Balls Town, was on her way to the British Army camp to be with her sweetheart, when two Indians attacked her and her aunt. It was an unprovoked murder and scalping. Miss McCrea carried a wedding cap and a letter from Captain Jones, according to her aunt.

Captain David Jones later recognized Jane's hair hanging from the belt of the Indian who killed her. She had exceptionally long and beautiful hair. The Indian with the scalp is identified as a scout for British General Burgoyne. Jane McCrea's body was found in a shallow grave near the abduction. Her aunt survived the attack shaken but unharmed.

When the British army officers learned of her death, they tried again to order the Indians not to attack civilians. But they did not punish the Indians who now had scalps hanging from their belts. Some British officers were afraid the Indians would refuse to fight the Americans if they were punished for scalping.

When Major Gordon heard of Jane McCrea's death, he saddled his fastest horse and rode to the mill. Jane's brother was a member of the Balls Town militia. Calling Matthew away from the din of the noisy saw, he instructed Matthew to take his horse and ride from farm to farm telling of the attack and murder.

"Warn them. Men should carry their muskets when they are in their fields, and women and children should not stray from their cabins," ordered Gordon. "Tell them to harvest their crops. There will be no muster in August, but to be prepared to battle somewhere near

161

the banks of the Hudson River north of Albany in September. We have orders not to let the British take Albany."

Matthew took the reins of Gordon's prized mare and kicked the horse into a full gallop. He raced up the lane to warn his brother first. Joseph was in the field cutting a second crop of hay. His sister had the rake and was spreading the green hay out to dry. Dressed as a boy, she could be easily overlooked except for her long hair. Matthew was alarmed. Matthew rode into the field trampling the hay. Joseph knew there was trouble.

"John McCrea's sister, Jane, has been murdered and scalped. Seems she was in love with a Tory and refused to evacuate to relatives in Albany. Instead she and her aunt rode into an Indian raiding party near Fort Edward." Matthew looked at his sister. Lucy had paled. "The British have no control over the Indians. It's bad. Joseph, carry your musket with you when you are in the field. Anne and the children should not stray from the cabin. Lucy, tie your hair back and hide it under your shirt."

Matthew turned the horse to leave. "Gordon will send me again if there is more news. Pray to God we are spared a battle in Balls Town, brother." Matthew kicked the horse into a gallop.

Major Gordon was somber; no powder was wasted on target practice and even the cannon was silent. The men knew this would be a serious muster. "On August 19, General Washington ordered the replacement of General Schuyler by General Horatio Gates. Here is more information that I learned yesterday. Someone, bring me a bench." Gordon sat down and told his men to get comfortable. "You have got to hear the entire story to understand just what's happening. This fellow General Horatio Gates is not a young man – maybe 50 years old – and his nickname we've been told is Granny Gates, because he wears his spectacles low on his nose. He comes to us from England, but he's no nobleman. His father was said to be employed as a Duke's housekeeper in England. General Washington trusts him, and the New England Army has agreed to fight under his leadership. We'll be taking our orders from General Gates, who will be in daily contact with General Washington." Now he paused. "As you know, the death of John McCrea's sister was a terrible thing. Our families have much to fear from the Indians."

Joseph and Matthew thought of their Indian boy living not far from the cabin. After Matthew's visit in the field, Joseph had sworn to himself that despite all the kind things that had occurred on the hill, he would defend his family from Indians.

"When you are packing your gear, remember your canteens and food. You are responsible for taking care of your own needs. You probably won't want much of a blanket now, but since we don't know when this battle will end, bring one. Jerky and hard biscuits would be good. We'll have no fires or kitchens where we are going. Bring some of your stores to the fort. We will need to have flour, meat, and cider for Washington's troops. If each of you brings what you can spare, we can feed a few of the Continentals."

While Major Gordon was speaking, ten men came into the fort. Joseph and Matthew recognized two of the men. They were the same two who had torched their field and tried to burn down the cabin.

"We have come with our muskets to fight for our land," said the tallest man, the one with a slight limp. "We know that the men along Scotch Bush are determined not to fight and many of them have deserted their farms, but we will not. We aim to fight alongside you."

Major Gordon had paused when the men approached. Slowly, he walked toward the men, but stopped to pick up his musket and shove a pistol in his belt. He motioned to Matthew and Jacobus to do the same. "Take their muskets and knives and hold them prisoner outside the fort until we are finished here." He knew this was serious business. If they were telling the truth, it was good news. If they were lying, his militia would be in grave danger. He turned back to his men when the Tories were out of ear shot, and told them to return in three days prepared for battle and tell no one of their plan to gather.

"Your families can come to the fort, but they must bring their own supplies. Again, bring what food you can spare. We will load wagons and take the stores with us to Bemis Heights. Militia dismissed." The Major saluted his men, and they returned the salute.

Major Gordon ordered the ten men imprisoned. Matthew and Jacobus marched the men to Slade's barn on Middle Line Road where they would be held with the other Tory prisoners. He would decide later what to do with them.

CHAPTER XVII

Battle of Saratoga

Meanwhile, England's Army was running short of food and many of her men, horses, and women camp followers were sick and weak from hunger. Their crates of food from England were moldy and spoiled. The Indians traveling with General Burgoyne's Army sensed an approaching disaster. They had sent out their own scouts who reported counts on the gathering American militias that were joining the ranks of the Continentals.

The autumn weather was changing the scene, too. September nights left frost on the tall grasses and heavy dews in the mornings. The trees were flames of red, orange, and golden yellow against the deep blue sky. The still warm Hudson River was blanketing the valley in a dense fog each night continuing into early morning. Conditions were right for the Indians to slip away into the woods unseen. They left with as much loot as they could carry and began the long trip to their tribes in Canada. The cold winter weather would come even sooner there than in New York. As they traveled north, they stole horses and weapons as they looted American farms and headed back up the Hudson Valley to Lake Champlain and on to Canada and home.

America's General Gates, after much deliberation, consultation and touring of nearby Freeman's farm, had chosen the open fields of Bemis Heights to make his stand. The farm lay directly in the path of Burgoyne's march to Albany. For two weeks the gathering militias and the Continentals had been setting up their camps on the Heights and digging trenches for protection during battle.

With the newspaper stories of Jane McCrea's death now circulating throughout the colonies, militias from as far away as

165

Boston came to fight alongside the Continentals. Daniel Morgan's sharpshooters from Pennsylvania, Putnam's force from the New York Highlands, and John Stark from New Hampshire recruited more men from the ranks of those who had declined earlier. Since Jane McCrea's death and all the publicity, the call for Patriots to fight had focused on the impending battle in the small village called Saratoga. One of the militias was from Balls Town – the 12th Regiment of the New York militia commanded by Major James Gordon.

"It's been three days, and I must go to the fort and join Gordon and the other men. Matthew has been racing around to the other settlements passing the word of the probable battle and need of food. Pack me a double ration." Joseph said to Anne. "It looks like it will happen at a place called Bemis Heights near the village of Saratoga," he explained. "I shall fight the British and the Hessians, Anne, and do my best."

Anne just stood by the door. She already knew all that Joseph was saying, but didn't hear any of it.

Joseph kept talking. "Francois will stay here at the cabin. He's a good shot, and he's volunteered to protect our cabin; all the same, I wish he would go to the fort, too. We can build another cabin if it comes to that, but we could never replace such a loyal friend. The Indian boy knows about the sleeping den under the tree, but the Canadian Indians will not. Francois said he will stay hidden most of the time in the sleeping den, not build a fire, and stay awake at night. He knows the ways of Indians."

Anne had been slow in packing. She was not ready.

Joseph looked at his boots. "I want you, Lucy, and the children to pack a few more things into the wagon and we will leave after dinner and go to the fort."

Anne nodded.

"Lucy will bring Matthew's old musket. He's taught her how to load and shoot," finished her husband.

Sam was around the back of the cabin and heard his father talking to his mother. He was scared.

Lucy loaded up the wagon with their kettles and a few more possessions. They took their warm clothes and quilts, and candles. Not knowing if the cabin would still be there when they returned, Anne took her trunk containing her mother's Bible and the looking glass Joseph had given her. Francois lifted Anne's sewing chest and Thomas's crib into the wagon.

Sam had a leather bag with his books, the knife Francois had given him, and the spy glass from his father. As the family was loading up, he ran back for his fishing pole. Lizzie packed her doll and doll bed. Even though the wagon was full, there was so much left at the cabin. The tools and furniture would be left.

Sam ran over to the Liberty Tree. He ran the needles through his fingers. He thought of his grandparents and took a deep breath. He would not be scared.

Joseph, seeing his tools, picked them up and buried them in the cold cellar. He called to Sam to help him barricade the opening with firewood. It would take a while for a man to break into the cellar. He poured a pail of water on the fire. "No sense giving them a flame!"

They said good-bye to Francois with tears in their eyes and loaded up in the wagon. Riding down the hill, Sam looked back as his home and Francois disappeared behind the trees.

The next morning the families said good-bye to the Balls Town militia. After Sam kissed his father good-bye, he ran into the fort and up to the look-out. Husbands, fathers, and brothers were marching down the road towards Saratoga. When they were just specks, he watched them with his spy glass. After the militia could no longer be seen, he just stood and listened for the drum.

"Sam, come down," called Lizzie. "Mother says she needs you to help with the fire."

Ten days later

General Burgoyne surrendered to General Gates on October 17, 1777 at Saratoga. The defeat of such a huge British Army was a turning point in the American Revolution. General Gates had food brought to him, and the opposing generals Gates and Burgoyne toasted Commander-in-Chief George Washington and England's King George. The next morning the American soldiers and militias formed a long corridor. The unarmed British and Hessian troops were marched through the corridor as a lone fife played "Yankee Doodle." They were taken as prisoners to Boston.

Most of the Hessians were captured at the Battle of Saratoga, but some had slipped into the woods and escaped. The rest spent the winter of 1777 near Boston and then were shipped to Virginia where more were allowed to escape. The Americans hoped the German prisoners of war would desert. This would clearly be better for the Americans, because as prisoners, the Continental Congress was required to feed and house them until ships could be found to return them to Europe. The local militias were told to allow the Germans to desert the British Army during the march across Massachusetts.

"I can see the militia coming," yelled Sam. With his spy glass to his right eye, he focused the lens on the returning men. He and his friends had stood watch day after day for just such a sight. "Some of the men have bandages on their arms and heads," he said. "Looks like some men are in the wagon."

Joseph could see the fort now. Proudly flying from a tall pole was a red, white, and blue flag – the flag of the Grand Union. Joseph knew Anne and the other women of Balls Town had sewn the flag and felt a deep stirring of pride for his wife.

Thank God, I am coming home, he thought over and over.

The women rushed through the gate, running down the road. Two men would not be coming home and five had wounds, but Joseph and Matthew had survived the battle uninjured.

Anne fell into the arms of her husband. Sam and Lizzie hugged them both and all were crying.

Lucy could see Rueben helping one of the men. He had his arm over his shoulder. It looked like Jacobus, but as they got closer she could see it was Jacobus's father. He was limping. Lucy started at the beginning of the group and looked again for Jacobus.

Matthew now came to her. "Dear sister, Jacobus is all right; he was not hurt. He was chosen to accompany the Hessian prisoners to Boston and will return in a few weeks." Lucy almost fainted in relief.

Matthew continued, "It was a loud, long, and brutal battle. Many men were killed, but General Gates had it figured right, and Burgoyne for all his boasting must now go home to England defeated."

Matthew drew a long breath and continued, "The Continentals fought courageously, and I will join them as soon as I can get to Schenectady. General Washington needs a few more battles like this one, and we will be rid of the British." Lucy hugged her brother, and he hugged her back.

By now all the men, wives, and children were talking and crying at once. Joseph told Anne he wanted to pack up the wagon and go back to the cabin as soon as possible. Joseph didn't want to even guess what might await them at the cabin. He was bone-tired and hungry. He knew that if there had been trouble at the cabin, he would have a huge decision to make. Would they come back to the fort, or should he take the family to Schenectady until the raids and trouble ended in Balls Town?

On the way home the family barely spoke above a whisper. Anne and Joseph sat so close together on the bench seat of the wagon that Sam didn't think a bug could crawl between them. Lucy had a funny look on her face. He guessed that she was still worried about Jacobus. Even Lizzie knew that they might come home to a burnt cabin and clung to Sam while Thomas slept in the crib. The movement of the wagon lulled him into a deep sleep. The noise in the crowded fort had been exhausting for the young children.

As they turned to their lane, even Yankee seemed to be reluctant to go the last mile. Joseph could not believe his eyes. There was smoke, billowing clouds of smoke coming from where their cabin would be. He almost turned around and headed back down the hill. Whatever was happening would be too much for Anne and the children to see. He stopped the wagon and got down.

"Anne, you and the children stay here. Lucy, come up and sit by Anne. I'll be back."

Anne watched him walk the rest of the way up the hill. His shoulders slumped, and he carried his loaded musket, ready to shoot. When he was out of sight, they all held their breath. It seemed forever that they sat in the wagon. Lizzie whispered, "Oh, Francois, Mama, Francois..." and Anne grabbed her daughter's small hand.

Then they heard a shout. It was Joseph. "Come along, Lucy. Come up the hill." As they rounded the top, they could see the cabin. Smoke was coming from the chimney and Francois was tending another smoky fire roasting what looked like a small deer. Everything else was pretty much the way it had when they left, except another wagon was now by the horse shed.

The cabin door flew open and their cousins ran out. "Sam, Lizzie, we're here! We came to your hill."

Lucy stopped the wagon, and the children jumped down. They raced to their cousins with shouts of relief.

Anne got down, Joseph picked up Thomas, and they walked together to the cabin. Once inside the dark cabin, Anne had to wait a minute before she could see. Then she saw William and looked around for Sarah. William started to cry. She rushed to him. "Oh, Will, where is Sarah?"

William's voice broke into great sobs; he had held them in for so long that they now poured out of the depths of his being. "The baby came too soon, she was so tired and sick from caring for the soldiers. I begged her to stop, but she said they were so young and far from their homes...she couldn't watch them starve and die of their wounds."

Lucy was standing at the door. "Oh, Will." She ran to her brother and hugged him tight.

Then William reached to the table and picked up the Bible. Joseph recognized whose it was in an instant. "No, it can't be," he cried. Lucy let out a small cry and ran to her oldest brother. Joseph was numb with shock. William began with long sad sighs and pauses, "They stayed with the house...I found them after we came out of hiding in the woods...They said they would be right behind us, but father stayed. He must have fired at the British a couple of times...I think mother died when she saw him fall. She was lying close to his body with her head on his chest. "The troops passed by quickly, I don't think they even stayed at the house. General Howe's men were charging after Washington's troops. We learned later that Howe and his army have taken Philadelphia. They are living with the Loyalists."

"Oh," cried Anne, as she slumped into a chair.

The rest of October was sad. SR

Sam wrote in his *Almanack* almost daily. It seemed to be the right thing to do. He watched his father and mother as they went about their chores. Everything got finished and stories were read before bed, but there was a deep sadness in the cabin. Uncle William's children slept with them in the loft. His little cousin, Abby, quietly cried herself to sleep each night. He would take his cousin Jack to see the fox den. Maybe by Christmas, they could read *Poor Richard's Almanack* together and have a good laugh. And then he thought of his Grandmother Phebe and Grandfather Samuel.

Francois walked down to the Mourning Kill with Sam. Soon Francois would be leaving to set out his traps, and they wouldn't see him again until spring. They had long talks as they sat by the creek. Francois knew all about people dying. He had once had a family, but while he had been away trapping, his family had died.

"Sam, you're old enough to know that we shall all someday die. The thing to do is to build upon what your grandparents achieved and take the next step while you live. That's what your father is doing. Your father has big plans for this hill."

Sam looked at Francois, but didn't say anything.

"If Joseph had just wanted to be a farmer, he could have stayed in the low country of New Jersey where the dirt is thicker and richer and the summers are longer. Your father, just like your grandfather and grandmother, wants to push a little harder and try something new." Francois threw a stone into the bubbling creek water. There would be another time to explain the naming of the Mourning Kill and his family to the boy. There had been enough sadness.

"Your father is tired, just home from the battle, but he will tell you sometime about his plans for this hill, and you and Lizzie and Thomas and the new baby that will be here in the spring..."

"What new baby?" demanded Sam.

"Oh, I talk too much! Maybe you haven't noticed how your mother looks, all rosy and flushed? You just wait; she'll have an announcement one of these days. It's not the right time just yet, maybe after Christmas. I think I've said enough, maybe way too much."

Francois looked at the sunrise, "I think we're in for a change in the weather. My guess is our long Indian summer is just about over. I'll be heading north. Say, let's go have a peek at the fox den. I wonder how big those kits are by now. This time of day the vixen would be off looking for food."

Sam would never stop wondering how this Frenchman always had something up his sleeve to talk about. Maybe it was because he just talked to horses all winter. *LuLu and Bess wouldn't have much to say*, he said to himself.

Yankee Doodle

Yankee Doddle went to town,
A riding on his pony.
Stuck a feather in his cap
And called it macaroni.

Yankee Doodle keep it up,
Yankee Doodle dandy,
Mind the music and your step,
And with the girls be handy.

Origin of the word YANKEE

There are many versions of how the word Yankee came into being part of the English language. Here are a few of the explanations I have found in books and on the internet.

The music and words of "Yankee Doodle" can be found in 15th century Holland as a harvesting song that began, "Yanker dudel doodle down." In England the tune was from "Lucy Locket." "Yankee" was a mispronunciation of the word "English" in the Dutch language and "Doodle" refers to a dumb person, according to the British leader Oliver Cromwell. *Taken from "Ben's Guide to United Sates Government for Kids."*

Joseph Fennimore Cooper, author of the "Last of the Mohicans," wrote that the word Yankee was a corruption of the word "English" in American Indian, Yengees.

173

CHAPTER XVIII

Barn-raising

Joseph and William took about an hour to develop a plan. It was pretty simple; they needed to enlarge the cabin and organize a barn-raising. Joseph would ask his neighbors if they might help, then he would help his neighbors with their barns. But, first they would add an addition to the cabin. It made no sense to build a separate cabin and keep two fires going all day. Plus, the children would be spending most of their time together, and it would be easier for Anne and Lucy if they were all in one cabin. William, for the time being, would sleep in the den with Francois. He wouldn't mind the Frenchman's company, and he needed time to think. After the cabin was finished, they would start on the barn. Jacobus and his father had already offered to help. If they could get a few more neighbors and maybe some of the men in the militia to help, they might have the frame up by the end of November. Then they could shingle the roof with fewer men and the siding by themselves.

Friends and neighbors gathered on the chosen Saturday. The yard was filled with wagons and children, women, and babies. The children were all sitting on top of the cold cellar, where they had a good view. The women were gathered by Francois's large fire pit. Two small deer were roasting on a spit.

Even though it was late November, the men were stripped down to their breeches and tying their ropes to the beams lying on the ground. Teams of horses were dragging huge flat sided boulders to the places Joseph had marked for the cornerstones. Joseph now ran from one bent to the other, making sure that the men knew what they were doing. Some of the men were joking and not paying attention, but as he ran from joint to joint of the bent, or the beamed side of the

174

barn on the ground, they took notice. He did not want this to come out badly. The beams were heavy, and the pegging of the first two sides was very important to keep the joined beams from twisting crooked and falling before they were in place or worse, tearing the joints apart. He told the men to tie their ropes well; lives depended on this being done correctly.

The lightest bents would be drawn up first. The side of the barn with the large door opening and the end side with the big loft door opening were pulled up together and pegged at the corner joint. It took real manpower to lift the heavy frame of beams off the ground to a standing position on the cornerstones. The men pulled with grunts and groans on the ropes. The strongest man now climbed up the junction to do the pegging. The others held their ropes steady, knowing a man's life depended on their strength to hold the heavy bents in place. With the huge, heavy beetle mallet, he pounded the beams into position and then secured the joint with square pegs.

With two sides now standing, the men retied their ropes on the third bent. The other end of the barn was raised, pounded into position, and the joint pegged. Joseph again ran from corner to corner, making sure that the fourth and final bent would be raised in the right place to complete the rectangle.

Once the pegs were driven through the beams, the tie beams were fastened onto the ropes and hoisted up to the top of the frame and secured. They would become the supports for the floor boards of the hay loft. By now, men had climbed onto the beams, ready to receive the rafters and the ridge pole that would run along the peak of the barn. The barn's skeleton was huge, and it dominated the yard. As the men jumped clear, they agreed that Joseph had done a good job and were slapping him on the back.

Sam could see that his father and the other men were sweating. His father was still running from side to side, checking the joints and pounding the lower beams securely with the beetle. More and more pegs went into the matching joints. The men now stepped back, coiling their ropes. They were anxious to get the work finished so they could begin the wrestling matches.

Joseph waved to Anne that the men were done. The children leaped off the cold cellar and raced to the framed barn. Reverend Ball knew that it was now or never to say the blessing. By the time the keg was tapped and the men started their wrestling matches, it would be too late. He ask the men to remove their cover, and for everyone to be quiet.

Dear Lord,

We are gathered here together to thank you for your bounty of forests and food, of family and friends. Bless this barn that it may protect the animals that will dwell within and the food it will store. Let this barn withstand the blows of the storms to come and be safe haven for God's creatures.

We gather here this beautiful November Saturday in thanksgiving and fellowship. We thank you for bringing these men home from battle, and we mourn those who died. May the wounded heal and be restored to good health. Winter will soon be here and we will be isolated on our farms for a good many days. Let us be good neighbors and care for each other and share our provisions.

We thank you for the safe journey of William Rue and his children Jack, Jonas, Louisa, and Abigail to this new land. We share in the Rue family's sorrow at the death of Sarah, their mother and infant sister Lena. These are hard times for a family to be without a wife and mother. We also share in the sorrow for the loss of Samuel and Phebe. In God's name we pray. Amen.

The roasted meat, squash, potatoes, and corn were served. Most of the women had brought food. Some of the dishes were made from recipes that Anne had never tasted before. The children gobbled down the waffle cookies, and there were apple torts and blueberry pies. There were so many children now eating and running around on the top of the hill that Anne said it looked like a town.

"No," said Joseph, "It's a city! Hop City!"

Everyone laughed, but Sam looked hard at his father and knew he had to write some of this down. His father was back dreaming again, and Sam wanted to be part of that dream.

Now the children were racing around the big boulder and playing hide-and-go-seek. Anne was talking with the other women, and Joseph was with William and the other men. No one was watching as Lucy and Jacobus left the group and walk down the back hill to the Mourning Kill. Lucy wore her best clothes, and her hair was shining and pulled back with a blue ribbon. Jacobus had on his work pants and boots, but he now wore a clean, dry shirt. After his return from Boston, his mother had trimmed his hair and he had shaved his whiskers, unlike the other men who were unshaven. His hair was tied back under his new three-pointed hat. He carried his musket, powder horn, and bullets wherever he went. The memories and sounds of battle at Saratoga and the forced march of the Hessian and English soldiers to Boston still gave him nightmares. His lack of concentration at the mill had alarmed his father.

"It will take more time, Jacobus, before you feel like yourself again," said Lucy with deep concern for the young man who now meant so much to her. "That was a long march, and you have probably not eaten well for over a month. Your mother heaped your plate, did you notice?"

"Yes," he sighed. "I guess mothers can tell when you aren't sleeping and eating well. She has been asking me if I feel all right and I guess I do; there's nothing wrong."

"Would it help if you told me about your trip? I've never been to Massachusetts. What is it like in Boston? Did you see the harbor and the tall ships?" Lucy asked.

"The Colony is just as beautiful as New York. We marched the men over the Berkshires without much trouble. There was little food for us to eat, but as the march continued the men were strung out over miles. Sometimes we could hear the Hessians singing and shouting their military drill sounds, and sometimes even the English prisoners broke into a song about beating the French or us, of course."

Jacobus paused and then began again. "It was a strange battle. We fought hard, and men were killed, but it was like we were fighting our English cousins who looked just like us except they had on those itchy red wool coats. And the Hessians were well-trained and good shots, but on the march they pointed at the trees and orchards that we passed. They seemed to think the sky was something special, and their eyes grew large when they saw fields of bundled corn." Jacobus shook his head as if he were still on the march and not believing the Hessian's surprised, envious looks.

"After the third day, the Continental officer in charge of the prisoners walked alongside me and under his breath said, 'Let the Hessians escape if they try to leave the march. The Continental Congress has no food for prisoners, and the ships in Boston are not ready to go to England. In fact there aren't enough ships, and they probably won't leave anytime soon, if at all.'"

"After that, in several towns in Massachusetts, farmers came up to the prisoners and speaking in German, would you believe, asked the men if they would help them with their crops? It was a strange war, Lucy. Those men were well-trained fighters; it's hard to think of them now as farmers. That's why I carry my musket with me." Jacobus shook his head as if he were still on the march observing the Hessian soldiers' envious looks as they saw the piles of cut hay and fields of corn waiting to be harvested.

Lucy listened, and so did her heart. Until Jacobus had worked out this experience of battle, he would not have thoughts of her. She lowered her head and stopped. "Jacobus, remember when you surprised us with the ham while I was sledding with the children?"

"Yes," Jacobus smiled.

"Well, winter will soon be here, and we will be sledding again. Please remember us and come to our cabin for lunch. It will be a long winter, and I will miss seeing you."

Jacobus took her hands in his. "I will try to remember."

Lizzie ran down the hill as fast as she could. "Lucy, Aunt Lucy. We were looking all over for you. You promised to give us rides on Yankee this afternoon. It's getting late."

Across the field and hidden in the tall grass, the Indian boy and his mother watched the celebration. They could smell the roasting meat and see the orange pumpkins tossed on the hay around the tied corn husks. The Indian boy could not take his eyes off Sam.

As Sam was just about ready to climb into the loft, his father asked him to go out and make sure the cooking fire was out. The wind had come up, and Joseph worried that it might fan the coals back to life.

Sam put on his short deerskin coat over his sleeping shirt and barefoot left the cabin. He was happy, happier than he had been in a long while. He had watched his mother and father smile and laugh. When the dancing started, he had sat with Jack and watched the adults dance in the deep-shadowed setting sun. Now, the sky was dark blue, the air clear and crisp, and he thought the hill the most beautiful place on earth. In this still dreamy state, he approached the fire pit. As he bent to feel the heat of the coals, he saw the shape of the Indian boy outlined against the pale sky. He called out "Hello, Yoo-hoo."

The startled boy jumped up and then turned to run, but stopped. He turned back to Sam and said, "Hello, hey."

"Hey," responded Sam.

Sam smiled and reached into his coat pocket for the smooth rock from the creek. With the stone in the palm of his hand stretched out in front of him, he slowly walked toward the boy.

The Indian opened his leather pouch tied to his waist, reached in and pulled out a rabbit's tail. As the boys exchanged their gifts to each other, big smiles broke out on their shadowed faces. At last, they met again. Sam felt a thrill run down his back. Francois had been right. The exchange of the stone and rabbit's tail meant Sam understood the ways of the Indians, if only a little.

Sam tried to "talk" with the Indian. "Sam," he said and pointed to his chest.

"Lone Fox," said the Indian boy said in English as he pointed to his chest.

Sam was surprised and let out a laugh. This truly was a happy day. He must get his father. He was sure Lone Fox had come for food. He thought, *there was so much food left from the dinner they could share with the Indian family ... the corn and pumpkins had been from the Indians ... now we can share them back.*

Sam made signs to show the boy he was going to the cabin for food and for Lone Fox to wait. As he ran to the cabin he turned twice to see that the boy had not fled, without hesitation, he raced to the cabin and whispered to his father to come out.

In his night shirt, Joseph lurched out of the cabin and looked to the fire. "Is the fire out?"

"Oh Father, I didn't even look at the fire. The Indian boy is here. I think he must have watched this afternoon, and he may be here for food. He spoke English and his name is Lone Fox." Sam felt his pulse throb with the excitement.

Joseph paused what seemed to Sam as a very long time, then said, "We shall give him corn and pumpkins."

Sam raced to the cold cellar and returned with two pumpkins and a sack of corn. Together they walked across to the barn. Lone Fox was gone. They put the food by the cold fire, and Joseph put his arm on Sam's shoulder. "He'll be back. I think you have a friend, Sam."

Sam knew he had a friend. He looked back again and again as he walked back to the cabin, but Lone Fox was not there. Then he reached into his pocket and fingered the rabbit tail. *Yes*, he thought, *I was as ready for the encounter as Lone Fox was,* "I have an Indian friend, Father, named Lone Fox." The next day Sam wrote is all down in his journal, but he knew he would never forget sharing tokens with Lone Fox.

December 18, 1777

Commanding General George Washington declared a Universal Day of Thanksgiving, celebrated with roasted pig at Valley Forge.

CHAPTER XIX

Christmas stranger

The temperature had warmed, and the snow had turned to sleet, then rain. It didn't seem at all like Christmas. Sam quickly dressed and whistled to Jack. They left the cabin. This was their special time to be together. It was still dark as they headed down the back hill to the creek to look for fresh animal tracks.

Sam and Jack shared their days and their secrets with each other. The biggest secret was in the barn. For the past week they had noticed that some animal was sleeping in their barn. They could see the matted hay, even though the animal who had slept there tried to hide the evidence. Sam was a tracker, and he could tell a sleeping den when he saw one. First, Jack thought it might be the Indian boy, but Sam explained that the Indian boy would never stay in their barn. Indians would prefer a sleeping den like Francois's or a long house if he lived with his tribe. Indians would never sleep with animals in a barn. Then, Jack thought it might be a bear, but there were no bear tracks. Sam knew Jack was still just getting the fundamentals down on tracking. He had a long way to go before he even came close to reading tracks!

The boys found no tracks by the Mourning Kill. Without snow, tracks were almost invisible and hard to read in the pre-dawn light. They hid behind trees and were very still, but heard or saw nothing. Their talking must have spoiled their hunt or maybe the martin and fox had a good idea the boys would come each morning and waited for them to leave before venturing out of their dens.

Now, climbing up and around the far side of the hill, they stopped at the Liberty Tree. Even in the foggy low light of dawn, they saw something that shocked them both. This morning there were funny disguised tracks near the Liberty Tree. But that's not what

181

caught their attention. Sam and Jack got down on their hands and knees and stared at the little tree with their mouths open.

Someone had decorated the tree. There were tiny carved wooden ornaments and others made from corn husks and a string of berries looped over the branches. But the most remarkable decoration was the Star on top tied with a vine. The star was embossed on a brass coat button.

The boys ran to the cabin shouting to their fathers. William and Joseph followed them back to the Liberty Tree. As the men and boys encircled the small tree, a voice behind them said, "Tannenbaum, tannenbaum."

Startled, they turned and looked in amazement. There was a tall skinny soldier in a blue coat standing not six feet away. His high leather boots gave his identity away. William and Joseph said together, "Hessian."

Joseph didn't know whether to run to the cabin for his musket or fight the Hessian to the ground with his bare hands. Shocked, as they stood staring at each other, Joseph's fists were ready, but his legs weren't. The man was grinning, didn't appear to be threatening, and he looked unarmed.

As the Hessian spoke, Joseph stared, still in shock as the stranger over and over tried to explain his presence in a loud and rapid cough of German words. Joseph's memories of the battlefield flashed through his mind and now his jaw stiffened. He could see again the charging Hessians as they fought and killed at Saratoga. His pulse was racing, and the anxiety of having the enemy soldier on his land made his heart thump in his chest. He put himself between the Hessian and Sam and held up his hand to stop Anne and the rest of the family now running toward them.

William was speaking in English to the stranger and then trying to understand what he was saying. William remembered little of the German language he had heard his parents speak years ago. Phebe had clung to her family heritage the longest and recited little poems to them in German and sang songs in French, but their schooling had always been in English. Samuel had often said one of the first things that newcomers to America did was to learn English. Then they tried hard to cover their foreign accents as they now wanted only to blend with the other immigrant Americans.

Sam looked around his father, waiting for the next explosion of words. The soldier appeared to be telling Joseph his name and that he meant no harm but was very hungry. He kept pointing to his whiskered face and slapping his stomach. It made a hollow empty sound. *He is hungry,* Sam thought.

Joseph seemed to have no trouble understanding this either, and told Anne, Lucy, and the children to go back to the cabin; he and William would deal with the Hessian. Not understanding who the stranger was, the children wanted to look closer at the decorated tree. Sam wanted to stay, too, and Jack hadn't budged from his father's side, neither had Jonas, so Sam didn't move either.

Complaining, the children followed the women back to the cabin. Anne quietly said to Lucy as they walked back, "Looks like there will be another plate to fix for Christmas dinner." The children spoke in whispers about the ornaments on the little Liberty Tree. They begged to look at it again, but Anne hustled them back to the cabin.

Joseph then loudly spoke to his brother, "Do you believe it! Six months ago Father was shooting at Hessians out the window of the saltbox. And I was facing them at Saratoga. Now here's one begging for food, his uniform in rags, thin as a fence post, shivering and sleeping near our barn."

Turning to the Hessian, Joseph shouted, "You should be on a ship going back to Germany!"

The boys jumped. Sam had never heard his father's voice spoken with such anger.

The Hessian stood his ground and kept pointing at the Liberty Tree. A cold wave of emotion flowed over Joseph as he again felt the fury of the discovery. Here, not a short walk from the cabin, a Hessian solder was probably sleeping in their barn and most likely eating their food. He and his brother had been so preoccupied sawing more siding and roofing and so relaxed about the threat of more war that they had let their guard down. He knew now they had put the family in danger with their complacence. Other soldiers as well as Indians could be near the cabin, and they, too, would be hungry and, as he looked at the smile trying to form again on the skinny Hessian's face, maybe not so happy. Where had the Hessian been since he returned from Saratoga? It was like a bad dream that this shell of a man was now standing by their barn.

The Hessian dropped his head as if he could read Joseph's thoughts and let out a mournful deep groan.

As he looked at the soldier more closely, Joseph now spoke in quick nervous sentences to his brother, "He's starved and as mangy as any poor critter I've ever seen. He has to have been watching us as he knows it's Christmas. He sure has good timing. And take a look at those carved ornaments. How long do you think he's been in the barn, if that's where he has been hiding? Don't you wish he'd stop smiling?"

William relaxed a little after Joseph acknowledged the smile. "I guess he figures we might shoot him if he stops, but he can see we are unarmed."

The brothers shared a nervous laugh, and the Hessian's head looked up and his grin reappeared.

"Herman Wehner on East Line Road speaks some German. If the weather is mild in the morning, we can ride over to see him tomorrow." More in control of his emotions, Joseph sent Sam and the cousins back to the cabin. "Tell your mother the Hessian will need a bowl of oatmeal for breakfast."

The boys ran to the cabin. "I figured he'd stay," shouted Jack. Jonas nodded to his brother.

Sam thought of the cold cellar. He needed to check for missing food. The Hessian had been around at least a week. Jack hadn't connected the Hessian with the matted hay in the barn yet. He wasn't as smart as he thought he was. In the same instant, Sam realized he should have mentioned their discovery to his father.

The remainder of Christmas Day was quiet. Nothing could compete with the excitement before breakfast. Lucy made a batch of cookie dough, and all children sat around the table rolling balls of dough into snakes and shaped them into little ornaments like they had seen on the Liberty Tree. Lucy stacked the cookies on shelves in their temporary oven next to the fire. If they didn't burn, the children's cookies would be presents to each other.

The Hessian was given Christmas dinner, too, and told he could stay in the barn for the night. Joseph went through their bags of old clothes and gave the Hessian warm socks, an old coat, and a horse blanket. Joseph began the blessing with a prayer:

Dear God, we are gathered together this Christmas to celebrate your Son's birth so many years ago. Like those in the stable in Bethlehem, we, too, are living in a new and sometimes dangerous land. This Christmas is especially sad for our family as we are still grieving for four family members: wife and mother Sarah and baby Lena, Grandmother Phebe and Grandfather Samuel. We pray that they are with you in heaven.

Dear God, please watch over and protect Matthew as he spends the winter with General Washington's troops in Pennsylvania. He will be in danger, and we ask that you protect him from harm and when the Revolution is over, bring him home. We miss Anne's family and pray that they are safe and well. We know not where our sisters Patience and Susanna are today. We know not how to find them and we pray that they will find us.

This Christmas we thank you for our health and this abundant food that we have harvested from your land and ask your blessing.

Oh, and we pray that this stranger who is now seated at our table will not harm us or we him. Amen.

The family, with a sniffle from little Abby at the mention of her mother, quietly chorused, "Amen." The Hessian was visibly moved. Anne saw sadness in his eyes.

Later, the family read the Bible and retold stories about Jesus since it was his birthday they were celebrating. They ate the little pale cookies that had shapes of bugles and drums, angels and bells, and pine cones and stars.

The weather was mild and damp with a heavy fog at night, not at all like a typical northern Christmas. There had been no snow, and added to the sadness of missing Sarah, Phebe, and Samuel, the families now had a stranger living in their barn. They said their prayers and Joseph banked the fire and blew out the candles.

The day after Christmas, Joseph hitched up the wagon and the three men drove to East Line Road with the Hessian riding in the back. They knew about the deserters and the Hessian's smile and Christmas ornaments had tempered Joseph's anger. The more Joseph and William talked, the more they agreed that having an extra man for cutting wood and ploughing in the spring would be good. The Hessian had written his name; it was Kaspar Kessel. They were now driving in silence.

William, trying again to break into his brother's dark thoughts, said, "It seems to me that he should help with the food since we know he's going to be eating plenty of ours. Should we trust him with a rifle?" Then after a long pause, he added, "We need meat and the Hessians soldiers were good shots."

Joseph didn't answer his brother.

CHAPTER XX

Happy snow

Kaspar stayed. He was so grateful for the food and equally grateful for refuge, he willingly agreed the next day to work at the Rue farm for food and asked to shelter in the barn until the end of winter. Joseph and William had learned from their visit with Herman Wehner that they were not alone in harboring deserters. And there were probably still more Hesse and Redcoat deserters in the woods, along with horses and oxen that had been driven off farms ahead of Burgoyne's advancing troops.

Herman Wehner had also heard that British immigrant farmers living near Saratoga, Cambridge, and Stillwater who remained loyal to the English Crown were now in a terrible state and had either been jailed or had fled to Albany, leaving their cabins and barns abandoned or reduced to ashes.

Sam's Almanack:

> *We are now feeding a Hessian soldier named Kaspar. He is sleeping in the barn and wearing some of father's old clothes. His high leather boots are in bad shape, but he cares for them and seems to favor them. He will work for father. I wonder what Francois will say about having a Hessian living in the barn?*

> *January has been very cold, not like December's warm spell or last year when we all were sick. Still without much snow, father is worried that the water in the well and the food stored in the cold cellar may freeze. He explained that a blanket of snow over the well and on the roof of the cold cellar would be good. The cabin is very crowded, and the sleeping loft*

is a mess. With all of our clothes and things, there's hardly room to sleep. Mother is going to have a baby. SR

That wasn't the only entry in *Sam's Almanack*. Joseph had asked him to write about his grandparents. During one of the long, dark January nights Sam wrote:

Grandmother Phebe was always busy with her loom. She said she had learned to weave from her mother in the Palatinate. There was never a day she didn't weave or sew or knit. Grandmother wove my blanket. She knitted us all caps and mittens. She sang to us and took us berry picking.

Grandfather Samuel was a farmer, my father says, because they had to eat. But he did lots of other things. He made my fishing pole. He also could carve beautiful chair legs. And he was a carpenter. He made all the doors for our house in his workshop. Some day we will go back to our house and take it all apart and bring it to Hop City and put it back together. SR.

Joseph and William looked up as they heard Sam read his journal aloud. It seemed like years ago that they had built the saltbox. So many things had happened since then. They didn't say a word. Sam caught his father's glance, but didn't know what it meant.

Joseph wanted to tell his son that right now bringing the house to their hill was not important. It was winter, and there were more trees to cut and boards to mill. They needed fresh meat for the kettle. Anne was cooking soup, not roasts. There was an unsaid worry about having enough food for five adults and seven children. A baby was due in the spring. A German soldier was living in their barn.

Sam was trying to understand his father's serious look, when his mother interrupted his thoughts and sent him to the cold cellar for another heavy pumpkin.

188

Sam's Almanack:

The weather is cold and windy. Mother is tired of gray days. We all want snow. There is not enough snow on the back hill to go sledding. Jack and I packed hay around the pumpkins and squash in the cold cellar to keep them from freezing. Father and Uncle William have cleared another field and taken the good logs to the mill. With Yankee and Uncle Will's horse, the wagon trips are fast. Our lane is clear of snow and the ground is frozen.

Father sold some of the wood at the sawmill, but the good logs are to be sawed for paneling and floor planking. Father has a plan. That's all he said.

Kaspar is helping with the wood. He eats with us, but says little.

Mother made us pumpkin soup and Aunt Lucy likes to make corn soup. We all have talked about ham and eggs and how good that would taste for a change. Lucy would like to see Jacobus; maybe he will come with a ham when it snows and go sledding with us on the hill. Cousin Louisa says if she were living back at the house, she would be ice skating with her best friends. She forgot her skates.

The cold cellar has two bare shelves. Mother has the crib ready and has been making little clothes for the new baby. Lizzie is hoping for a sister. SR

Jack woke up first. He ran to the outhouse, then, burst into the cabin waking everyone.

"It's snowing!" he yelled.

"It's snowing!" chorused the girls, as they huddled, looking out the crack of the open door.

"At last," whispered Anne to Joseph, as she rolled her heavy belly to the side and looked at her sleepy husband. "The children can all go outside today. Lucy has been so good keeping the children busy with projects, but she's just about at her wit's end. It will be wonderful to get everyone out of the cabin for a couple of hours."

"And, oh," she continued, "I'm thinking that when the baby comes, I should like Lydia here with me for the birth. Will you fetch her? And I was thinking if you could make William's side of the cabin all in bunks, we could make that a room for men and boys. The girls can stay in the loft with Lucy, and I will sleep here in our bed with the baby. I will be up during the night several times and will wake you."

Joseph didn't say anything while Anne was speaking. He knew that the new baby would wake him no matter where he slept, and he wanted to stay with Anne and keep an eye on the fire.

"We'll see when the time comes," was all he said.

Joseph was glad it was snowing and already thinking ahead to spring. They needed a good snow pack to wet the fields for growing good crops this summer. The rocky land on the hill drained quickly after a rain. He hoped that his seed was not freezing or rotting in the cold cellar. There would be money from the timber to buy more seed, but there were so many other things they would need.

The mild January had given him and William and now Kaspar an extra month to cut timber for a hay field west of the cabin. With two horses, they would need twice the hay. His mind was still planning as he built up the fire to warm the cabin.

Breakfast was especially happy. The girls were sitting on the bench at the end of the table like peas in a pod. Their oatmeal topped with maple syrup was quickly being scraped out of their wooden bowls, and they were talking fast and furious about the snow and what they would wear sledding and who would go first down the hill.

Lizzie now had playmates. She was the oldest girl, but only by a year over Louisa who was six, then came Abby who was four. Lizzie liked being the oldest girl; she could usually explain the rules to her girl cousins without protest. Because the boys now outnumbered the girls, the girls rarely won when voting. But, Aunt Lucy always seemed to be one step ahead of the boys, and the girls had plenty of time to draw pictures on the school slates or get a fairer deal in the settling of arguments.

Sam, on the other hand, had to deal with Jack who was eleven, and two years older than Sam. This was a big problem. Jack had his own ideas about everything and didn't know anything according to Sam. Whenever there was a decision, Jonas, eight years old, sided with his brother. This was usually after his brother gave him a hard stare or a shove. Sam's brother, Thomas, was three and too young to go out by himself or with the bigger boys, and he was not included. Sam liked his cousins most of the time, but it was hard to share his hill and his mother with them sometimes.

This morning, however, all thoughts were on the snow that was still falling from the dark overcast sky. They wiped the foggy window pane and looked out at the garden fence. Little piles of snow dotted every fence post and blanketed the rails. In a second, the wind whipped blowing snow past the window, and the fence posts disappeared from view.

"The chickadees must be outside waiting for us to bring them their breakfast," said Abby.

"Don't be stupid," said Jack, "birds don't fly in snowstorms."

"They do too." said Abby, with tears forming on her long eyelashes. "They always came to my mittens for bread crumbs when it snowed at our house. Mama always saved our crumbs for the birds."

"You always were Mama's favorite, and she just saved the bread crumbs for you because you were such a baby," scolded Jack.

"Why do you always have to spoil everything, Jack? She's your little sister." said Lizzie.

"Lizzie," interrupted her father. "You all need to be careful today when you play on the hill. The stumps are still there and until the snow gets deep enough, you could bump into one sledding and that would hurt. Since this looks to be a wet snow, it would be better for snowballs."

The boys started to yell and the girls yelled back. Anne looked at her husband and shook her head.

Lucy just laughed. "Just like back home, right? Don't worry, big brother, we know what to do with this snow, don't we girls?" And the girls cheered. They didn't have a clue, but their Aunt Lucy had figured out something.

Before the men left for the barn and the woodlot, Joseph tied a rope from one corner of the cabin, almost over the table, and into the opposite corner. "Have fun in the snow, and then hang your clothes to dry."

By now, Kaspar had learned their names and with his ever-constant smile, the children had accepted him as Joseph's hired man. This morning at breakfast, he looked as excited as the children and wished them all "happy snow."

It took hours to get everyone ready. Anne got out all the mittens, hats, jackets, sweaters, and woolen leggings and laid them out on the table. The children tried on everything that William had packed in the wagon when they left the house. Some of the clothing was very old and had holes from the moths and was put aside for patching. Leather boots too big for the wearer had their toes stuffed with wool. The rest of the clothing that was too small or too big was carefully folded and put away, but there wasn't much left over when they were done. Lizzie would have to wear an old pair of Sam's breeches and boots and pass hers on to Louisa.

> *Sam's Almanack:*
>
> *Kaspar is learning to speak English, happy snow. We built a fort with Aunt Lucy's help and made snowballs and had a great time today. The stumps are still showing on the back hill. No sledding on the bark scraps, but they are ready. The men worked in the barn all day. It's still snowing. SR*

After the first heavy snow, life in the cabin settled into one crisis after another. There were so many children in such a small cabin that tempers flared and boredom set in. Abby still had tantrums when Anne or Lucy did something different from what her mother would have done. Whether it was about who would comb her hair or cutting her potato just right, the little girl was letting her grief over her mother's death slowly seep out. The family all lent their shoulders for a good cry and William, stoic as he was, would often hold his children tight with his strong arms and cry with them.

Jack and Louisa, on the other hand, worked out their grief by picking fights with Sam and Lizzie. The table had been knocked over during one of Sam and Jack's fights, and Lizzie and Louisa fought over hair ribbons and the best place to sleep in the loft almost every night.

William understood what was happening as he was still missing Sarah terribly, but he couldn't seem to comfort his children or promise them that they would someday be a family again. Instead he told them they needed more to do. Lucy suggested that he help his children make *Almanacks*.

So William encouraged Jack and Jonas to make *Almanacks* like Sam's. Louisa refused, saying she had decided to make hers a diary like Lizzie's *Elizabeth's Diary,* and it wouldn't include the weather like Sam's. She had so much to write about. She missed her old life and friends and thought living in a cabin in the wilderness was awful. Hers would be a secret book. Because she had barely learned her letters, she would mostly draw pictures in her *Diary.*

Bending and stooping over the cooking fire was getting harder and harder for Anne. She was much more comfortable sitting in one of Samuel's chairs. So Anne asked Lucy to do the morning chores, while she started school every morning after breakfast at the kitchen table.

Little Abby would ring the make-believe school bell by banging the huge iron kettle hanging by the fire with a spoon. The children would draw straws to see who could use the two overworked slates first. The older children helped the younger ones with their reading and somehow, the volume was kept low enough to hear the new readers sounding out the words.

Lessons always began with a prayer and ended with the children singing "Yankee Doodle." The ending of the lesson and the singing became a celebration. The children beat their fists on the table pretending it was a drum, and Lucy would put aside her apron and marched around the table pretending she was blowing on a fife. The children laughed and cheered. The men could hear the shouts, and Kaspar recognized the song.

Kaspar was falling in love with the land. He was already making plans to find a farm nearby. He thought the deep woods were beautiful, even in the bleakest month of the year, and he knew he wouldn't be disappointed come spring.

If there was good weather, everyone went outdoors after their lessons. Anne always walked around the foundation of the cold cellar and watched as the children played. Lucy, Sam, and Jack took turns exercising the horses.

If it was storming, the boys cracked the hard hickory nuts while the girls learned how to crochet little doilies. Lucy said if they crocheted enough round discs from the scraps of wool yarn, she would crochet them together into a blanket for the spool crib.

Keeping the cabin clean and wood box full was a family task, and all of the children had their chores. It would be spring before the women could wash the heavy clothes and quilts. But many days, the lighter wash hung on the clothes line inside the cabin in everyone's way. The children took turns sweeping the cabin floor. The poor broom was worn down to a hard stub.

At bedtime, Joseph and William took turns reading from Anne's Bible by candlelight, giving them all something to think about as they went to sleep. It would be another month before they would go back to church on Sundays.

CHAPTER XXI

Big trouble

The second big snowfall finally blew in, this one from the northeast. Sam and Jack were arguing as they came in the door from the outhouse.

"A Nor'easter," insisted Sam. "This storm is coming on soft winds that will build to a howling gale! It sneaks up on you. The wind blows straight from the northeast. I know! Aunt Lucy and I were in a Nor'easter last year and only made it home because Yankee knew the way."

Jack didn't believe a word, but Jonas knew his cousin would never lie about something as serious as getting lost in a snowstorm, so he didn't nod his head in agreement with his brother as the discussion reached a fevered pitch.

At the height of their argument, Kaspar came into the cabin with a load of firewood and saw the empty water pail. He said "pail." Then he glanced at the boys and saw them punching the air between them. He was covered with snow and had an excited grin on his face. "Blitz! Blitz!" and he was out the door with the pail to get water from the well.

The boys stopped hitting each other. "Kaspar's speaking Gerlish again. Is he trying to say blizzard?" asked Jack, and the boys laughed.

Lizzie asked, "What is Gerlish?"

"Blitz, blitz!!" said Abby, imitating Kaspar's pronunciation. The boys laughed even harder. "Blitz, blitz!"

"Gerlish is German/English, don't you know?" smirked Jack with a stupid grin on his face.

Anne raised her voice, "That will be enough, boys. Put on your coats and tend to the horses."

As they searched for their mittens, Jack said, "We have plenty of time to feed the horses. Let's go down the back hill. Maybe there's enough snow to go sledding." And then Anne heard Jack yell to Sam as they raced out the door, "Let's check the fox den across the creek, too. Maybe there are fresh tracks or something."

But Sam knew the ice was too thin to cross the Mourning Kill to the den and it was snowing too hard to see tracks. Calling ahead to his cousin, "Let's go to the barn instead," but his words were blown away from the cabin, and Anne never heard her son's shout.

Jack still didn't want to go to the barn, until the snow-filled wind sucked his breath away and he angrily agreed with his cousin. Jonas gripped his coat and turned his back to the wind. He followed Sam.

They tugged at the side door, pushing aside the snow, and the wind whipped the door closed behind them. The horses were happy to have some company. They had plenty of hay, but loved to be brushed. The boys climbed about on the horse stalls and on the horses' backs.

The rest of the afternoon, the three cousins played "fort" in the hay loft. There were imaginary Redcoats marching toward them, and Indians circling around them or hiding in the hay. When they tired of that, they lay back and buried themselves in the hay to keep warm and told ghost stories, with each boy trying to outdo the last with more horrid tales of witches and ghosts, bloody heads, and puss-filled wounds.

By late afternoon, it was already dark inside the barn. Yankee whinnied and snorted as the wind gusted against the barn. The wind pushed against the huge roof causing the timbers to creak, and little snow piles now grew inside the barn as snowflakes flew through the cracks in the siding. Hungry and a little spooked, they raced to the door to return to the cabin. Jack raised the door latch and pushed, but the door didn't budge. The three boys all pushed at once, but drifting snow had piled against the door.

Jonas was scared, but Jack said it was nothing. They would just go out the other door. But the hinged doors that were wide enough to drive in a wagon were securely fastened from the outside, and snow would have drifted against them, too. Sam knew they were trapped.

"Someone will come to the barn. Father will come to check on Yankee," thought Sam aloud.

"I'm hungry, and this place is dark. I don't know how Kaspar can stay out here," said Jonas. "Let's call again." The boys called until they were hoarse, but the wind and blowing snow carried their shouts into the woods.

It's time for dinner, thought Sam, *and the barn is cold.* "Let's get the horse blankets and just wait for help," said Sam as he tried to calm Jonas.

"Kaspar has a blanket, too. I'll get his," said Jack.

As Jack went to the third stall where Kaspar slept and was feeling around in the dark for the blanket and picked it up, they could hear someone calling. Something heavy dropped out of Kaspar's blanket and struck Jack's leg as it fell. Blood streaked down his cut shin as he raced back to shout with Sam and Jonas.

"Kaspar has a knife." Jack whispered to Jonas.

Soon they heard the shovel scraping outside the door. When it finally opened, the boys were greeted with a serious shout.

"Blizzard," said Kaspar.

He scooped Jonas up with his strong arms and headed out of the barn. He turned to the older boys, "Latch the door."

With Jonas now on his back, the strong Hessian bent into the wind and blowing snow. Jack and Sam trudged through the drifts, trying to follow in Kaspar's footsteps. They could not see the cabin but could smell the smoke from the chimney.

As they stumbled into the cabin with frozen feet and hands, William and Joseph shouted stern words of relief. Their fathers' wet boots and jackets hung by the fire. They had walked beside the half frozen Mourning Kill to Gordon's sawmill. With fresh snow covering tracks, they had worried that the boys might have been playing on the thin ice and come to harm. They had called, again and again thinking the boys might have gotten lost and had wandered away from the hill.

William told the boys to sit on the bench in front of the fire and take off their wet boots. The girls and Thomas didn't say a word, but sat at their places even though they had long ago finished their dinner. As soon as the three stopped shivering, Anne served them hot corn mush with maple syrup and big chunks of baked squash. Then, Joseph sent them to bed. "Not a word tonight from any of you, do you understand?"

The sorry boys answered in unison, "Yes."

When all the children were in bed, they could hear the adults whispering. Then they could hear them praying, thanking God for the safe return of their sons. Sam turned his face into his pillow and sobbed. His mother was crying.

A day later, the cut on Jack's leg was red and swollen. Jack had not shown it to his father or washed the dirt and hay from the knife wound. His leg hurt, and he cried in pain as his father now put hot wet towels across the cut. William said the leg must be hot packed often until the redness was gone and the puss stopped oozing. Jack was shaken, and the other children quietly observed the steamy soakings.

Sam and Jonas walked to the cold cellar without Jack. As soon as they left the cabin, Jonas started crying. He told Sam he feared his brother's leg would have to be cut off like the soldiers' legs in the war. Sam was worried too. He wished he and Lucy could ride to the trading post. Marie, Nicholas McDonald's spooky Indian wife, would know what to put on Jack's cut to make it heal. But that was impossible today. The wind was blowing the snow into huge drifts, and they had been sternly told to go no farther than the cold cellar or out of sight of the cabin. There would be no travel until the storm passed.

Sam reached for the latch on the cellar door only to discover it was already unlatched. He cautiously opened the door. As his eyes became accustomed to the dark, he had a feeling they were not alone. Hoping beyond hope that he knew who was in the cellar with them, he pretended to blindly reach for the familiar shelves, searching under the hay to find a squash, talking all the while with Jonas.

When his eyes became accustomed to the darkness, he saw the Indian boy crouched in the corner. At last, he said to himself, at last.

"Yoo-hoo, Lone Fox," he shouted.

"O-ho, Sam," said Lone Fox saying the Indian response to the hailing call. *Next he would use the friendly Indian "hey" or maybe the American "hello."*

Jonas gasped and shrieked and hid behind his cousin. Sam turned and grabbed him by the shoulder and said, "He's my friend."

Jonas's eyes grew even larger. Sam walked toward Lone Fox and stretched out his arm. The Indian held out his arm in return and stood. Then they started to "talk," hands waving, fingers pointing, stomachs patted. The boys' delight in being able to communicate clearly overshadowed any fear as now both were laughing.

Then Sam was serious and talked in English. Jonas watched as Lone Fox seemed to understand that Sam was telling him about Jack's leg. The Indian heard the words knife and wound and that Jack was injured. Sam said over and over, "Puss, puss" and made a gross face and pinched his nose while pointing to his leg.

Watching and listening, Jonas figured that the Indian boy lived somewhere nearby and that he knew all about their family and had come to the cold cellar before. He also figured that his cousin Sam had kept it a secret from his brother.

Sam was handing Lone Fox potatoes and filling a sack with corn. Jonas couldn't believe his eyes. Now, Sam was giving away their food. In a second, the Indian boy was out the door and disappeared into the storm.

Sam's Almanack:

> *The Nor'easter has covered the back hill with snow. The sun is shining most of the time and the wind is not blowing hard anymore. We have been rolling*

down the hill and having great fun packing a trail for the bark sleds to run.

Father told the story of the Indian corn and pumpkins planted in our field. Now the cousins know all about the Indians in the woods.

Lone Fox brought a leather bag filled with moss to the cabin. He told us it was for the "puss." Uncle Will bandaged Jack's leg with the moss covering the red-hot wound. By the next morning the swelling was down. Uncle Will said they will hot pack and wrap the cut with moss until Jack's leg is healed. Jack has been very quiet and says his prayers every night without being told.

Mother and Aunt Lucy were glad to finally meet the Lone Fox and gave him cornbread and some of their jam to take to his mother SR.

The men were now busy in the barn all day, and the children were told to stay away. The boys had no idea what might be going on, but they quietly walked by the barn several times a day trying to hear a word or any clue as to what might be happening.

Two weeks later it snowed again, and the men were shoveling away the drifts in front of the big barn doors. Lizzie was the first to notice the open doors, and called to Sam. Jack limped to the door and walked behind the cabin where he could watch. The horses came out harnessed together. Yankee did not look happy with the new, stiff harness on her back. She much preferred the soft wagon harness or no harness at all. And Boots was rearing and trying to escape from the leather straps. Kaspar stood in front, between the horses heads, holding their bridles, and slowly leading them out of the barn. He spoke quietly into their twitching, pricked ears. He voice was calming, and he showed no hurry moving them out of the barn.

By now the rest of the children had their coats on and were standing in the shoveled path to the barn. The yard was a maze of topless tunnels. The wider ones led to the outhouse, cold cellar, well, and barn. But there were smaller beaten trails to the back hill and to the Liberty Tree. The lane was just a smooth, wind-swept, snow-covered open path down the hill with no tunnels or tracks.

Then the children let out a whoop! Emerging from the barn behind the horses was a sleigh. It was skidding from the hay covered barn floor to the trampled snow. The horses were being led toward where the lane would be if not covered with snow, slowly breaking a trail and taking short steps into the drifts. Yankee whinnied and showed the whites of her eyes. Kaspar spoke again to the horses and both she and Boots went heads down, snorting with huge puffs of hot breath billowing around their heads like clouds in the cold dry air. The children cheered and jumped up and down, not believing what they were seeing.

Joseph was in the sleigh and had the reins in his gloved grip as William now guided the sleigh past the opened barn doors. The horses were moving toward a wind-swept part of the road and out of the big drift, and the children could see the profile of the sleigh. It had a high back with tapered sides. There was a little side step and a door cut for the passengers to step through to enter the sleigh. The most beautiful parts of the sleigh were the two carved wooden runners that curved in the front then onto the snow straight back.

Anne and Lucy hugged and cheered as the horses pulled the sleigh on to the crest of the lane. They knew the men were building a sleigh, but had not been permitted in the barn. It was to be a surprise.

Joseph and William were smiling, and Kaspar grinned from ear to ear. He tried to contain his throaty laugh, fearing it might scare the horses, but the laugh surfaced as he heard the cheers from the family. The children ran to the barn then followed in the tracks behind the sleigh, stumbling and ploughing through the snow shouting their delight.

Sam's Almanack:

The men made a sleigh. It's beautiful and wonderful to ride in. We have been up and down the lane several times. The horses have not had such exercise since the Nor'easter. We are so happy. Jack is smiling again and his leg is better. He rode in the sleigh with us.

Kaspar told us, using his Gerlish, that our sleigh is like the sleighs in his homeland. He carved a picture of his village on the back of the sleigh. There are houses and a church and a tall tower with a magical clock. His grandfather told him an old story about the clock. One time the clock sang and warned the people of the village of danger in time for them to hide from robbing horsemen.

Kaspar misses his parents and brothers and sisters; he has no wife or children. He likes our hill very much and wants to become an American. SR

Jack, Jonas, Lizzie and Louisa all wrote or drew pictures of the sleigh in their *Almanacks* and *Diaries*. Abby and Thomas drew too, carefully writing their names below the pictures of the sleigh, and Anne hung their drawings by the window.

Kaspar continued to carve runners in the barn, and one by one he made small sleds for each of the children and a toboggan. Firewood stored in the barn was now loaded on the toboggan and pulled to the cabin by the boys. Sam used his sled to haul the big pumpkins. And the younger children played on their sleds near the cabin on the small hill by the cold cellar, while the older ones packed new trails and ran their sleds down the steep back hill.

Everyone seemed happier. Even the horses were happier. Lucy said that Yankee had never looked as beautiful as she did pulling the sleigh with Boots. The children could hardly wait for the school lessons to end so they could go outdoors.

Anne was awake before Joseph. As soon as she heard his deep breathing turn shallow, she turned to him. Whispering, not to wake the children, "Isn't it time to build bunks and move our boys into the sleeping room with your brother?"

When Joseph, who was pretending to be still asleep, turned to the wall, Anne continued. "Joseph, the baby will be here in another month. We must make a plan. Thank goodness the sleigh is finished, and you will be able to fetch Lydia in time. This baby will come quickly."

Joseph didn't answer. He wished with all his heart the house was here and that his family was safely settled in the saltbox. Anne would have a big cooking fireplace, the children would be in beds, and they all would have room to move about. And, Anne would have the borning room for the birthing. He remembered his mother walking through the saltbox saying, *"Joseph, a woman needs a borning room....."* Joseph choked. Anne knew her husband was thinking.

The men had worked hard. More siding, floor planks and roofing were cut and ready for the house. Extra shingles were neatly stacked. They would do without windows until Joseph could get to Schenectady and have a glazer make them. He thought "nine over nines" would be so fine. He could imagine his father's delight in seeing the big windows and shutters complementing the thick double cross door he had masterfully hung with iron hinges.

How he missed his parents. His heart ached when he thought of them. They had protected his home to the last, and now he was feeling powerless to bring the house to Balls Town. Over and over, his dreams of rebuilding the house on top of the cold cellar turned into nightmares as he slept shouting and watching as the house burned to the ground.

He and William had thought of every conceivable way to get the house to the hill. But now that America was at war with England, what plan could they use? Who was winning the war? Who was living in their house or had the saltbox already been torched by the Redcoats like so many of the cabins near Saratoga?

Anne had stopped talking. Her husband had become quiet, not just in bed, but quiet all the time. He rarely smiled and was sometimes gruff with Sam and short tempered with her and Lucy. She had seen Joseph and William arguing, and once they had come to blows out by the barn, only to end their fight with hugs and tears.

Where was Matthew? Was he still alive or had he died fighting with General Washington's Army? And, what about Joseph's sisters? Had Patience married? Was she living in the house? And what had become of Susanna?

And what of *her* sisters? Anne felt in her heart that her family's strong ties to England would turn them against the American rebels. Her father, Thomas, had been so proud to be an Englishman living in an American colony. Her sisters and husbands, too, thought of themselves as English citizens. Caroline loved her shopping trips in Manhattan and dealt with the garment traders just like her father had when he had his business in London. Now their beautiful quilts were sold only in English shops. Even at the last quilting bee, they were all still drinking English tea long after it had been banned by the Continental Congress.

The thought of never seeing her sisters again was too awful to think about. She pushed that ugly thought to the back of her head, gripped her pillow, and let out a weak moan. She began her silent morning prayer with a plea to God for her family's safety.

As if to bring her thoughts back to her own needs, the baby was now kicking and stretching, moving and ready to get out into the world. Her body told her that this would probably be a normal birth and soon there would be another child to smile at her. Her pregnancy had gone well and there had been no sickness this winter except for a few sniffles. She went back to her interrupted prayer and thanked God for his protection from illness and for the sleigh. Lydia would be here for the birthing, coming either in the sleigh or the wagon.

Her thoughts and her prayers were now all mixed up. Now she was thinking about the sleigh. The sleigh and sleds had made winter a happy time. Joseph took the children with him in the sleigh to McKnight's for the milk and Lydia's for eggs. They now churned the cream for butter for their bread and oatmeal, and twice a week they ate eggs for breakfast.

Joseph and William had taken wagon loads of big logs to the mill, and Major Gordon had eagerly bought all of them. Now that the British Army had been defeated at Saratoga and the Northern Indians had gone back to Canada, he felt sure that new colonists would come to Balls Town to settle and build houses and barns.

The farms along the Scotch Bush road had been abandoned by the Tories, and Gordon's men had boarded the cabin doors and windows. Gordon had told Joseph the United States would sell the abandoned farms in the spring. Now Anne thanked God for protecting her husband and the other men who had fought at Saratoga and then of the men who had given their lives at that horrible battle.

The American flag was still flying over the fort last Sunday when they came home from church. It had been a cold clear day, and the wind had whipped the flag. Thomas had told her, "The flag is talking to you, Mama." Then she remembered the women whose husbands had been wounded or died at Saratoga. They had been at church with their children. After the baby is born, I shall do something with them. Two of those wives had been part of the group who had sewn the flag. Would they like to join her quilting bee?

Sam was up. She could hear him slip on his boots and head out the door. He had been such a help while they had waited for word of the battle. At the fort, he had stood on the lookout platform and watched for the men's return with the spy glass to his eye, always reassuring the other children and telling them not to give up hope; to have faith that their fathers would come home. On the next bright sunny day, she would sew white stars on her son's blue and red quilt. *Thank you, God, for my children, for Sam who watches over the other children. He has much more to learn, but has already shown such wisdom for being only nine years old.*

Anne next thought of Francois. She then said a silent prayer for his safety and prayed he would be coming soon. She would be glad to see him and so would Sam. In fact, the trader would be a welcome sight to all the Rues. She laughed as she thought Yankee would be glad to see Lulu, too. *Amen, amen. Now I'm praying for the horses.*

Joseph turned on his back, then towards Anne and reached for her. His warm hand gently rubbed her swollen belly and a smile formed on his lips even though his eyes were still closed. "What shall we name this big fellow?"

"How do you know it will be a fellow? I have plans for a darling daughter who will wear pretty dresses and have ribbons in her hair and fly around this hill with flowers in her fist, laughing and playing with Thomas. I looked in my trunk, Joseph. Someday Lizzie will want to be called Elizabeth, and she will want pretty party dresses. She wants a little sister like Abby."

"If the baby is a she, she will be as pretty as her mother, wear party dresses and have flowers in her hair, and I shall proudly carry her about as I carried Thomas when he was a baby."

Anne laughed. This was so unlike Joseph. He never used those words or said those thoughts. What had gotten into him? Anne sighed, but continued her practical thoughts. Things would be all right today, but tomorrow the boys must be moved to the side room and a curtain hung between the two rooms. "Joseph, we must reorganize the cabin, and you must trust Kaspar with the rifle; a nursing mother and growing children need meat!"

Kaspar was given Joseph's musket and had been gone for more than a week when he returned with large buck strapped to the toboggan. For days afterward, he talked of the land. His love for America was growing to include the wilderness north of Balls Town. He talked of the hot springs and herds of deer just to the north and the elk and moose in the old rounded Adirondack Mountains. He had been in country Joseph and William had yet to explore.

The roasting venison filled the cabin with a most wonderful aroma and drifted out the chimney. Anne was still enjoying the aroma of the roasting meat as she walked around the cold cellar. She checked the foundation where their house would be. Joseph had piled even more snow over the planking that would be the house flooring. Today her children were sledding and rolling down the hillside of packed snow. Their little bellies would be puffed up after dinner tonight. Anne gathered apples for a cobbler from the cellar. Then she went back for squash. This would be a feast with buttered vegetables and meat with gravy. She felt wonderful, full of energy and a smile broadened on her face as the sun came out from behind the clouds. The cabin did not seem so confining after William and the boys were settled on bunks in the side room. Today the three men were cutting logs for another addition on the other side of the cabin for the girls.

April wind blew open the cabin door, and the downdraft from the chimney blew smoke and ash onto the cabin floor. Lucy slammed the door and grabbed the broom.

"How many times must this happen before spring really arrives, and the sun warms the ground and dries up some of the mud?" she muttered under her breath. The quickly melting snow left trails of mud. The children were tracking mud into the cabin, and everyone's shoes were wet. They would not wear their boots.

Lizzie calmly spoke, "Aunt Lucy, it is spring. I have put away my boots for another year!" The boys refused to wear their hats and gloves saying it was warm outside, but their hands were now raw and chapped. The girls were cranky. Their clothes were dirty, and the air was so damp that when they did wash clothes, it took forever for the clothes to dry.

Anne sat by the fire. Lucy was making breakfast and snapping at the children to wash up for breakfast. As Anne fingered the locket which hung around her neck, she thought of her mother. For a moment she closed her eyes and felt such a loss for the woman who had borne her and then died. She would not have understood how Anne could be happy in a cabin in the wilderness, as Matthew had described Balls Town. Yet it seemed so right for Anne. She turned to go to the table and wait for Joseph's prayer to begin their day. As she turned she looked to the floor. The boards were damp.

"Joseph, please look under the floor and see if my trunk is still dry."

Joseph removed the loose board and reached for the trunk. Anne opened the lid only to find one of her favorite dresses on the bottom was wet and the rest damp.

Upset, but holding back her anger, she asked Lucy to hang them all outside in the air to dry. She didn't want them to smell of smoke.

"Joseph, it's time to rake away the leaves from around the cabin. The water must run down the hill, and we need air to circulate under the floor."

Joseph knew this, and it was time to move the outhouse, fill the stinking hole, and dig a new hole, this one farther from the cabin.

"Boys, rake away the leaves behind the cabin and spread them over the garden. We shall plough them into the dirt before planting." Then to his brother, "Shall we give a toss for who gets to do the outhouse?" The brothers laughed.

Lucy was tired, tired of being indoors, tired of wiping sniffling noses, and tired of cooking and washing up. She didn't appreciate her brother's humor this morning. She longed to get away, maybe take Yankee for a long ride. Above all, she was unhappy that Jacobus had not been to see her. There had been no visits all winter. After the Nor'easter when he had not come with a ham, she stopped tying her hair and just braided it down her back. The roads were now passable but only by horseback. Lucy thought Jacobus might ride to their cabin and have lunch with them. But he had not come. She was beginning to give up hope that he would ever ride up to the cabin with his happy smile just to see her.

"What's the matter, Aunt Lucy?" asked Sam, "You don't usually slam the door."

"Quiet, Sam. If I want to slam the door, I will, and wipe your feet, and eat your oatmeal...and...." And the tears began to fall. "I was hoping Jacobus might stop by, that's all."

"Oh," said Sam, pausing with his mouth wide open, then with courage he said, "Remember good 'ol *Poor Richard's Almanack*, Aunt Lucy, 'He that lives on hope, dies farting,' I mean fasting."

There was a moment of silence and then everyone in the cabin started to laugh, including Lucy. Sam, too, began to laugh at himself. Later Anne took Lucy aside and put her arm around her shoulder. "He will come when he's ready. Have faith, he will come." But Lucy was not so sure.

William tapped the maple trees, and the sugaring was going well. Daily routines changed to adapt to new spring chores. Now the children would quickly dress and go out to check all the pails hanging from the spouts on the trees. The older children cracked the surface ice and poured the watery sap into the two big kettles while the men built up the fires. Anne could hear Abby and Thomas run from tree to tree shouting, "There's more, there's more over here," as they raced around the yard. The temperature was still dropping below freezing at night, and often the trees did not start to drip until midday, but it continued long after the children went to bed. They were rewarded each morning with new sap. Then they would rush into the cabin with red cheeks and chapped hands hungry for breakfast. School now began after lunch.

Lucy was cooking again this morning. It would be oatmeal, and she had softened some dried apples. They were running extremely low on both salt and oatmeal, two foods they depended on every day. Having William and his children with them through the winter had run down the supplies. The cold cellar was looking very empty. A ride to the trading post might be a good excuse to take Yankee for a ride. And she could check for mail.

As the apple slices plumped up in the warm water and their sweet smell filled the cabin, Lucy wondered what she would do this spring. She needed a project, and she knew it should involve food. With three men, the garden and fields would be quickly ploughed and planted. What would she plant?

Maybe she would raise chickens this summer. More eggs would be good; the children were always so hungry in the morning. She would ask her brothers if they could build a chicken house. And without fail, today she must bake more bread in the hottest coals of the fire. The boys were eating almost as much as the men.

Lucy asked Anne if today might be the day. Anne said she thought not and had made a list of supplies they needed. Lucy put on her jacket, then ran her brush through her long hair one more time, and tied it back with a red ribbon. "I shall have quite a load to bring home, and Joseph said the road is too muddy for a wagon. Shall I make two trips, Anne?"

Kaspar overheard the conversation. "Miss Lucy, I will ride along. Carry the heavy bags. Ride Boots. After lunch do my chores."

Lucy looked at Kaspar. He was serious and not smiling. She agreed that she could use his help and it made sense, but she longed for solitude and hoping that she might see Jacobus. Still, being sensible, she said, "If it's all right with my brothers, I would like the help." The shopping trip was uneventful as there had been no mail for the Rues, and Lucy and Kaspar had made it back to the cabin well before dinner.

CHAPTER XXII

Fear and joy

Anne was restless and walking past the Liberty Tree. She thought about walking down to the Mourning Kill, but decided the climb back up to the cabin was not a good idea. That thought was replaced with a cramp as she rounded the cold cellar foundation. She called to her son. "Sam, go find your father. He said he was going to the barn. Tell him to fetch Mrs. Palmer. I think the baby will come today."

Sam heard the words and looked at his mother. He handed Jack his pail of water and ran to the barn. Anne slowly walked back to the cabin. Lucy took one look at Anne and knew today could be the day. Anne sat by the fire and had a cup of warm cider. Then she smiled. "This will be a short wait; I hope your brother doesn't take his time fetching Lydia or you may be my helper! After Lydia comes, you better plan on spending some time outdoors today. Maybe you can take the children on a long walk this afternoon. Thank goodness it's not raining."

"I'll pack a basket lunch, and we'll watch William and Kaspar fill the pot holes in the lane." Lucy was glad that this was the day. Her brother could tend to the chores around the cabin while the others were outdoors. "Sometimes," she said almost to herself, "things do work out." Now, it would be up to Anne, and Lucy prayed that Anne's labor would be short and the baby healthy. Lucy called to Jack to get more potatoes. There would not be time to make bread this morning, and there were so many mouths to feed that a meal without bread would need plenty of potatoes. It seemed like she had been cooking her whole life.

Anne looked at her young sister-in-law. Lucy had become a true friend, and they had spent so much time together in the little cabin that they knew each other's moods and emotions without even speaking. Today she saw a change in her sister-in-law. Lucy had washed her bloomers, and her hair was neatly pulled back. Anne saw a woman; Lucy was seventeen.

Joseph burst into the cabin, "The snow is gone so the sleigh is of no use." He mindlessly told the women. "The lane is so muddy and has washed out in several places from the rain last week, so the wagon will not work either." Anne smiled as Joseph nervously rattled off his thoughts. "Lydia will have to ride. I will ride Yankee and take Boots for Lydia." And he was gone. Lucy started to laugh, and then both women were laughing.

Anne looked about the cabin. She had sewn sacs with draw-string bottoms and tiny caps for the baby to wear to keep its head warm at night when the fire was banked. She was confident that she was prepared. The girls had crocheted enough little circles that a warm blanket now covered the firm mattress of straw and wool. The spool crib was ready for the new baby Rue.

The next best thing, thought Anne, was that the cabin was ready. It hadn't taken long for the men to enlarge the cabin with another room. The second addition was even better than the boys' room as it had two south facing windows, a sturdy plank floor off the ground, and bunk beds across the north wall. William had made shelves for the girls to keep their books, and Kaspar had carved hooks for their clothes. The men had made a table and benches, and the girls now boasted that their room was the neatest room in the cabin.

By evening Jack was pacing and could not work on his *Almanack* or read his book. Finally he burst out of the cabin and stood in the dark. William followed. "I can't bear to be in the cabin with Aunt Anne. What if she should die like Mama?"

The men had planned to take the children to Lydia's in the wagon when Anne delivered the baby, but now with the lane impassable, the wagon was still in the barn. It was evening, and the baby still had not come. "Jack, your mother was exhausted from nights of tending to the sick soldiers in our barn. Your aunt is healthy and well. When the time grows near, you and any of the other children who are still awake will dress and come out with us to tend the bonfire. We will burn up the rest of the sugaring wood and some of these wet leaves and branches. It's a beautiful night, the stars will be out, and we will be warmed by the fire." William put his arm around his son's shoulders.

The younger children slept through it all. They were so exhausted after their walk with Lucy that they almost fell asleep before they finished their dinner. Lucy had sung songs with them as they marched down the lane and watched the men shovel dirt and small stones, then dig ditches to channel the water from the soggy hill to the Mourning Kill. It had been a long walk for the younger children, but exploring the hill had been fun.

Sitting on old logs out of the wind, they had soaked up the warm rays and cheerfully played for most of the afternoon. The boys had explored a new area of the hill and found more big boulders and followed animal tracks going from the woods down to the creek. The girls and Thomas had picked a bouquet of trilliums and lady slippers to take to Anne, and Lucy had woven little garlands of violets into the girls' hair.

When they returned to the cabin for dinner, Lucy smelled the rich aroma of her soup. Lydia had brought spices with her, and she had made a thick bread pudding from stale baked bread she had stuffed into her basket before leaving home. Lydia was happily singing when the girls brought the flowers they had gathered and gave them to Anne.

The baby was born before midnight. It was a normal birthing, but had required some hard pushes from Anne. The infant was now washed and dressed with soft lamb's wool for a diaper and wrapped tightly in muslin. Anne was tired but much relieved, and she and Joseph were now together in their bed. Both too exhausted to speak, they quickly fell asleep.

William let the bonfire die down, and the older children came into the cabin exhausted and quickly fell asleep. Later as William lay in his bed he thought, Anne had been right, it had been quick at the end. He thought of Sarah and how brave she had been, and how quietly she had died holding his hand after their tiny baby was born. His sorrow washed over him, and he prayed that God might help him sleep; the same prayer he said every night.

Abby and Thomas were on the bed with Anne as she nursed the infant at day break. "My sister?" asked Thomas.

"It's a brother, Thomas," said his father building up the fire. "And, your mother and I have decided that he looks like a Charles. Your mother had a grandfather named Charles that for all we know is still living in England. What do you think of that name?"

Thomas nodded to his father and then snuggled under the covers close to his mother.

Abby was so happy to see the baby that she hid her disappointment that it was not a little girl. "I love babies. Aunt Anne, I will help take care of little Charles." Anne thanked her sweet niece who had tears in her eyes, but a brave smile on her round little face, "I will need lots of help."

Joseph was washing up during all of this. "I better fetch the preacher. Today is a wonderful day, and he needs to get here and bless our new big fellow."

Anne smiled and gave Charles to Lydia. "Better clean the big boy up. Reverend Ball will be here in no time. In fact, all of you straighten the cabin and get dressed. Joseph, please hand me your mother's Bible." Anne carefully cleaned the quill of the pen and wrote:

Charles Joseph Rue
Born March 30, 1778, Balls Town, New York

"Breakfast's almost ready, and Kaspar went hunting last night. We shall have meat tonight if he's lucky," said William.

Thankfully, Reverend Ball arrived the next day. He rode up on his horse with his black coat buttoned to his neck as he braced his body into the wind. "God save us from this wind! It pierces my coat right down to my flesh!" yelled the huge man still gripping his hat. "Rue, this hill is steeper than I remembered, and my horse has not been getting the exercise he needs. I had to stop twice to give the poor beast a rest."

Sam poked Jack in the back as he looked at the preacher, and then whispered to his cousin, "He's been sitting at the table a little too much, too."

The children held back from the man dressed in black from head to toe. He could shake the Church's candle chandelier during the service, or else it was the presence of the Almighty that did the shaking. Both Sam and Lizzie had noticed the chandelier swaying during his sermons, and they had moved closer to their father.

Today, the adults were all smiles. "Another good day for the Lord and Balls Town," said their preacher, "Let's get on with the baptism. Whatever Lydia has cooked up, sure smells good."

Lydia's husband arrived after breakfast with two plucked roosters that, added to the cornbread and gravy, had everyone's mouths watering. He had balanced a beautiful crumb cake their daughter had made on his lap as he rode up the hill and had also brought a bottle of elderberry wine for the baptismal celebration.

Reverend Ball carefully took baby Charles from Joseph. He held the sleeping infant in his arms and recited the words they had last heard while the family was living in the saltbox when Thomas was born.

> *"Dear Heavenly Father, we come together today to baptize this baby in your name that he may grow in love to know you and to do your work in this new land. Charles Joseph Rue I baptize you in the name of the Father, Son, and Holy Ghost. Amen."*

Then he continued, "You all know, of course, that this will have to be part of a service at church. We shall welcome him into the congregation and introduce him to everyone. He will need a godfather, too, Joseph. It's time you were all back to church on the

Sabbath. Easter is in two weeks, if Anne is feeling well and the lanes are not too bumpy, I'll expect to see you all at the service." Reverend Ball turned and looked at the serious, staring children's speechless faces.

Joseph cleared his throat. "Reverend, we hope you were planning on staying for dinner."

"Good gracious, yes, but then I must head down your hill."

Lydia and Lucy dished out the chicken. The girls ate at their table to make room for the preacher. The noise now woke Charles, and he started to cry. Anne picked him up from the crib, took him into the girls' room and put him to her breast.

As Reverend Ball stood to leave, he called to William and asked him to join him outside. "William, I know that it has been just a short time since your dear wife Sarah departed. But God's work is never done, and you should know that He has work and plans for all of us. I want you to come to church on the Sabbath, too, and bring your children. We need to see you, and you need to be a family once more." He pulled himself up onto his still tired horse. "Downhill is much preferred! See you on the Sabbath."

William nodded, but made no promise.

Rue Family Tree

Samuel Rue *m.* Phebe Martin
    Joseph Rue *m.* Anne Ducker
        Sam
        Lizzie
        Thomas
        Charles
    William Rue *m. Sarah d.*
        Jack
        Jonas
        Louisa
        Abby
        Lena d.

    Matthew
    Patience
    Susanna
    Lucy

CHAPTER XXIII

Oxen

It was two weeks since Kaspar had taken Joseph's musket to hunt. William had made excuses that maybe he had to go a long way, or maybe he had become lost. Joseph had darker thoughts, maybe Kaspar had left, or worse, died.

They didn't share any of their thoughts with the children, but the boys talked about it too. "Remember, he's not one of us," said Jack. "He doesn't have to stay."

"But he has father's musket," reminded Sam.

Sam tried to put himself in Kaspar's place. It wouldn't be good to be away from your home and family. "Maybe he went to Boston to be with the other prisoners, and he has boarded a ship to return home."

Jack thought not. "Haven't you seen how he looks at Aunt Lucy? She tries to avoid his smiles, but he always carries the milk to the cabin for her. He helps her down off Yankee's back, and we both know she can do that herself."

"Kaspar's back!" yelled Lizzie. Everyone rushed out of the cabin. They crowded around the big man as he slipped off the horse. Kasper had returned with two oxen, three half-starved cows, and was riding a black stallion. They were all tied together in a caravan. The oxen were dragging a wooden sled packed with hay and a boney sow securely tied to the frame that scraped along, digging huge channels in the mud from the weight of the thin logs and pig. The unhappy sow had ridden on the sled at that curious angle and was now squealing in pain. She was thin, but appeared to be healthy.

"The mud, slow." he beamed. "Too slow, I'm very hungry."

Now, everyone was admiring the horse. It was black and larger that Yankee or Boots. It, too, was thin, but Joseph could see

218

that this was a fine horse. Might it be a British officer's horse? Joseph kept his thoughts to himself and shook the Hessian's hand.

Anne and Lucy joined arms and cheered, then, realizing they looked silly, they quickly stopped and just laughed. Anne said with a smile, "How did we know Kaspar would be hungry?"

Joseph and William could hardly contain their surprise. The children gathered around Kaspar with questions, and he answered all with pats on their heads.

Later, after the animals had been led to the barn and fed, Kaspar's story unfolded. He had gone back to Saratoga and searched around the farms where he had been during the battle. Then in a stroke of luck, he found an abandoned farm tucked in the woods that had been spared the torch.

Knowing the consequences, Kaspar shouted a warning before walking through the smashed barn door. To his amazement, he found the animals. Two cows had died, and the smell had been terrible, but the rest had wintered in the barn, eating hay that was now almost gone. He thought the horse had broken into the barn. He could see that the door was pushed in and the hinges were broken.

"As long as there was snow on the ground and hay in the barn, they stayed," offered William.

Kaspar had stopped on his way back to the hill at Herman Wehner's farm and talked with the German farmer. Kaspar said Wehner now had two horses and a pig in his barn. Wehner had assured Kaspar that it was all right to bring the cattle to Balls Town and looked with envy at the two oxen.

"The Rues will be pleased. The oxen would have just wandered off as soon as the new spring grass appeared anyway," he had told the young German. Herman fed Kaspar, gave him the hay, and helped him build the sled for the pokey pig.

Sam's Almanack:
The oxen have changed everything. Father says they
will build a sturdy wagon and fetch the house. SR

"Anne, I have spoken with William. We shall fetch the house. We cannot stay in this cabin another winter. I have spoken with Kaspar, too. He has agreed to stay here with us a little longer, and Francois will be coming soon."

Anne looked down. She would be left behind, this time with infant Charles. She longed to see if her sisters were well and would have jumped at the chance to visit them. Now with the lanes clear...she had to have time to think.

"Joseph, please go to Schenectady and read the papers. Try to find out what is going on in the Colonies. See if there are any letters for us that haven't made it to McDonald's. Our sisters would write if they could. Would Matthew be able to send letters? It's been so long since we had word. We need to know more before we decide that you should go. Maybe the house is not there."

"I just wish that I knew if the house is unharmed," agreed Joseph. "If we knew it was burned, we would start another. But if it is standing, the doors that father made and the beautiful moldings he carved...Anne I could never replace those."

His voice choked. Anne knew that Joseph would go regardless of what she said. To keep the peace, she would postpone his leaving a few days. She wanted to convince herself that she agreed to the trip, too. She was tired and not getting enough sleep, and would warm weather never come? She missed being around people. It had been a long winter in the cabin. She was cranky and felt cooped-up, and she would like to go, too.

Joseph was considering her ideas. "That's a good idea to go to Schenectady, and we do need supplies; make a list."

"I will. You know I can do that! You must promise to keep to the list and trust me to know what we need. I have plans, too."

"I'll do my best," promised her husband.

Wistfully, she put little Charles to her shoulder, "Joseph, how I would love to go to Schenectady and shop. It's been so long since I was in a store. I have no idea what might be there; it will be hard to make a proper list."

"Make your list of the things you need, and I promise before the summer is through, you and I shall go shopping in Schenectady." He smiled at his proposal that had just flowed out of his mouth. It made him happy, too. They would dine and spend the night at the inn by the Mohawk River. He had enough money for that. The baby would have to come with them, but that would not matter.

On the morning that Joseph was to ride Yankee to Schenectady, Anne was propped up in their bed with a hungry Charles greedily nursing when Joseph awoke before dawn.

"How can I sleep with all that slurping?" teased Joseph.

"You wanted a strong boy; I remembered your wish," Anne said with a smile. "Oh, and Joseph, I was thinking..."

Joseph let out a sigh. When Anne was thinking, it was always a good idea to listen. There would be no way of living with her if he didn't acknowledge her ideas.

"Why don't you take our big wagon and Yankee and William's horse? Then you will have plenty of room for the supplies and bricks."

"Bricks?"

"Regardless of whether there are letters waiting for us about the house, I will need an oven this year! Didn't you love the crumb cake Lydia's husband brought to the baptism? Oh, I had forgotten how good a baked cake tastes. The beautiful bread pudding Lydia made for us here would have been so much better if it had been baked in a real oven. And we could have real bread. Think Joseph, real bread. My mouth can just taste a good crusty slice of bread as I think about it."

On and on she went about puddings and pies, cakes and crusty bread.

"Joseph, just because we live in the country, doesn't mean we have to eat like poor farmers. We can build the oven outdoors by the cold cellar, and it can be my summer kitchen even after the house is built. I can build the oven fire outdoors on hot days when I'm putting up food and when the girls and I dip candles this summer. Candles, I forgot to put candles on the list. But, then again, we can buy candles when you and I go to Schenectady. But then again, we have the new animals and can dip our own candles."

Joseph smiled. He knew his wife well enough to listen through her words. She was already packing for their trip to Schenectady. "Yes, we will go, and yes, we are not poor farmers. We live in Hop City! Be sure to put hop seed on your list. We shall need barley seed as well. I hope that Kaspar can help us with this new project. I must talk with him. Maybe that will be reason enough for him to stay a while longer."

Just minutes before he had been speaking of bricks, and now they were building a brewery. Joseph had to agree; he had missed baked bread, custards and pies. He would freshen the big Holstein this spring, and there would be cream for custards. This year would be so different than the last. *Anne was right, why hadn't he thought of an outdoor oven before? They had been living like peasants with their smoky fire.*

"Right, we shall have a brick oven, and I will see about buying bricks this trip. I will need more bricks for the house too, but we shall get those bricks after the house is built. I will bring back your supplies, information, and bricks…and hop and barley seed!" He carefully patted the warm child at his wife's breast and stood to rekindle the fire. It would be a good day.

The whole cabin had been listening. Sam was excited. He had heard his father say a trip to Schenectady! Maybe he could ride in the wagon with his father.

As Joseph and William were washing up by the horse shed, William said, "As we drive to town, why don't we stop at Gordon's Mill? I was thinking we might pick up our load of cherry planks. They might sell for a better price in Schenectady."

Joseph grunted. It was one thing to admit to your wife that the bricks were a good idea, but another to admit that your younger brother had a good idea. "I'll give it some thought."

Sam rode with his father to Schenectady on the bench of the wagon. They hitched Yankee and Boots to the wagon and had not brought any of the fine cherry boards to sell. They would do that later. This would be a trip for supplies, information and bricks. His father had told him he could come along if he helped to load the bricks and saw to it that they didn't forget anything on his mother's list. But Joseph did stop by Gordon's sawmill and collect his money for the white pines.

Sam could hardly contain his happiness at being chosen to travel with his father. For the first mile, Sam talked of just about everything he knew, until his father gave him a stern look.

"Son, it's always wise to be brief. You never know when you might need to listen, and if you're talking all the time, how will you hear someone talking to you?'

Sam closed his mouth and gave what his father said some hard thought. After several minutes Sam asked, "Father, what do you think we shall find out in Schenectady?"

"Not much," replied his father, "unless there are letters."

"Father, are we going to buy anything else beside the items on Mother's list?" asked Sam sitting straight back and looking straight ahead just like his father.

"Yes. We're going to buy something for your mother, but I don't know what that will be. She wants bricks!" laughed Joseph.

Then Sam began to laugh, too, and he decided that not talking too much was much more interesting than he thought.

Lucy watched the wagon roll down the hill. Her brother and Sam would be gone for at least three days. Joseph told her that he wanted to have time to talk with people in Schenectady who may have recently traveled from the lower Hudson and ask them about lane conditions. There was no sense in trying to bring the saltbox's heavy beams to Balls Town if the lanes were rutted or impassable.

Joseph also told her that he wanted to visit with men in the Schenectady militia. Was there news from soldiers traveling with

General Washington? Matthew had made many trips to Schenectady on Major Gordon's behalf; the locals would recall his name.

Standing by the lane, Lucy was eager for news, too, news from Jacobus. He could have at least sent word to the trading post if there had been trouble or sickness in his family. When she had mentioned Jacobus's name when she and Kaspar had ridden for supplies, Sally McDonald had only told her that people were taking their grains to his father's mill, and there had been no problems. She had not seen Jacobus, but Lucy had just missed seeing Reuben.

Now, walking back to the cabin, Lucy recalled her shopping trip. The short break away from the hill and the never-ending demands of the children had proven to be the respite she needed. Riding the horse at full gallop past the fort had somehow erased some of the tension she had felt.

What was the unsettled jumpiness she was feeling now? One restless feeling had been replaced by another. She recalled how Kaspar had easily ridden Boots alongside Yankee. Whenever she glanced at him, he returned her glance with a reassuring smile that spurred her to quicken Yankee's gait. By the time they reached the trading post, both horses were lathered and breathing hard. Lucy had loved the wind blowing in her face and the rocking horse beneath her. For now, Lucy had promised her brother she would stay close to the cabin while he was gone, and that she would do. In a few days, Yankee and Boots would be hauling bricks back up the hill for Anne's new oven.

Kaspar had said she could ride Blitzen, and again she was taking him up on his offer this morning. This would be the fourth time she had ridden the big horse that was always ready for a gallop. He had quickly learned to follow her light commands, and the two made a spirited picture of horse and rider as they raced around the fields.

Lucy walked into the barn, reached for the bridle, and said the horse's name. Blitzen greeted her with a whinny and shook his massive head. He was more than ready to be let out. The horse followed her back to the cabin, nibbling at her jacket. It would be a short trip today, just down the hill to fetch milk. Any little trip would give Lucy a break from washing clothes. Their bedding still smelled of smoke despite the airing, and mattresses needed to be replaced with new hay as soon as it was grown and cut. In the mean time, she and Anne had washed clothes until their hands were red and chapped.

It would be a good idea to take Abby with her, thought Lucy. Thomas didn't like it when Abby told him what to do. He was no longer the baby in the family and the two young cousins had been fighting. Thomas was a big brother now and didn't need Abby's help. Plus, thought Lucy, it should be time for the lambing to begin. Abby would love that.

Lucy brushed Abby's hair, made sure she was in cleaner clothes, and then asked if she would like to go with her to the McKnight's.

"Yes, Aunt Lucy, yes, yes, yes."

Lucy took Blitzen to the fence, and using the fence as a ladder, climbed on the Blitzen's back. William was walking back to the cabin from the wood lot. He lifted Abby off the fence and onto Blitzen's back in front of Lucy.

"Hang onto the mane, Abby. Don't fall off!" he cautioned.

"I won't, Papa. Aunt Lucy is hanging on to me," said his little girl, as she headed down the hill.

William had left the older children with Kaspar, picking up stones from the fields yet to be planted. They carried the smaller stones to the edge of the field and added them to the existing wall. The men would later roll the larger boulders with the help of the horses. When that was done, they would move to the newest field and make burn piles from the discarded branches that had been strewn about when the logs were taken to the mill. This was boring work, but the day was so beautiful; it was just wonderful to be outdoors. William could hear the older children laughing and playing games with Kaspar as they dug out the stones and piled them along the edge of the new field.

But William wasn't in a laughing mood. He, too, was unsettled this morning, more than usual. Anne was resting in a chair by the open door with her eyes closed letting the sun warm the pale skin on her face and arms. He poured himself a cup of coffee.

"Joseph didn't ask me if I wanted to go to Schenectady." William let out a sigh.

"I guess he felt a man should stay at the cabin," Anne countered. "He also needed to spend some time with Sam."

"Yes, I appreciate that, but I would have liked to have gone, and Kaspar is here."

"Will, maybe I'm wrong, but perhaps it was Joseph's way of giving you a little time by yourself."

"Funny, I thought of that, too. Anne, I haven't been good company lately; my life seems to be standing still. Soon we will be ploughing the new fields, then planting, then harvesting.... over and over, again and again."

Anne rose, walked to her brother-in-law and sat next to him at the table. "We have good neighbors in Balls Town; maybe you need to get to know them. Will, maybe it's time you took the children in your wagon and went to church. When we all go and you stay home, you don't have an opportunity to meet other people in the congregation."

"First it's the Reverend, then Joseph, and now you. Must I go to church? I'm happy when you leave and take all the children. I can find things to do here."

She waited until he looked up. Then she started to smile. "Next Wednesday I'm quilting at the Gregory's cabin. Isaac Gregory was killed at Saratoga. His widow, Nellie, and her neighbor Molly Cooper and I will be meeting on Wednesdays from now until the snow flies. These two women are friends that I see only at church. Nellie and Molly helped me sew the flag that's flying over the fort."

Anne continued and walked to the window. "Molly's husband is getting better. His wounded leg is healing, and he's getting around pretty well, but I'm sure he'd appreciate a visit or two from another man beside Reverend Ball."

Anne now remembered her conversation with her friend. Lydia had understood. The two women had talked about what they could do for their friends without making a fuss. No one needed that at such a terrible time. What they needed were good friends and a sprinkle of normalcy in their unhappy lives. Lydia confessed she had more than enough to do this summer, and she and Anne could get back to quilting on Wednesdays in early winter. Lydia hugged Anne and said she was doing a wonderful thing and would help by stopping by to visit Nellie and Molly whenever she could. Anne had responded that she hoped Will thinks the same. The women hugged and laughed in relief. "We can only do our best and it can't hurt, right?" her friend had answered.

William still hadn't responded. Anne took a deep breath and continued. "I have an idea. Maybe you could offer to take me and Charles to Gregory's cabin, visit with Molly's husband, and then bring me home mid-afternoon. I'd like you to meet Nellie; she's a fine woman, Will." Anne sat down again.

William finished his coffee. He'd heard this same message from his brother. His year of mourning was ending, and it was time to find a wife. As uncomfortable as it was for him, he needed to make a move, and Anne had come up with this idea. He wondered if she had recently thought of the plan or had been just waiting for an opportunity to speak with him.

Regardless, William would give it some thought. Nellie Gregory would be at church this Sunday. He guessed he could go to church. He and Jack, Jonas, Louisa, and Abigail could go to church on the Sabbath. Was there a woman alive who would take on four additional children? William was prepared to be both mother and father to his children, and he held little hope of having a wife again.

But this woman had children and had suffered a deep loss, too, Anne had told him. It had been a long time since he and his children had been together as a family. He hadn't given it a thought, but he could take his children to Schenectady some day, and Anne was right, his mourning time was ending. When his brother returned with his horse, he would take his children to church. Then, he would consider taking Anne to the quilting bee at Nellie Gregory's on Wednesdays.

Jack was first to spot the loaded wagon coming up the hill. "They're coming. I can see Sam and Uncle Joseph."

The children ran to the lane and then part way down the hill. Joseph slowed the horses, and the children climbed onto the wagon for the ride to the cabin. Now the wagon was loaded with children and bricks. The horses labored up the hill.

Joseph pulled into the clearing by the old horse shed and put the brake on the wagon. He asked Sam and Jack to unharness and feed the horses.

On the way to the barn, Jack was blurting out questions so fast that Sam could not answer but the first. "Yes, we had a good trip." The horse needed no encouragement to go to the barn; both Yankee and Boots had given their all to get the loaded wagon up the hill on the soft roadbed and were ahead of the boys trotting to their stalls.

Joseph gave Anne a huge hug and then scooped Lizzie and Thomas into his arms.

"Quite a trip! Quite a trip! Sam and I had no trouble on the road going, but the added weight of the bricks slowed us coming home. The roads are soft. We had the ferry across the Mohawk River all by ourselves with this heavy load."

Joseph looked with pride at his laden wagon. "Thank goodness it didn't rain while we were traveling; some of the lane is still washed out by Scotch Bush, and I didn't think to take the shovel."

Joseph looked at the burning piles of limbs and stumps in their new fields. "This good weather has everyone out in their fields ploughing; I need to see what our oxen can do."

Anne could hear the excitement in her husband's voice. She smiled and looked expectantly at the wagon. The trip had been good? Was there news from home? But as she started to speak, her husband was already talking again.

"First, word from the militia in Schenectady is that Matthew, as did all the Schenectady men, survived a very cold winter at a place called Valley Forge, Pennsylvania. General Washington did everything he could to keep his army supplied with food, but they ran short of both food and fuel before the snow was gone. It was bad. General Washington's wife, Martha, even came for part of the winter, bringing stores from their Virginia home and lending a hand with the cooking." Joseph slapped his hand on his leg, still bursting with information.

"But now that's old news. The Continentals are headed south. I mean way south. Matthew is heading for the state of North Carolina, maybe even Georgia."

Anne could hardly believe what she was hearing as Joseph continued! The British had blockaded the entire east coast of the United States. The fight for independence was now in the southern colonies, too.

"Were there any letters for us? Was there news from my family? Did you post my letters? Did you read any newspapers? What is happening in the New York Colony...in Manhattan?" Anne's voice faded as she said Manhattan.

"No, there were no letters and yes, I posted your letters to your sisters and mine as well." Joseph said with a sigh and as gently as he could. "I did read the newspapers at the hotel and did a lot of talking with the shopkeepers as I worked on your list. Supplies and mail are not getting through to the states; we're living in New York State." He gently corrected his wife.

"The British naval blockade and the destruction of the salt works in New Jersey have seriously depleted our country's salt supply. The Schenectady store was rationing salt, and we must ration the small amount that I was able to buy. Albany has little to spare."

Joseph continued, "There's no trade with the English, but Americans are building shops and producing many of the things we need. We're even building sailing ships, and the Untied States has a small navy – five ships. French merchant ships are smuggling in arms and provisions for the Continentals from the West Indies, and Congress is paying for the goods best it can, some with hard money and some with promises.

229

"The Schenectady tradesmen are doing a great business; people are bartering supplies for goods and goods for supplies...so many new shops...clock makers...printers...carriage makers....the boat builders on the Mohawk River are doing a terrific business with so many people going west. And bricks...down by the Bline Kill there are piles of bricks and people lined up waiting to fill their wagons....and we brought you and Lucy new Schenectady brooms made to last!"

Anne sat down; first no letters and now new brooms? "What else did you buy?" she weakly added, mostly to herself, but heard by her husband.

Joseph gave a hearty laugh, "Anne, we brought everything on your list and then some."

Joseph called to his son. "Sam, bring in the presents for your mother."

Sam went to the wagon and returned with a package wrapped in brown paper and gave it to his mother. Anne's hands shook as she undid the twine. She unfolded the new dress that was spilling off her lap. It was bright and freshly starched. The white linen bodice was embroidered with flowers, and the neck and cuffs had lace trim. The skirt was made of cornflower blue muslin with deep pockets covered with more embroidery. With the sun shining on the clean blue fabric, her dark skirt looked even more worn and dirty.

Anne was thrilled and pulled the dress around her. "How beautiful!" she repeated again and again. "Thank you, Joseph. Do the women of Schenectady all have pretty dresses? The embroidered flowers are Dutch. Am I right?"

"I was told your dress was made by a Dutch seamstress, and there are more dresses to look at in the shop when you and I go later in the summer." Clearly, Joseph was enjoying the moment.

Then Sam returned with an armful of flowers for his mother. "Tulips, mother, tulips! And we had the farmer dig them up so you would have the bulbs to plant this fall, and they will bloom again next year."

Anne took the basket of red and yellow tulips from Sam and touched the stiff petals to her face. They were so beautiful and smelled so fresh that her heart felt it might burst with love for her husband and son. Happy tears flowed down her cheeks. Passing the tulips to Lucy, she hugged her proud son, then stood and embraced her happy husband.

The rest of the day was spent unloading the wagon. The children unloaded the bricks like a fireman's water brigade. Jack took a brick from the wagon and handed it to Jonas, who handed it to Louisa, who handed it to Lizzie, who passed it to Abby, who handed it to Thomas who grunted as he gave it to his big brother Sam, who stacked it in a neat pile where the oven would be built. The children laughed and counted the bricks as the wagon was unloaded and the pile grew on the ground.

Joseph brought in the supplies. "What's this bundle?" said Anne.

"That, teacher, is a package of books and lots of paper and ink. You have new school supplies, and the children will have new stories to read. Sam knew just what books he wanted. He chose books that Ben Franklin had written about in *Poor Richard's Almanack.* We found all but two on Sam's list. You should have seen him looking over the books. I suppose I was just as bad poring over the newspapers from Albany. I brought some of the local papers for you to read and one from Manhattan that a traveler had left at the brick works."

Anne looked through some of the books: "*Seller's & Sturmy's Books of Navigation, Cocker's Book of Arithmetic, Greenwood's English Grammar.*" Reaching for another stack, "Ah," said Anne. "*Blackbeard, the Pirate, John Bunyan's Works,* and *Pilgrim's Progress.* And look at this, a book of maps."

Anne looked worried. "These books must have cost a fortune, Joseph."

"They're not new. The bookseller was quite taken with Sam who talked and talked about Ben Franklin. The shopkeeper could not refuse our son and said he would save books for Sam's next visit. He told Sam to bring back the books he had read and borrow new ones. It was Ben Franklin's idea, and the idea is catching on. Sam must be careful not to damage the books."

"We shall offer quite a schooling for these country cousins. Oh, Joseph, I never even thought of school supplies or reading books when I made my list. I thought only of having enough food for this big family."

"Don't worry; we shall make frequent trips to Schenectady. If I have forgotten something, we shall fetch it on the next trip." Joseph lifted his wife from her chair at the table and hugged her close. I missed you, wishing you had come along, too. We shall travel together next time," then breaking away, "and find more to buy, I'm sure."

"Yes, I'm sure of that, too," she laughingly agreed.

Joseph turned and shouted to all the children, "I have an oven to build. Seems the lady who lives on this hill desires an oven, and the man of the hill demands baked bread!" They hugged again, and the children laughed at their silly father and uncle. William smiled, but clearly he was jealous of his happy brother.

By Sunday, William had cleaned his wagon, and Boots was groomed and waiting in the old harness. Will had asked Anne to cut his hair. He had shaved and put on a clean shirt. His children were ready too; they were excitedly racing around the cabin anxious to go to church with their father.

With a shout, the William Rue family was loaded into the wagon and heading down the hill, while the Joseph Rues were still closing up the cabin. Lucy rode with Joseph's family, and Kaspar stayed at the cabin. He had been invited to join the churchgoers, but was still afraid of the welcome he might receive. "I will stay on the hill," had been his answer.

CHAPTER XXIV

Lucy's woes

June's weather was warm, and the ground was damp and ready for planting. The oxen proved to be patient pullers and seemed not to mind the tug of a stone or the snag of a root when the plough dug deeply into the new field. Anne's vegetable garden was planted, and the families would be eating peas and beans soon. The fruit orchard had lost one tree over the winter, but the remaining trees had sent out new shoots, and Lydia had sent a replacement sapling to Anne with Lucy. Lucy's new project for the summer would be to raise chickens. Lydia made a trade with Lucy, fertilized chicken eggs for the promise of riding lessons later that summer for Lydia's children. In addition, the cows had been bred with McKnight's Holstein bull, and Joseph was asking around for a boar for their nasty tempered pig. Kaspar joked that the sow was still mad at him for the long trip tied to the sled. The Hessian had made no mention of leaving the hill.

A week later, Kaspar was building the hen house, and Lucy was rearing the hatched little peeps to the delight of Abby and Thomas who had named the fuzzy chicks A, B, C...all the way to Q. They had written down the letter names, and as the feathers sprouted, guessed which chicks would be hens and which would be roosters. The older children didn't interfere with Abby and Thomas's science project as it was obvious to all but them that A looked just like B and C looked just like D...

Anne had suggested to Lucy that she exercise Yankee every day. A good ride was good for the horse and good for her sister-in-law too. Kaspar sometimes joined her. The horses had shed their winter coats and now looked sleek and strong. Both horses were in

233

their prime, but Kaspar's horse was taller with longer legs. Kaspar never went ahead of Lucy, but held his horse's speed in reserve. Yankee never resisted being harnessed to the wagon but clearly was always ready for a gallop with the stallion.

The Balls Town militia met once in June. And it had voted in favor of a Fourth of July celebration at Long Lake which Major Gordon promised to be a celebration like no other. He had suggested three-legged races and swimming for the children. The men all wanted a wrestling match, and someone suggested food competitions for the women and girls. Major Gordon thought it fitting to have the grand finale culminating in a horse race around Long Lake. He would start the race with the cannon, just to make sure it still worked, he had said with a shy grin.

Lydia had understood when Anne explained she could no longer quilt with her on Wednesdays. Anne's Wednesdays were now promised to the two women who had suffered from the battle at Saratoga, and William was her driver to the Gregory farm. William would spend the day doing chores at the farm or at the Cooper farm. The three women, Anne, Molly Cooper, and Nellie spent the day quilting, talking, and laughing together while their needles flew along their patterned pieces of muslin. After the third quilting session, Nellie invited Louisa to come along with her father. She wanted William's daughter to begin a sampler. Louisa was old enough to learn her stitches.

Nellie had drawn a school girl sampler for Louisa on a square of fine muslin, and Louisa was already embroidering the letter "G." Abby sometimes tagged along to the quilting bee, too, and played with the kittens. She stayed in the cabin with the women, being shy about playing outdoors with Nellie's children. William visited with Molly Cooper's husband, helping him with the heavy farm work in the morning, and then all would gather for lunch.

It was Wednesday, and William had just left with Anne, Charles, and Louisa. Joseph looked at his sister. Lucy had not fixed her hair this morning and had on an old shirt. He saw the pail and knew that today she would be cleaning the cabin while so many were gone. It was a bright sunny day and the floor would quickly dry.

He carefully phrased his question. "I wonder why we have not seen Jacobus. Tell me again what Sally McDonald said that day you went to the trading post."

Lucy washed up the last of the breakfast bowls. "Sally just said she had not heard of any sickness and that people were still going to the mill as usual."

"Was Kaspar with you in the store?" asked her brother.

"Oh yes, we had just ridden the horses hard, and we all needed water. Kaspar was so happy; I guess we both were."

Lucy recalled the moment again when Sally had looked at the Hessian, first at his smiling face and then down at his boots. "Joseph, do you think people are saying bad things about us because Kaspar is staying on the hill with us?"

"I haven't heard any comments from our friends at church, but you know the people of Mill Town have their own church. But that might be a reason we have not seen Jacobus. People have long winters to think about things, and sometimes they get to thinking about the wrong things. Jacobus certainly knows about the Hessians and how they loved America enough to stop fighting at Saratoga and desert the British army. He would understand if a Hessian soldier was working on the hill with us. But, he might not understand the two of you riding together and hearing that news from Sally McDonald or one of the men in the militia."

"Like Reuben?" asked Lucy. "He may have seen us."

"Maybe," responded her brother. "What if we ride up to Mill Town with this nasty pig of ours and ask if Jacobus's father would be willing to let her spend a few weeks with his boar? That sure was a good ham Jacobus brought to us that first winter. After the barn-raising," Joseph stood to go back to the field, "I thought Jacobus would come again this winter, ham or no ham."

Lucy had barely heard the last sentence. "Oh Joseph, that's a wonderful idea. When shall we go?"

"How about Saturday? We'll have to check with Anne. Wait, Friday might be a better day. She depends on you to help with the baking on Saturday, and I need to make sure William and Kaspar will be here, too. Kaspar has been talking about riding to Schenectady to see about work this winter. When I told him about the carriage shop that made sleighs, he sounded interested."

"William's spending Saturdays over at Gregory's." He didn't even need to say this, as they all had happily watched and teased Will as he put on a clean shirt and took the children to Nellie's every Saturday. "Yes, how about Friday," smiled Joseph.

Friday came, and the crabby pig was persuaded to climb into the wagon with an ear of corn dangling in front of its head. The children all laughed and were giving the stubborn pig encouragement. "Come home with piglets in your belly," shouted Thomas.

The older children laughed. Now Jonas repeated Thomas's sentence over and over, laughing at his cousin and poking him in the stomach until Thomas was laughing, too.

Joseph helped Lucy, who was wearing her best skirt and fullest petticoat, into the wagon and waved good-bye. Sam wanted to go too, but Joseph had told his son that he was to stay at the cabin this time and help his mother.

This was one trip Joseph had been looking forward to making. He had been south to Schenectady and now he would go in the opposite direction to the north. Ever since he had climbed the sugar maple when he, Anne, and his brothers had come to the hill, Joseph had looked forward to the day he could explore the land to the north. The road was rough, and the sow was squealing every time the wagon gave her a jolt. "Remind me, dear Lucy, that this was my idea." His sister just nervously laughed.

They would need to travel at least two hours to reach Mill Town. The only road that was passable for the wagon was to go south down the hill, east past Gordon's sawmill, and then turn north up Middle Line Road. They would pass Major Gordon's home and his gristmill on Gordon Creek, and then follow the road north to Mill

Town. The road was well traveled by farmers, but a much longer trip than Joseph usually took to the small gristmill on the Mourning Kill. There was much to be said for short trips.

When they had been on the road only an hour, they came to a spring. Joseph slowed the wagon. They could see the milky water bubbling from the ground and moved closer to get a better look. Yankee pulled the wagon to the edge of the spring and licked the wet rock. Joseph and Lucy got off the wagon and wet their fingers with the flowing water. It tasted salty and was a little smelly.

They were now on the road Francois had told Joseph would continue on to Mill Town. Going north, they passed several farmers returning south with their milled grain. He recognized a few from the militia and waved, but most were strangers. Joseph had to pull his wagon off the narrow road to let the faster southbound wagons pass.

By mid morning they were following the Kayaderosseras Creek going upstream to the falls at Mill Town. Joseph was not sure which of the gristmills belonged to Jacobus's father. They stopped for directions, and learning the mill was nearest the falls, continued on.

When they pulled into the mill, they were the fourth wagon in line. Joseph drove the wagon out of the line and under the shade of a tree. It was obvious to Joseph that Jacobus's father's mill was the busiest mill on the Kayaderosseras, at least in Mill Town. Leaving the sow, now asleep in the wagon, Lucy and Joseph walked into the mill.

Men were shouting, as the rushing water spilled over the wheel, and the gears and timbers groaned under the weight of the millstones. Farmers were watching as their wheat or corn was ground into flour or meal. They shouted to one another; always aware of the wheel and the millstones, and very careful not to get too close.

Jacobus was loading flour into a sack when he first saw Lucy. He quickly looked back to his work with no measure of a response. Lucy swallowed hard. There was something wrong; there was no fondness at all in that look.

Joseph had left her in the mill and sought out Jacobus's father. They had gone out of the mill where they could have a quieter conversation. Lucy remained and watched Jacobus work for a few more minutes, hoping he would again look up, but then she joined her brother at the wagon where the men were in a humorous discussion about the pig.

"Fine looking sow, good size to her. Bet she's a brut when unhappy," laughed Jacobus's father.

"You're right there! Ever since the Hessian brought her to the farm, she's done nothing but complain. I was hoping your boar could take care of that for us. What kind of a deal can we make?" offered Joseph.

As the men talked, Lucy went down to the Kayaderosseras with her carefully prepared lunch basket. She would wait there for her brother and Jacobus. But, Joseph and Jacobus's father came and sat with her.

Lucy welcomed them, but there was a chill in her greeting that was felt by the men.

Jacobus's father hesitated, stammered a bit, and began, "My son's not a worldly sort, Miss Lucy. He has only known the mill and the battle at Saratoga. I'm afraid you'll have to excuse his rudeness. I will have a talk with him, you can be sure."

Trying to change the subject he asked, "Are you going to the Fourth of July celebration?"

Lucy said yes, but it was clear that she had hoped to at least talk with Jacobus. Now she was disappointed and angry. With her back straight and her jaw proud, she answered, "Yes, I am baking a special cake, and I'm entering the horse race." Lucy closed her mouth in surprise. What had she said?

"I will tell my son. I wish you well, Miss Lucy. You sure look fine on this beautiful day."

He stood to leave, turned and hesitated, then turned back to Lucy. "I don't think there will be any women in the race. Horse races can be dangerous. You might not want to do that, young lady. I know your special cake will be a winner if it is as good as this lunch. Thank you."

Joseph said he would be back for the pig, and the brother and sister drove home with little more said.

Lucy didn't know what had gotten into her. She had no idea what she might bake and the thought of entering the horse race had not even occurred to her. She only knew she was very angry. Joseph had not questioned her on the quiet trip back to Balls Town. She was thankful for the silence.

Preparations for the Fourth of July celebration began soon after the men returned from the June muster. Now the celebration was all the women talked about at quilting bees and discussed after church. The women were planning what they would bring for the noon dinner, but not about what they would enter in the baking contest. Their entries would be a secret until the day of the competition. And the judges, Reverend Ball and Major Gordon, were already enjoying the added attention by the women at church.

There was so much to do. First, Anne wanted her children to look presentable, but when she thought of the foot races and contests in the mud by the lake, she decided that she would look good, and the children would wear clean play clothes, not their Sunday best. She had put their shoes away until fall. Even Joseph was now barefoot, and if he decided to enter the wrestling contest, he would not leave the cabin in his best clothes either. Anne, on the other hand, would wear her new dress.

William announced he and his boys would be helping Nellie cut hay and store it in her barn. Also, they were planning on going to the celebration together. Nellie was baking a cake for the baking contest. That was all he knew. Anne knew that Nellie was very talkative at the last quilting bee, but she hadn't mentioned a cake. None of the women were talking about their baking entrees for the contest.

Lucy had come home from Mill Town resolved that Jacobus might not be "the one" and regardless of the outcome of their

239

friendship, if there was a friendship, she would not be anxious to marry. Now, marriage was far from her thoughts. There were other things to do and more places to see, and there was the race. Her brother had not discouraged her. To enter the horse race would be her decision.

She brushed and rode Yankee everyday. The horse seemed to know from the tone in her voice that something was about to happen. The farm had no wooden fences so the horses, cows, and oxen were free to graze anywhere on the hill. Yankee often came to the cabin seeking Lucy when it was time for the daily exercise run, and Blitzen was always by her side.

Two weeks before the celebration, Lucy was in a panic. She remembered and was painfully regretting her conversation with Jacobus's father. She would race, but her boast to bake a special cake was now becoming more than worrisome.

The new oven was working well, and Anne had decided to enter a loaf of her sweet pumpkin bread, but Lucy still had yet to bake a good cake, let alone a special cake. She had to build a fire in the oven each time she baked and it took eggs, flour, and sugar. Their only cake pan was large and she had to double the recipe. Each day that passed without a successful cake made her more anxious. Now the deadline was keeping her awake at night and she was grumpy.

Aware of her dilemma and with a caved-in cake again for dessert, Joseph added a short prayer to the blessing. *"Dear Lord, please help Lucy with her cake. Amen."* Everyone burst out laughing except Lucy. She ran from the table and out the cabin door in tears!

The next morning, Lucy had another setback. Her brother had come to her with the news that he thought Yankee was going to have a foal. Her race horse was pregnant. Lucy could stand it no more and ran into the field to escape Joseph's terrible news.

Sam's Almanack:
> *Aunt Lucy is in the hayfield crying. Yankee followed her and they trampled down the new hay.*

Father is not happy. He came in and told us that Yankee will have a foal this winter. We are all very excited. Now we will have chicks, piglets, a foal, and Mrs. McKnight has promised us two lambs when they are weaned, in exchange for maple syrup. Father is building a hold for the lambs and it will be Lizzie's job to make sure they are in the hold before nightfall so the wolves don't eat them. Thomas and Abby will help Lucy feed the chickens and gather the eggs.

I'm so happy that father bought new paper for school and my Almanack.

We have one new problem. The animals all like to eat from the garden, and Mother is not happy. We shall have to fence in the animals or the garden. I'm hoping we fence in the animals; it will make it easier to find them in the evening when we put them in the barn.

Francois still has still not come, and Kaspar has ridden Blitzen to Schenectady to see about working at the Carriage and Sleigh Shop that Father and I saw on our trip. Kaspar told me that he needed to work during the winter to earn hard money.

Uncle Will spends a lot of time at Nellie Gregory's.

The Fourth of July Celebration is coming next week. I hope Lucy can make a good cake. She has been baking cakes for two weeks, and they all sink in the middle, which makes her very angry. They taste good but are soggy in the middle. We eat the outside and give the middle to the pig.

I can't wait to play the games at the Celebration. I think I can out-run Jack, and he's pretty fast. Jack has been very boastful about Nellie Gregory's farm. He says the cabin is much nicer than our cabin, and their land is flat. He has admitted that when his father ploughed her garden, there were a few small stones, but he and Jonas quickly put them on the stone walls.

We have no school during the summer, which I miss, but mother is too busy, and I guess I don't really miss it that much. I don't talk about school much. I have been reading Blackbeard, the Pirate *in the sleeping den. The sun doesn't go down until after nine o'clock. I miss Francois. SR*

Lucy's cake looked good and tasted good. "Finally. I think I have the mixing figured out. The eggs are the worst, you just beat them and beat them; there's no hurrying baking a cake, but it's still not special," she moaned.

Anne whispered an idea into Lucy's ear. Lucy smiled. She knew she could do what Anne had suggested, but since the baking contest was such a secret, they dared not tell the children or the men. This would mean that Lucy would have to do it right the first time. It may be the last time, too, and she grinned secretly to herself. If she couldn't ride in the race, at least she could win a prize for her cake.

Lucy had given up the plan to race Yankee around Long Lake. Joseph had told her it would be her decision, but he was confident his sister would make the right decision, and she did. So now it was up to this cake and the new blouse she had sewn for her old skirt and bloomers. She would not have time to make everything new. Her blouse and hair ribbons would have to do. The fiddlers will be at the celebration.

Lucy told Anne that she and Yankee were going walking behind the hayfields. She had an idea, and Anne gave her a hug.

CHAPTER XXV

Fourth of July

The family was up before dawn. Joseph and William had the horses harnessed, and the children were picking at their breakfast and excitedly talking. Anne was sure they would be hungry before the noon meal. William was taking Jack, Jonas, Louisa, and Abby to Nellie's in his wagon, and they would go together with Nellie's children.

Anne was glad when his wagon left; now she could get her surprise ready. Lucy's cake had come out of the oven perfectly baked, and her bread had a dark brown crust and a zig-zag crack down the middle revealing the orange inner bread. While the children were tending their chores, she would surprise her sister-in-law as soon as the cake was completed.

Lucy's hands shook as she slowly brought the milk, sugar, flour, and egg mixture to a boil over the fire. This was taking more time than she had remembered. It was the same pudding she always made, but today it seemed to take the milk forever to boil because she was in a hurry. When it had thickened, she put the pan in cold well water to quickly cool the pudding. Then she split her cake into two layers and spread the cooled filling on the bottom layer. Carefully, she arranged half of the tiny wild strawberries she had picked in the field on the wet pudding and covered the pudding and berries with the top layer.

Anne told her she better put three short wooden splints through the cake, so the top layer would not slide off. Then Lucy carefully lowered the cake into her newly woven basket and stood back.

243

The two women hugged and giggled. Lizzie ran into the cabin to hurry the women. She looked at the two baskets and grinned. "You are both going to win. Mama, Aunt Lucy, you are both going to win."

"Lizzie, take your father our lunch and make sure it gets into the wagon," said Anne, "and come right back."

Then Anne reached to her shelf and gave Lucy a package. "Here's a little something from your brother and me."

Lucy opened the brown paper. The fabric unfolded as Lucy held the waist band. Speechless, she held up the beautiful black riding skirt that was trimmed with red piping and pockets embroidered with red, white, and blue flowers. She reached for Anne, and tears of happiness flowed down her pretty young cheeks. Lizzie raced into the cabin and now looked at the two most beautiful and happy women she had ever seen.

Anne laughed and said, "Quick, dry your tears, get dressed, and let's finish getting ready. I have to bundle Charles before we leave. Lizzie, tell your father we'll be ready in a short while. And remember, not a word to anyone about what we have brought for the contest. Our bread and cake must be a surprise if the other women are not to talk about them in front of the judges."

Lizzie flew out of the cabin, her new hair ribbons bouncing on her long braids.

Lucy brushed her hair one more time, put the blouse on she had made, and then the new black riding skirt. She couldn't believe how the material felt as she smoothed the skirt over her slender hips. She lifted her basket and Anne's while Anne carried Charles, and the two women walked out of the cabin and faced the family and Kaspar.

The men and boys were silent and then cheered. Joseph beamed at how beautiful Anne looked and gave her a kiss. Kaspar helped Lucy onto the wagon. The children quickly loaded up. Joseph handed Charles's bag to Lizzie and Anne's bread to Thomas. "Don't peek. Don't drop them, and don't tip Aunt Lucy's basket," ordered their father as he handed Lucy's basket to Sam.

Kaspar was riding Blitzen. He had decided to come. He explained he wanted to talk with Herman Wehner and meet the two other Hessians now living with families in Balls Town. Kaspar had shined his boots and tied back his long brown hair.

Gripping the side rail on the bench seat of the wagon, Lucy urged her brother to go slower. She was also making Sam nervous as she turned and looked over her shoulder, watching his arm swing back and forth holding her cake basket level as the wagon wheels went in to and out of the pot holes in the lane. Slowing almost made the motion of the wagon worse. Finally, since they were going at a snail's pace, Joseph asked Kaspar to carry Lucy's basket. The wagon went faster after that, and Sam breathed a sigh of relief.

As the wagon pulled into the field by Long Lake beach, the crowd turned. They recognized Joseph and Anne, Lucy and the children, but who was the man on the black horse, and what was he carrying? The crowd of women whispered as they first looked at Anne's new dress, then at Lucy's basket decorated with red, white and blue streamers. The men looked at the black horse.

Joseph had a good idea what was going through the men's minds as he steered his wagon under the big shade tree by the lake. "Sam, unhitch Yankee and tie her to a tree where she will have shade this afternoon. Don't forget to fill her water pail."

The other children climbed out the wagon and raced to be with their cousins. Joseph followed Anne as she walked to the judging table placing her pumpkin bread, safely covered with a muslin doily, on the table. She turned and reached for Charles. Lifting the sleeping baby from her husband's arms, she quietly spoke, "Joseph, did you see our neighbors' glances?"

"Sure did! The women stared right at your new dress and the men couldn't keep their eyes off Kaspar and the stallion. Now, look at that group of young bucks standing around Lucy! We sure made a grand entrance, Lady Rue!"

"Shush," Anne touched her husband's sleeve at the compliment. "Joseph, that's English talk, Mrs. Rue, Mrs. Rue! Go about your business. We are all settled here. I'll see you at noon for lunch." Anne walked over to join the other women.

The children's games and swimming went well, but there was no arguing the tenseness among the women that kept them from truly enjoying the day. Finally the time came for the judging of the baked goods. Anne, Lydia, Nellie, and Molly were surrounded by family as Reverend Ball and Major Gordon walked around the judging table. There were breads, pies, cakes, and berry cobblers. Each entry now had two small tasting slices resting on cloth napkins.

The judges slowly went down the table, taking a bite from the samples. The women nervously watched and waited. It took Reverend Ball the longest. He finished each sample, leaving not a crumb or berry on the muslin napkins. When the sampling was done, the two judges slowly walked over towards the wagons with their heads together, mumbling quietly. Then Major Gordon's arms shot up in distress, and it was obvious to the women that the Major didn't like what he was hearing from his father-in-law Reverend Ball. They were clearly arguing, and their conversation was getting louder.

Reverend Ball's wife and Major Gordon's wife, the Reverend's daughter Mary, rushed to their men. The men stopped talking and listened. Then there was a nodding of heads as the women spoke and the men looked at each other in agreement. "Why don't you explain to these women what we have decided?" tactfully ordered the Major to the Reverend.

Reverend Ball cleared his throat, then, asked for a glass of cider. After slowly drinking from the mug, he carefully wiped his mouth, cleared his throat again, and began.

"Dear women of Balls Town. You have done this young community proud. I don't think I have ever been tempted by such delicious and sweet desserts." He nodded to his wife, "Mrs. Ball, you have made me wonderful desserts, but never in such quantity, and for that I am grateful." He cleared his throat and resumed his delivery. "Getting back to the judging, I'm afraid that James and I cannot come to an agreement. Major Gordon prefers pies and I, myself, am a cake and cobbler man."

The women were not happy. Now, what were these men thinking? Certainly there was one or two desserts that were far and above better than the rest and would be declared the winners.

"So our wise wives have decided we must put the desserts in categories and then decide on the best bread, pie, cobbler, and cake. That is what they are doing right now at the table. I think we can make a better judgment as to the winners."

The men were losing interest and drifted away to continue their wrestling matches. There would be no problem determining the winner of their contest. It would be the man who won all of his challenges and was still standing. The older boys went to watch while the mothers of the younger boys kept their sons at the tables.

Lucy watched as her basket was moved to the end of the table with the cakes. Anne's bread was in the first group. A blue ribbon was placed on the loaf of hickory nut bread. Anne was disappointed.

The pies were next and the strawberry rhubarb won easily. The pie tin just oozed with the sugary pink syrup and was now stuck to the table. The cobblers were next. This was the hardest as there were more cobblers than any other dessert. After a quick refreshing nibble, and a nod from the Major, Reverend Ball declared the elderberry cobbler the winner. He mentioned to Major Gordon that it was a shame that they hadn't included a competition for elderberry wine. Gordon laughed and said, "Next year."

Now they were down to the five cakes: apple walnut, rum sponge, black walnut, pound cake, and Lucy's cake. Lucy's was the last cake on the table and the smallest, but the judges had taken big bites of the pudding-filled cake a second time. They again walked over towards the wagons. Their wives ran to bring them back to the table with stern words that they must choose.

The men discussed a bit longer, then returned to the cakes, and Reverend Ball placed the blue ribbon on the apple walnut, his personal favorite.

Anne didn't look at Lucy. She just couldn't bear to see her sister-in-law's disappointment. Lucy's head fell to her chest. This was the crushing blow, first Jacobus's estrangement, then Yankee's pregnancy and no chance to race, and now her cake was last, the very last of all the other entries.

Major Gordon cleared his throat and got the attention of the chattering women. "Because this event has taken place on July 4th, the pudding filled cake in the basket, decorated with red, white, and blue ribbons, deserves recognition."

Lucy couldn't believe what the major was saying. She looked at Anne, who smiled back in relief.

Adding to his delight in the success of the contest, Major Gordon continued with his chest puffed out as if he was displaying the colors, "This final entry so patriotically displayed will be called Washington Creame Cake after our commanding general."

The contest was over. The women politely clapped and then raced to cut and serve their desserts to the impatiently waiting younger children and each other. They would taste the entries and decide for themselves the real winners.

Lucy lifted the pewter plate, with the remains of her gooey cake and loose strawberries, out of the basket and then put it back. It looked better in the basket. She hadn't won a blue ribbon, but her cake had been named for George Washington. She was thrilled and the children, now pushing to see the cake name for Washington, loved her messy cake and were satisfied to touch their finger to the plate and taste the creamy filling.

As friends and neighbors were eating the sweets, James Gordon drove his wagon onto the grounds. The children scattered, and the adults only wondered if the good major may have lost some of his good sense or had a little too much "celebratory cider." But the wagon rolled to a stop, and Mary Gordon, who had been gripping the seat of the wagon and almost losing her hat, pulled back her quilt covering the cargo. People stared at the tin canisters wrapped in burlap. Mary Gordon waved to her parents as she patiently waited for her husband to help her down. Major Gordon then climbed into the back of the wagon so all could see him, and in his booming voice, announced that they would be serving iced cream to the children.

The crowd immediately started talking.

"Form a line, a proper straight line with the youngest first," the Major loudly barked. "If there's any iced cream left, the adults can line up behind the children." Gordon cleared his throat and puffed his chest. "As you know or maybe don't know, George and Martha Washington serve iced cream when they entertain." The children squealed with delight, although they did not even know what they would be eating. The crowd then began with polite applause, but soon broke into wild cheering.

The horse race began at four o'clock. That was Major Gordon's idea too. He was into building traditions, and today was the Fourth, so the cannon should fire at four o'clock. No one could argue with that.

The race course ran the perimeter of Long Lake. It roughly followed over the swampy outlet, a few inlet streams, a stone fence or two, woods, and fields. The wooded lot came right to the edge of the lake. All the riders would have to slow their horses and walk through the woods. If any horse was seen cutting the course short by running in the lake, they would be seen by the crowd monitoring the race from the swimming beach and be disqualified.

Lucy watched as the men who had been wrestling went to the lake and washed the sweat from their heads and arms. The water was not cold in July, but still refreshing after a hot and sweaty fight. Gordon was calling his men to prime and ready the cannon. There would be no shot or ball to load, just a good charge to boom out the beginning of the race.

Lucy walked over to Yankee and ran her hand over the horse's back. The horse returned the affection with a gentle nose rub on her skirt. "You'll have quite a foal, Yankee Lady, you sure picked yourself a stallion."

Lucy was rubbing the mare's slightly swollen belly when Kaspar and Blitzen walked up to the tree.

"Kaspar, are you going to race?" asked Lucy.

"I don't think so. The other Hessians are encouraging me to race, but I think it would be better if just the... people... from Balls Town were racing."

Lucy heard Kaspar say people, not men. Her hand dropped to her side. She felt the soft firm fabric of her new riding skirt. Kaspar caught her in her thoughts. *He can read my mind*, thought Lucy. Blitzen now moved between Lucy and Yankee.

Blitzen is talking to me too, she realized. She looked up at her friend and knew she didn't even have to ask. Kaspar offered her a lift up, and the next thing Lucy knew, she was mounted on the black stallion.

Kaspar gave her that smile that flooded her with confidence. He believed she could ride as well as any man. Major Gordon was calling the riders. It was now time to join the other racers. She gave Kaspar a determined look that broke into a grin, a grin almost as wide as the German's. Lucy walked the horse to the starting line.

The men turned as Lucy approached. Jacobus was not riding, but he was standing by Reuben, who was mounted and ready to race. She could not even look at Jacobus. Reuben welcomed her and promised to dance with her after the race. The other young men looked at Lucy and the big stallion and figured they better not give this girl a chance at winning. It would be important to forget she was a girl and make a mad dash when the cannon fired. Their girlfriends would be proud if they won and very cross with them if they let a girl win.

A rope was pulled across the field making a starting line. The riders all vied for a good position, and Lucy had a hard time working Blitzen into the line. Major Gordon was now giving a final warning and held the smoking puck high in the air. Lucy's legs were being squashed by the horses and men on either side of her, and the sweaty smell of the men so close to her gave her stomach a bad feeling.

She looked to the side and caught a glimpse of Joseph. Her brother held his arms in the air, just like Gordon was holding the puck. She searched for Kaspar, but could not find him. Joseph lowered his arms.

"BOOM!"

The rope dropped, and the horses were kicked into action by the riders. The horses began the race, but Blitzen reared instead. Lucy felt his body shudder at the sound of the cannon. She knew instantly that Blitzen had been at Saratoga. The horse was remembering the battle.

Lucy dropped her head to the horse's neck and calmly spoke. "You're safe, big horse, you're safe. Let's go and win this race!"

Lucy barely touched her heels to the horse's side. Blitzen leaped forward, almost unseating her. She gripped with her legs, her hair flying behind her, her new riding skirt flat against the horse's side. She was far enough behind to gather herself before they would reach the boggy end of the lake. She couldn't believe she was racing.

Ahead she saw two horses already slowed to a walk up to their hocks in the swampy mud. She would go around the marsh with the other riders. Horses were now spread out along the route. A few had balked at stone fences and had to be led around. No one would risk injuring their horse for a race.

Blitzen glided over the first low wall and Lucy steered him around to a gate in the second wall. The riders took the open field at a full gallop that was visible from the beach. The crowd was wildly cheering, and Sam could see his aunt about halfway back from the lead horse.

The first stream was filled with small rocks and Lucy slowed Blitzen to a walk. The horse picked his way across the stream bed and resumed a full gallop. Lucy passed three riders. Their horses were lathered and breathing heavily. They had slowed and would drop behind.

Four horses were in the lead, and one was Reuben, she recognized his shirt. The second stream bed was next. Again Lucy was prepared to slow to a walk, but Blitzen seemed to be giving her another message. The horse was running at a full gallop.

Lucy leaned close to the horse's neck and gave the stallion his head. Blitzen cleared the brook and Lucy felt the power of the horse's leap beneath her. As they landed, her hair ribbon flew off.

251

Now her face was wet from the horse's sweat, and her hair was streaming behind her. Having come around the south end of the lake, they were headed into the wind. Her eyes were tearing, and she was blinking to see.

They were gaining on the remaining three leaders. The thick wood lot was ahead. One rider was going down to the shore. The other two, one was Reuben, had slowed to go through the woods. She slowed Blitzen and followed behind Rueben. They were picking their way through the thorny brush that was catching on her new riding skirt and scratching her arms. Ahead were the big trees. Blitzen side-stepped around the trees with an easy gait, following Lucy's commands. It reminded Lucy of a dance. She moved with the horse and kept her balance.

There were now only two horses ahead of her, and Lucy was closing the gap. As the leaders broke into the open field together, Rueben shouted her name in surprise. It would be a sprint to the finish.

Again, Lucy dropped her head to the horse's thick neck and shouted, "Blitz, Blitz. Win it for Yankee." The horse only heard "Yankee." He was running at a full gallop, passing the second rider, now almost to the finish. Lucy could see the crowd moving away from the finish line. She lowered her head once more and didn't slow down.

Sam's hand shook as he wrote in his *Almanack:*

> *Aunt Lucy rode a wonderful race. She crossed the finish line with Reuben. It was thrilling. Aunt Lucy's hair was wet and blowing behind her head. She was hugging Blitzen's neck. We were so excited. After the race we ran up to her and jumping up and down, laughing and hugging each other. I shall never forget today. SR*

CHAPTER XXVI

Promise to keep

Sam could see dust rising from the lane, someone was coming. Then, he could make out a solitary rider with a packhorse coming up their hill.

"Francois! Francois!" yelled the boy, as he raced down the dirt lane.

The Frenchman waved in response.

When Sam reached the fur trader, the boy began a long string of questions. "Where have you been? What has kept you? I thought you might not come back to the hill." And after a deep breath for air, "Francois, I've missed you. I have so much news. The fox kits were born, just like you said; the Indian boy gave me a rabbit's tail, and I gave him my smooth stone, just like you said I should do. We're friends and his name is Lone Fox. And mother had a baby, just like you said, and Lucy raced Blitzen at the Fourth of July celebration..." On and on went Sam.

The Frenchman smiled at the boy. As he reached the peak of the hill, Francois noticed all the new sheds, animals, and fields. Soon he was surrounded by the family, and he met Kaspar. Joseph's introduction of Kaspar to Francois was cordial. Francois could see the Hessian had done much for the family that he loved. He might have been a little jealous of the fondness the women showed for the strong, young German, but Anne quickly dispelled all those thoughts. She warmly embraced Francois and said how glad she was that he had returned to the hill. He was months late. She looked forward to making him a good cup of coffee in the morning with fresh cream and serving him some good bread with a hard crust from her new oven. If anyone should feel jealous, it would be Joseph, but he, too, welcomed the Frenchman. Francois was family; that was the truth.

Francois unloaded his cargo of pelts and camping gear from his tired horses and stacked them in a pile inside the barn. Sam led Lulu and Bess out to the pasture where he imitated his father and made introductions of Lulu and Bess to Blitzen. The horses took little notice of the formalities.

Dinner that night was a celebration as Francois was welcomed back by the Rue family. Anne and Lucy cooked fresh green beans, new potatoes, and roasted a chicken over the outside cooking fire.

Just as Sam was putting a second piece of chicken on his fork, Thomas jabbed him in the ribs. "You're eating E."

"What?"

"You're eating E. Abby and I have known each chicken ever since it hatched. We have a book, too. It's our *Chicken Almanack*. We're eating E today," repeated his brother as he nodded to his cousin Abby, who hadn't eaten a bite of the chicken on her plate. Lucy lowered her head, hiding her face.

"But you can't write," argued Sam. By now everyone had stopped eating and was listening.

"I know my alphabet and I can draw chicken pictures; some are hens and some are roosters and they all have a name. This one's name is E, and he was a rooster." And Thomas looked again at Abby.

The family now had put down their forks, and no one spoke until Francois cleared his throat and said, "Umm, chicken and vegetables; one of my favorite dinners. E, you are very tasty."

No one laughed, all agreed, and dinner continued. Thomas was slow to eat his chicken, but eat it he did. Abby nibbled at hers. Dessert was strawberries served on warm biscuits drenched in sweet cream.

"Lucy picked the strawberries," said Anne, "from her garden."

Lucy laughed, "It's been a race to pick the ripe berries before the birds and rabbits eat them."

"Sam, your Aunt Lucy's strawberry patch might be a good place for another trap," said Francois. "Tomorrow I will show you how to make a snare trap."

Sam just nodded his head; his mouth was full of the sweet berries and biscuit and cream. He was so glad that Francois was back.

After the meal, Francois, now relaxed with a full belly, pulled his chair closer to where the women would be washing the dishes and lit his pipe. He had tales to tell, but they could wait. Tonight he just was content to be with the women and listen to their soft, gentle talk that he missed so much when he was in the wilderness.

The next morning after breakfast, Sam, Jack, and Jonas led Francois around the hill. They showed him the chicken house and the pen for the lambs that still were with the ewe at the McKnight's. Then they walked over to the orchard and examined each small apple tree. The newest field was next. The oxen were browsing, along with the cows and horses, among the stumps, stones, and weeds.

Francois approached Blitzen, and the horse froze. With some gentle French words, Blitzen slowly relaxed and let the stranger examine his eyes and teeth.

"Fine horse, fine horse. Yankee will have a handsome foal." Then he walked to Yankee and ran his hand down her side. "Won't be long, probably late fall or early winter before the really cold weather, and that's good," assessed the Frenchman.

The boys took it all in. Francois knew all about horses.

Lulu and Bess were in the field, too, and as they saw Francois approach, they raised their heads. Francois gave them a relaxing "bonjour" and they lowered their heads. There would be no loading up today. The trader's horses continued to snort their relief to each other, and when that was done, contentedly returned to eating the wild grasses and weeds while swatting flies with their long tails.

William called Jack and Jonas to the cabin, and the boys ran to their father. Now it was Sam and Francois walking the hill alone. Francois said he must take care of his packs. He had brought pelts and wanted to make sure that the furs he had unloaded in the barn the night before could be safely hidden. Was there room in the loft over the animal stalls?

Sam assured Francois that their barn still had plenty of room. Sam climbed into the loft, and Francois passed the silky furs to the boy one by one. Then Francois climbed into the loft and carefully hung the furs over a beam and covered them with his old blanket. Sam turned to Francois when they were done. "They will do fine. This is a good dry barn. There are few stains in the roof where the rain has seeped through," said Sam as he pointed to the roof.

Francois noted the darkened patches on the underside of the shingles and also the confidence in this young boy's speech.

Sam proudly explained to Francois that when the rain begins, the shingles swell and any little cracks quickly close up. Sam was proud of how well his father and uncle had shingled their huge barn. "We will hang the hops above the hay in the loft, too. Father thinks we will have enough hops and barley to brew beer this year. He plans on taking the wagon to Schenectady with mother in September. They are going shopping for supplies and will buy new barrels from the cooper."

"Kaspar should be able to help; Germans love their brew," joked Francois with a smile. "With a brewery near the creek, you will soon have a tavern in Hop City."

Sam nodded. He liked hearing Francois say Hop City. He must tell his father that Francois knows about the plans to brew beer. As they were climbing down from the loft, Sam said, "Lizzie thinks Uncle Will is going to marry Nellie Gregory before winter, and he will move to her farm."

"Ah. You will miss Jack and Jonas?" ventured Francois.

Sam nodded. He knew he would miss his cousins. They would see each other only on the Sabbath. "Father says they will be close enough."

"Ah. And what have you heard from your Uncle Matthew?" asked Francois.

"We have not received a single letter. Father talked with men from the Schenectady militia, and they have heard from Schenectady soldiers in General Washington's army, and all are well. The Continentals had a hard winter in Valley Forge and now are on their way south to fight the British in the Carolinas. Francois, do you know where that is? I have a book of maps, but it doesn't have a good map of America. Balls Town isn't on it, but Schenectady is."

Francois stopped by the pig pen. The sow was lying on her side with a greatly swollen belly and what appeared to be a smile on her face. "Soon there will be a row of pink piglets sucking on her swollen teats."

Sam nodded as Francois picked up a stick and drew a map on the dry dirt by the pen. "Here's the United States. Up here is Canada where I used to trade with the French a long time ago. Then you come south to the lakes, first Lake Champlain, then Lake George, and cut over going a little west, past the geysers and springs to Balls Town. Here's Hop City," which Francois marked an X. "Then farther south is Schenectady and the Mohawk River. My guess is that when Matthew traveled with the Army to Pennsylvania, they cut to the east from Schenectady to the Hudson River just south of Albany."

Sam knew that was how the family had come to Balls Town. They had followed the Hudson River north as far as they dared. They did not want to get caught in the British trade blockades around Albany.

Francois kept drawing his map. He drew Manhattan Island and Long Island, New Jersey, and Pennsylvania. He marked another X at where he thought Valley Forge might be and another X at Philadelphia, the first capital of the United States. Then he drew in Mary Land and put an X on Baltimore where the Declaration of Independence was now stored. Then he roughly drew the coast and named the southern states – Virginia, North Carolina, South Carolina, and Georgia. "These are the southern states, and they border the Atlantic Ocean. The British Navy has blockaded most of our harbors. That's why I brought my furs to the hill this year and why I am so late in coming. I'll not be trading with the English merchants, and I can't get to the French." Francois looked back at his map.

"But I've heard my countrymen are now fighting alongside the Americans. The British ships will have to do battle with the French Navy, and we have a fine Navy," the Frenchman proudly added. "Don't be too discouraged at not hearing from your Uncle Matthew," Francois continued. "He may have written letters, but the mail might have been lost. With troops and armies on the move, only the letter packets from the generals may be getting through."

Sam could tell from Francois's map that the Carolinas were a long way away. He asked Francois to help him draw the map again in his *Almanack*. He would ask his father where their house was, and he would make another X. He knew it had been built near the Hudson River north of Manhattan where he was born.

They left the map and started down the back hill. Sam told Francois how they had watched for the fox kits in the spring and then saw them playing outside the den. The quick animals were hard to track after the snow was gone, but they had watched the kits play from a blind.

Sam showed Francois the blind the boys had built of tree limbs on the hillside above the Mourning Kill. Using Sam's spy glass, they could see the kits soft fuzz change into thick reddish fur by summer. The boys had written in their *Almanacks* and noted when the den had been abandoned. They had crossed the creek to inspect the den and found it lined with the soft hair of the vixen.

Francois was proud of Sam and nodded his approval. "Let's talk about the Indian boy."

Sam reached into his pocket for the rabbit's tail and told Francois about meeting Lone Fox after the barn raising and later finding him in the cold cellar. Francois listened as Sam told the stories about the food that had disappeared from the cold cellar, then, sat on the hillside for a long time without saying anything to the boy.

Francois moved to stand and Sam did too. Together they turned and climbed the steep hill back to the cabin.

"Francois, how long will you stay?" asked the boy.

"I will stay until you are all safe in your real house. Your father is talking of going back for the saltbox this fall after the fields are harvested. I shall stay with you," said the Frenchman. "Think of the wonderful soup we shall have with plump chickens and roasts of crispy piglets. We shall have small, delicious feasts, and your mother and Aunt Lucy shall tease us with their breads and sweet butter. I found an elderberry bush loaded with berries. We shall strip the berries off the branches and we shall make wine. Sam, tell me, did Jacobus come this winter to see Lucy?"

"No, Francois, he did not come, and Lucy told Mother she was never going to marry."

"Ah," said the Frenchman. "The ways of love are often tortuous. Sometimes men are half out of their mind in love and then are half scared of love. Most men, even married men, don't understand women."

"Do you understand what happened?" asked Sam.

"I can only guess that when Kaspar came to the hill, Jacobus turned his anger for the war into anger for the Hessian. Remember, Jacobus's father was injured in the war. Maybe his father has something to do with it. If Jacobus is in love with Lucy, he will come, and now he will have to win her heart." Francois sighed. "Love is a very strange feeling, but your aunt will figure things out. Don't worry about that."

Sam laughed. The fur trader was a Frenchman. Ben Franklin had been to France and knew about such things, too. Sam had read about that. They were both laughing as they walked up the back hill. Sam could see his mother walking back to their cabin from the garden. She was holding the corners of her apron that Sam guessed was full of green beans and herbs. His mother's smile and waving apron warmed his heart.

Coming in from the far field, Joseph wrestled again with his nagging problem. He had promised Anne they would travel to Schenectady in September. For that he would need a horse to pull his wagon. Francois's horses had not been broken to a harness. Kaspar had ridden Blitzen to Schenectady, and he would not have asked Kaspar for the use of Blitzen even if the horse were still here. Will had taken his children to Schenectady to shop for new clothes for the October wedding, and Boots was totally unavailable now anyway. That left Joseph with a pregnant Yankee, not the right time for a horse to be hauling bricks. He almost laughed. Somehow, his world just never stayed under his control. Was it useless to plan for the future? How many times had his plans changed? Seemed to Joseph, he was constantly revising and making new plans.

Now walking across the orchard, he stopped and looked at the fruit trees. They had had a good year, but there would be no apples next year or the next. It would be years before they would bear fruit. He must trade for apples and cider again.

"That's what I do," he said talking aloud to himself. "I modify my plans every day to fit my situation." Now he did laugh and spoke aloud to his parents in heaven, knowing he was out of earshot of his wife.

"Father, you said I must plan for my future, and I have tried. But the best that I can do is plan for the day. And, Phebe, dear mother, I remember your dreams of living in a real house. I know Anne shares your dreams, but the house is still not on the foundation at Hop City." It was then that he felt the raw sorrow of losing both his father and his mother when they had defended his house, trusting that their actions would help other Americans be free to hope and plan for their futures.

He did not weep, but sighing, he thought back about what he had planned to do just a few short years ago; his dreams of building a place called Hop City seemed almost funny now. *Do I really need to create a city in the wilderness?*

Joseph's mind would not quit thinking. He had a future with Anne and four wonderful children. But, he realized, he and Anne could not create Hop City alone. He would need his grown children and their families and their families to achieve the dream. That was out of his control, too. He thought Sam loved his books too much to ever be satisfied as a farmer. Lizzie would be like her mother, but then she could be like Lucy. Thomas had a mind for figures, and Charles was too young. Exhausted with his thoughts, he would just try to survive and thank God every day for his blessings. That took a huge load off his mind.

Walking toward the barn and thinking of Yankee, his thoughts went back to the beginning. *What I really needed now is transportation to Schenectady so I can make good on my promise to my wife.* Anne had not mentioned the shopping trip recently, but he knew that she was looking forward to their traveling together. Joseph could not disappoint his wife.

Plus, as he could now see the bare stone foundation of the cold cellar, he needed to buy more bricks for the house. He would need bricks for two chimneys, and bricks mixed with hay to insulate between the siding and the interior lathe and plaster. He needed to make another trip for barrels if they were to brew ale, but building a brewery might have to wait another year. Forcing his mind to stay focused, *what I really need is a wagon and a horse.*

Then, in almost the same breath of thought, as he walked into the barn, he couldn't believe what he saw. Calmly eating hay were his two oxen. Why hadn't he thought of his oxen before? Although it wouldn't be as fast or as stylish a trip for a husband and wife, the oxen could pull a load, and he could buy enough bricks for the saltbox's fireplaces and chimneys.

After this revelation, he really started to think. *Maybe I can borrow the heavy duty wagon at the lumber mill. Maybe Gordon will exchange the use of his wagon for a delivery to Schenectady. I can take Gordon's rough cut boards to the lumber mill in Schenectady. Maybe I can sell some of my boards Gordon is storing at the mill.*

Then he thought about what needed doing in September before he could even think of leaving the hill. He and Lucy had one more hay cutting and the oats and barley to harvest. The children would be busy helping Anne collecting and storing the squash and pumpkins, and Sam and Lizzie were already shucking the Indian corn. The corn husks would feed the oxen on the trip if they were chopped. The pigs would get the rest this winter. Thinking of winter reminded him of the first hard frost that would be coming soon. He quickened his step towards the cabin; there was no time to lose.

There were hops to pull from the trees and stone walls to hang from the barn beams to dry. Sam could do that, and Lizzie could cut and hang the herbs to dry in the cabin. He would trade his barley for apples and cider as he had last year. And when all was done, the vegetable garden would need one final ploughing to turn the dead plants and hay mulch back into the earth before it snowed. This could all be done when he and Anne returned.

As he passed Francois's smokehouse, he gave thanks that the Frenchman was back. The trader was planning ahead for the sow's delivery and had rigged a smokehouse. He would have to wait, but they would have ham and bacon this winter, and now Francois was talking of making sausage. The lard would be rendered and welcomed by the women for cooking and baking. They would have pies from the brick oven that made his mouth water just thinking of them. The family would be more self-sufficient this winter with heartier meals and gravies. With William soon married and no longer living with them, cooking for the family would be half as much work for Anne and his sister.

His thoughts were running at top speed now, and he was planning again. He had lists of things to do, but he would get them done and then, when all was done, he would go for the house. He did not share his newest plan with Anne that night. Instead, as he held her in his arms, Joseph prayed that the trip with Anne to Schenectady would happen. Joseph fell asleep.

CHAPTER XXVII

Husband and wife

Anne was seated on the rough bench seat of Gordon's logging wagon. The oxen were not happy pulling the load of planks from the mill, but they would toughen to the job. Lugging lumber and bricks would harden the beasts, and Joseph would soon know if they would be strong enough to haul the saltbox timbers in November.

Anne had little Charles on her lap as they traveled. She would ask Joseph to stop while she nursed the baby, and that would give the oxen a rest. As they approached the Mohawk River, the gently sloping bottom land was beautiful to behold. Farms dotted their route, and the wooden fences and dried summer flowers, played well against the blazing maple and oak trees.

The ferry ride across the Mohawk River went well, and Joseph headed straight for the finishing mill. The mill workers tossed Gordon's rough cut planks to the ground. They would deal later with Gordon for a fair price on the board feet. Joseph was simply the driver, and the unloading went quickly. Gordon had bought Joseph's lumber outright, and given Joseph hard money in payment.

Now, Joseph was anxious to settle Anne and the baby at the inn. The plan at first had been to drive the wagon to the brickyard and together they would walk the short distance back along the river to Schenectady. But it was late in the day, and Anne was tired from the bumpy ride. Charles was fussy.

Joseph maneuvered the huge empty wagon down Front Street and stopped at the doorway of the inn that he had seen when he and Sam had come to Schenectady. With his hungry and thirsty baying oxen and oversized wagon blocking the street, people stopped and stared at the roughly dressed farmer. Not minding the stares, Joseph thought only of Anne and that she soon would be settled and could rest with the baby. He would go to the brickyard, place his order, stable his oxen, and walk back to the inn.

Anne, however, could hardly contain her excitement as they drove into Schenectady and never saw the stares. Overwhelmed with the activity, she saw great numbers of people and carriages moving quickly along the streets. Joiners were building new houses all along their route. Stores and shops had flags and brightly colored signs. In fact, color was everywhere. Women wore long skirts and big hats in dear, rich shades. Summer flowers growing in window boxes had not yet been touched by frost. Bouquets of blooms cascaded from the sills. Her simple wildflowers could not begin to compare with the blooms hanging from baskets.

"Joseph, the Dutch have brought their flowers to Schenectady. Could any street be so beautiful?" exclaimed Anne with joy.

Joseph turned to his wife and kissed her. "I'm glad we're here."

Their room was on the second floor. The innkeeper provided a wooden cradle for Charles. He explained to Anne that there was a footed cast iron tub down the hall. It would cost extra, but she would be able to bathe if he had enough notice to heat the water and have it brought up. Joseph quickly paid the innkeeper for two nights and hot water for a bath. After seeing Anne and Charles safely to their room, Joseph left for the brickyard.

Anne hung her shawl over the stand by the window and saw the setting sun. Then she stretched out on the feather bed, loosened her bodice and nursed Charles. She hoped that this would keep him content while she and Joseph later ate their dinner in the room below. She had glimpsed the inn's small dining room that overlooked the Mohawk River. With the long rays of the brilliant fall sun now streaming into their room, she felt as if in another world. A young woman brought her cool cider and a pitcher of warm water for the basin on the stand. Charles would have a bath, too.

Soon Anne could hear the clatter of kettles and chatter of the young girls setting the tables for dinner. Newly laid fires were snapping in giant hearths to take the fall chill from the room. She had to pinch herself to believe that the comfort the inn provided was real. She vowed that she would encourage Joseph to make the trip for their house. They, too, could enjoy these luxuries at Hop City, if only they had their saltbox.

Anne had come home tired but excited. She now longed for her house and was certain that her husband would fetch the saltbox's beams before Christmas. They would have a real house next summer. She would travel again to Schenectady and buy the beautifully woven white muslin she had seen. Yards and yards were needed for the nine over nine windows Joseph would order.

The Wedding

Lucy's chickens laid enough eggs for three cakes, and the stored eggs were brought from the cool shelf down in the well. Anne and Lydia met to bake, what they hoped, would be a beautiful wedding cake for William and Nellie. The cake would have three layers, currants and black walnuts in the bottom layer, and be decorated with a silky white icing. Lucy built the fire in the outdoor oven and excused herself from baking. She agreed with her sister-in-law that three women baking a cake were too many. She would watch Charles.

New clothes were hanging in the cabin. Anne had bought Lizzie a new frock in Schenectady with long sleeves and stockings to match. It would be her first real dress. There were embroidered flowers around the sleeves and hem. Joseph had thought a collared shirt would be appropriate for Sam and a simple buttoned shirt for Thomas. Charles would wear his baby clothes. Anne had found dresses for herself and Lucy in the same dress shop that Joseph had bought her cornflower blue dress. These were sewn from fine wool and would serve them well at Christmas, in fact all winter, she had told Joseph. After much protest, Joseph had bought a new shirt.

The women of the church were determined to out do each other with good food for the reception. As weddings were held on Sunday afternoons, families came prepared to be at church all day. That way, weddings and other church events didn't cut into farming time and everyone could look forward to a whole day of worship, socializing, and rest. Hoping that the weather would be fair, they would hold the reception outdoors. If it should rain, it would be in the church, which nobody wanted as there would be no keg.

The event demanded haircuts and baths for everyone. On Saturday afternoon, the children lined up outside the cabin on benches, and Anne went down the row snipping their hair. Now the boys had halos of white skin that had not tanned under their long hair. William had heated enough water so the children would have a bath in the wash tub, girls first, and he had saved warm water for a final rinse of every ones hair.

Jack, Jonas, Louisa, and Abby were packed and ready for the big event. In fact, they had been packed for a week. William's shopping trip to Schenectady had been successful. He had bought his children new clothes with the money his brother had paid him from the timber profits: navy blue long dresses and white stockings for the girls, and dark wool breeches and white collared shirts for the boys.

William asked Joseph to stand up for him at the ceremony, and Nellie asked Molly Cooper to be her witness. Joseph decided that Sam, Lizzie, Thomas, and Charles would be in the second pew with Anne, Lucy, and Kaspar. Kaspar wanted to sit in the back, but Joseph said he was their guest. Jack, Jonas, Louisa, and Abby were in the very front pew. Now, the last thought in everyone's mind was only that the sun would shine.

Sunday's sunrise was ominous. William hitched Boots to his wagon, and his children and all their possessions left the hill right after breakfast. Francois wished them all well, but said he would stay at the now half empty cabin as before. Lucy knew the natural odors of the Frenchman would not be appreciated, but no one had mentioned this attribute for a long time.

The late October day proved to be cloudy with a slight drizzle. Everyone had hoped for a late fall reprieve and one last good day of autumn, but it had started out badly. By the time the families arrived at the church, the men, women, and children were cold. Hair ribbons were limp on damp heads, and tempers flared when children ran from pew to pew before the church service. The sermon was long. The church stoves were cold. Reverend Ball called for a short recess before the wedding. He asked the men to build fires in the stoves and let the children run around outside while the men worked.

When all were again seated, a strong burst of wind pushed against the church roof. Men left their pews once more, and rushed out into the gusty wind to re-tie the horses and cover their belongings in the wagons. Then the women, worried that the food might be ruined by rain, left their pews and rushed to the wagons to oversee what the men were doing. Anne prayed the cake would be protected under their wagon seat draped with the tarp. Reverend Ball re-assessed the darkened altar, and decided the ceremony would need candles. The remaining congregation watched as candles were lit. One by one, the small flames mellowed the darkened room with a soft amber glow. People returned damp and wind-blown to their pews. Just as the wedding ceremony again was to begin, dark clouds poured huge drops of pounding rain on the church roof. Reverend Ball's voice was now muted, and his congregation watched as his mouth soundlessly moved.

Anne and Lucy could only groan; neither could look across the aisle at Molly and her family who were waiting for Nellie and her children to walk down the aisle. The weather could not have been worse for an October wedding.

Reverend Ball, however, seemed not to mind in the least. The church was full of his most favorite people on earth. As he looked out at his congregation, he beamed thanks to heaven for this blessed day and offered his prayers to the Lord that Balls Town was thriving. The men and women to whom he ministered were hard-working, God-fearing farmers. Their numerous children were sandwiched into every row, and their young excited voices filled his ears with happy melodies and his heart with gladness. God may have been the only one who could hear the Reverend.

Reverend Ball could hardly contain his joy. This was a wedding, a most wonderful wedding that would join two families into one. He was more than fond of both families and had prayed that such

267

a ceremony might happen. When William Rue and Nellie Gregory had come to him with their news of love and hopes of matrimony, he had held their hands in his and given thanks to the Almighty. This would be a blessed day.

As the congregation now came to their feet, Nellie Gregory, led by her young children holding hands, walked up the aisle. Molly Cooper left her pew and joined her good friend. William called his children to the altar and was joined by his brother. When all were standing, the wedding ceremony began and the pounding on the church roof abruptly stopped. By the time the vows were taken, the clouds and rain had moved on to the east. The sun was shining, and the delicious cool, dry air of new weather pushed the gloomy clouds away from Balls Town and out of the church. William encircled his arms around Nellie, and the children all clung to the kissing couple.

As Nellie Rue and William Rue walked down the aisle trailed by their children, the congregation stood and clapped. A new wind flew through the church, the dry air blew out the candles and the hungry congregation rushed from their pews following the wedding party. Standing by the front of the church, men were holding their wet shirts away from their skin and women were flouncing their damp and drooping petticoats to best advantage.

The children ran from table to table under the dripping trees, watching as the fruit, vegetables, and sandwiches again were laid out by the Church Women's Committee. The women gasped as the wedding cake was carried from Joseph's wagon and set on the main table for all to see. It was a cake that reminded the women of the life they had left behind. They had lived on the frontier and endured the bare necessities and were so moved that the sight of the beautiful cake nearly brought them to tears.

William's keg had been tapped, and the men were devouring the savory meats and cheeses pressed between thickly sliced dark breads with shiny hard crusts. Some men were suggesting a wrestling match, and their wives were shaking their heads and pleading a "no" with their eyes. The men had on their best clothes and they were in front of the Church.

The cousins stood together while they ate their sandwiches and then watched William and Nellie cut the beautiful cake. Thomas sidled close to his big brother. "Sam, I wish Major Gordon had brought the cannon to the wedding!"

Sam looked at his brother and smiled. He put his hand on Thomas's shoulder and continued smiling into the boy's beaming face. He must take Thomas down to the Mourning Kill and show him the fox den.

Rue Family Tree

Samuel Rue *m.* Phebe Martin
Joseph Rue *m.* Anne Ducker
    Sam
    Lizzie
    Thomas
    Charles
William Rue *m. Sarah d.*
    Jack
    Jonas
    Louisa
    Abby
    Lena d.
        m. Nellie Gregory
            Travis Gregory
            Laura Gregory
Matthew
Patience
Susanna
Lucy

CHAPTER XXVIII

Snowflakes, bells, & stars

Sam's Almanack:

 Uncle William is married, and Father has gone for the house. Mother is so excited that she talks of nothing except what she will do in her kitchen and how she will polish her new windows until the sun shines through with such clarity that they will be able to see sunsets and see visitors coming up the hill. She will have Uncle Matthew's long table and the chairs from the saltbox. Her family and guests will sit around the table in proper chairs. She will have her candle sconces that Grandfather Thomas made and her table linens from their wedding.

 Francois listens, but says little. We all know that the house may not still be standing. So many houses have been burned to the ground since the Revolution began. Our saltbox may be gone, too.

 But mother talks to Lizzie about the house every day. Lizzie will sleep in the north upstairs bedroom and have a little belly window to open on the hot nights to catch a breeze. Lizzie is as excited as mother. Thomas knows that father will return soon and that mother sings as she cooks and sews. Charles is a happy baby brother and seldom cries. I am worried. SR

"Today may be the day, Francois," Lucy said expectantly as she raised her eyebrows and looked across the table at the trader. "Yankee didn't eat this morning, and she is so restless. She looks like she would like to go for a fast run, not stay penned in her stall. I put down extra fresh hay and chipped away the ice in her trough and gave

270

her plenty of fresh water. But, she seemed not to notice the hay or me. She is not happy and not herself."

Francois was eating oatmeal with the family this morning. "Lucy, this may be a long day for the mare. She has much work to do if the foal is to be born today. I've not seen many horses as big as Yankee before birth, and this is only her first. You need to go to the barn often and reassure her that she can do this task that God has given all his lady creatures to do."

"I know we have talked and talked about this, Francois, but is there nothing I can do to help Yankee have her foal?" asked Lucy. Then she looked at her sister-in-law.

"Very little, Lucy," said Anne with a smile. "I can tell you from experience that birthing is up to the mother and the Almighty. When Lydia was here for Charles's birth, she did her best, but there's only the mother with God's blessing, who can push her child into the world."

Anne continued. "Let's make a stew this morning and maybe a good bread pudding from the crumbs and crusts. Sam, bring in potatoes and lots of onions for the venison. Thomas, you can help bring in the vegetables from the barrel. Let's have apples and hickory nuts in the pudding. Sam, you crack the nuts with the hammer, and, Thomas, you pick the nutmeats. Try to keep the shells off the floor. We shall cook up a feast to celebrate the birth. If the foal comes tomorrow, we'll eat what's leftover from tonight's feast tomorrow!"

"We may see a storm today, too," added Francois.

"A Nor'easter?" asked Sam.

"Could be," said the Frenchman. "The wind, what little there is, it blows from the east, and the sky is dark. Not much of a sunrise this morning. I will chop enough firewood for a week. That should keep me busy and sharpen my appetite for the stew and pudding. And I will bring in a bottle of elderberry wine to celebrate."

He filled his cup with more coffee and smiled at his adopted family. He didn't regret his decision not to go into the mountains. He had no desire to hunt or trap this winter. With Joseph gone with Gordon's wagon to bring back the saltbox beams, Francois was now the only man on the hill.

271

Francois had been glad to see Kaspar leave the hill to take work at the carriage shop and live in Schenectady. In a way, Lucy had felt that was the right thing, too. The family had helped him, and he had paid them back for their kindness and helped the Rues. Now he must find his own way. But she missed his happy smile and ways.

Sitting by the fire after dinner, Francois worried about Joseph. The plan had been for Joseph to send a letter to Schenectady as soon as he had reached the saltbox. The family needed to know that the men and his team of oxen had safely made the journey and that the house was still there. No letters had come, and Joseph had now been gone six weeks. With Christmas but a few days away, and the time for winter storms quickly approaching, the family would be isolated from news. Christmas was no time for a family not to be together. Francois kept thinking. Hauling timbers in spring would be even worse than winter. Even a fresh team of oxen would not be able to haul the timbers on muddy roads. If Joseph hadn't yet crossed the Mohawk River, he would be delayed until the melt and the river receded. What then? Where was he?

Anne knew all this, but was unable to speak a word of it aloud. Her heart told her that once she spoke of her fears, she would be doomed to despair. Each night as she gathered the children, she would read them stories from the Bible. Then they would form a circle holding hands and pray. Last night their prayers had been long.

Thomas went first. He prayed for the fox kits that would be born in the den across the Mourning Kill. He and Sam had watched every day through Sam's spy glass as the dog and vixen readied the den for the birth of their kits. He had learned to follow their tracks until the vixen had jumped into the Mourning Kill to lose the young tracker.

Lizzie prayed for the saltbox and her room and the new bed her father would make for her. She hoped that she might have a feather bed. She missed her father, and tears escaped from tightly closed eyes.

Sam had promised his father that he would help his mother while he was gone. He was doing his best, but often Francois had to help with the animals as the work was hard, and he was still but a boy. Drawing the water from the deep well was the hardest. Often Francois would come to him just as the pail reached the lip of the well and help Sam lift the heavy pail the final two feet. Sam missed his father and wished he had returned weeks ago. Sam prayed to God for his father's safe return.

Lucy prayed for her brother's return and Yankee. She loved the horse and worried for her now that the birthing time was near. She prayed for a healthy foal and Yankee's safety.

Anne prayed for each of her children, Charles, Thomas, Lizzie, and Sam, that they would grow up knowing God's love for them. Then she said a prayer for her husband's health and safe return. She explained to God and her children:

"Dear God, Our house is important, but the saltbox may be burned. You have provided us with ample forests and strong arms. A new house can be built on our hill. We ask that you protect Joseph in the storm. Amen."

Francois then cleared his throat and held out his rough hands to join the circle. *"Dear God, bless this good American family. They have proven their loyalty to this young nation. Please spare their good husband and father from danger and bring him safely home to Hop City. Amen."*

The children looked at Francois. There were tears of love for the man who was like a grandfather to them. Anne, too, had tears in her eyes as she hurried the children off to bed. Lucy and Francois went to the barn to check on Yankee.

Tired, but unable to sleep, Anne stayed up late sewing Christmas presents by the firelight wrapped in a woolen shawl over her fur vest. With each stitch she prayed for Joseph's safety and longed to be held in her husband's strong arms.

The next morning Yankee still had not delivered the foal. Francois and Lucy spent the night in the barn with the horse. Yankee was tired and Lucy thought the horse looked frightened. Sam ran to the barn before breakfast and watched as long as he could, but then ran back towards the cabin with tears spilling down his cheeks.

Now the snow was coming down hard, and the wind had picked up. He could see the smoke from the cabin's chimney twirling and whipping first northerly, then straight out of the east as he ran back to the cabin. *It was a Nor'easter alright*, he thought. *It's going to snow for three days.* He must bring in more firewood for his mother this morning and maybe get a big pumpkin from the cold cellar and ask about a ham, too. There hadn't been much left over from dinner last night.

He burst into the cabin. "Lucy and Francois are worried. The foal seems to be stuck and won't come out," explained Sam to his mother. "Francois has an idea and says that after breakfast, if the foal has not been born, he and Lucy will try to pull it free."

Anne was afraid. She knew pulling the foal from the horse would be hard work. She also knew it could be dangerous, as Yankee would kick. She sent Sam back to the barn to bring Francois and Lucy back for a good breakfast of leftover stew and pudding.

Sam's Almanack:

This was an exciting day. Yankee birthed a beautiful filly. She has big eyes and long legs. That was the problem; the long legs were all mixed up inside Yankee and no matter how hard Yankee pushed, the filly's legs got jammed up and wouldn't let her come out.

This is how it happened. After breakfast, when we went back to the barn, Lone Fox and his mother were there kneeling by Yankee. The boy's mother was stroking Yankee's head and talking to her. Lone Fox held some smoky weed burning in an iron kettle under Yankee's nose.

We watched as the Lone Fox's mother tied Yankee's bridle to the side of the stall. Then she slowly walked to the back of the horse, talking all the while in her Indian language. Then she reached deep into Yankee and found the foal's front legs. She tied a leather thong around the foal's legs and slowly, very slowly, Francois and Aunt Lucy tugged on the thong.

Reaching in, Lone Fox's mother tucked down the foal's head, she guided the little horse out into the light with her hands. Yankee let out a deep breath full of hot air and pushed.

Then it was over. The foal slid out and onto the pile of hay. Aunt Lucy and Lone Fox's mother quickly wiped the foal's nose and mouth, and then she called to me to untie Yankee. We backed out of the stall so Yankee could turn around; she began licking her baby. Yankee nudged and licked until the little horse was on her knees with her hind legs tucked under her.

Then it seemed like minutes went by before the little filly put out one front leg and then heaved with all her might and stood. Her legs wobbled, but she stood strong against Yankee's powerful licks.

In all the excitement the Indians slipped away before we could thank them. Francois thinks they will come back to check on the horses. He said to leave them gifts by the horse stall. What an exciting day! How I wish Father was here. SR

Lulu and Bess were glad that the foal had been born, too. The excitement in the barn had almost been too much for the pigs, cows, and the trader's horses. There had been so much heavy breathing and sympathetic mooing and groaning that the barn was now heavy with moisture and too warm. Francois told Sam to climb up into the loft and open the summer vent to let out some of the stale air. A farmer didn't ever want moldy hay, and the animals all needed some fresh air.

As Sam pulled the rope to open the vent, the hatch opened. Snow on the roof dumped into the barn. The icy flakes swirled as they fell from the rafters and danced around the animals. It was a celebration.

"Pitch down some clean hay for Yankee, Sam, and I'll clean out her stall," called Lucy, "Yankee's filly is already nursing." She would soon sleep close to her mother on clean, dry hay.

Sam then ran to the cabin to ask his mother if he might put out some of their food for the Indian family. Anne went to the cold cellar with Sam, and they filled a sack with corn, barley, dried apples, and a small piece of ham. Francois had told Sam that his Indian family loved pork. The boy went to the shelf and took down a beautiful round pumpkin.

"May I give them this pumpkin, too, Mother?"

"Yes."

Then Sam raced to the cabin and got out his pen and paper. He wrote the Indian boy a letter. It was written with pictures and words. He tucked his letter into the sack. He tied a hawk feather into his knot as he bound the gathered neck. He made two trips to the barn; the first with the sack, the second with the pumpkin. He pushed fresh hay against the gifts so they wouldn't freeze. Then he saw Lucy's new scarf tied with a hair ribbon and a small sack. Sam moved Lucy's gift close to the family's gifts.

Even though it was not night, the animals were quietly sleeping. The wind blew, and the hops swayed from the rafters. Sam climbed into the loft and pulled the vent closed. It would be a cold night. He thought again of his father and wondered if he was in the storm.

Sam's Almanack:

The Nor'easter lasted three days and left about a foot of snow on the ground. Most of the snow was blown into drifts, so there are places we can walk and places where the snow is very deep. Today the sky is deep blue, and the sun is warm on my face, and there is no wind.

Aunt Lucy says we will bake cookies today like we did last year. She said we will tie some on the Liberty Tree for the birds to eat. We will eat the rest.

Mother is not singing anymore, and Francois tries to keep her happy with little stories about his travels, but it's not working very well. We are all very worried that something bad has happened to Father. The roads may be closed from the storm, so he may just be a few miles away and the wagon stuck in deep snow. Or he may still be taking down the saltbox, or lost in the blizzard.

Aunt Lucy has cut pine boughs to make a wreath for the barn just like Father did last year. She said my Grandfather Samuel always put a wreath on the barn. She is decorating Yankee's stall with pine boughs, too. She spends much of her free time in the barn.

We have named the filly Liberty, Hop City's Yankee Liberty. It was Aunt Lucy's idea, but she said it was really Grandmother Phebe's Liberty Tree that made her think of the name.

The Indians have come to see Liberty. I know we have just missed them as I have seen their fresh tracks in the snow, and our presents are gone. I wish they would stay so I could talk with them.

Mother says that tomorrow is Christmas and we shall have a Christmas dinner even if Father's not here. We must celebrate Baby Jesus's birth. Mother has called us for dinner.

I almost forgot, Aunt Lucy had a visitor. Jacobus came with a Christmas ham from his mother and father. Lucy's hair was tangled and her apron a mess, but she politely smiled and said, thank you, and invited him to see the Yankee's foal. Jacobus will need to bring another ham. SR

The family was seated around the table eating potato soup dotted with small pieces of ham. Anne made oatmeal muffins, and the children were drinking milk that hadn't frozen the night before. It was Christmas Eve.

Thomas said grace and when he mentioned his father, he started to cry. Anne went to him and gave him a big hug and told him that his father has been delayed by the storm and would come up the hill just as soon as he could.

Sam thought he might cry too. He looked at Lizzie, and they knew that their mother was saying what she hoped was true, but she didn't really know when Father was coming home.

Anne asked Sam to go out to the wood shed to fetch a good long-burning back log for the fire as it would be a cold night. He didn't stop to put on his coat, but quickly opened the cabin door and raced to the old horse shed that now was filled with split logs. He wiped his nose with the back of his sleeve and blinked hard.

As he was poking through the pile to get a heavy log, that would last the night, he thought he heard bells. Sam dropped the log and raced back to the cabin and called to Lizzie. "Come out, come out, Lizzie. I need you to listen to what I'm hearing."

Lizzie grabbed her coat and stepped out into the dark night.

"Can you hear that?" Sam shouted with excitement.

"Bells? Bells? Am I hearing bells?" she shouted right back and squealed, "Visitors on Christmas Eve! Maybe it's Uncle Will and Aunt Nellie and all the cousins."

Sam raced to get his mother. Lizzie could see a light coming up their hill, and she knew for sure that she was hearing sleigh bells.

"Mother, Mother! Hurry! Come outside," shouted Sam into the cabin. "Thomas, get your coat on and come too."

Everyone came outside, even Charles, wrapped in a blanket, and they all could hear the bells and see the lantern coming up the hill.

Then Anne could hear a voice shouting, "I'm home, I'm home."

As the sleigh came toward the cabin, they could make out two shapes in the sleigh and a big black horse prancing through the drifts and blowing steamy breath into the cold night air. Now everyone shouted and knew at once it was Joseph and Kaspar. It was like a dream. The family ran to the sleigh.

Joseph carefully stepped from the sleigh. His right arm was under his coat and the empty sleeve tied down. They could only guess that there had been an injury, but Joseph was in good spirits and looked well. He face was red and chapped and his lips cold, but he was laughing as he hugged with his good arm and kissed Anne and the children. Lucy was next to give her brother a big hug. Then Lucy ran to the sleigh and welcomed Kaspar. He broadly smiled and returned her warm hug.

Francois couldn't seem to help himself and repeatedly asked him, "What kept you away so long?" But Joseph didn't answer as everyone hurried into the cabin.

Joseph then quickly explained that the overloaded wagon had broken an axle coming from Albany. When he and the other men tried to jack up the wagon, a beam from the house, "Roman numeral XII to be exact," said Joseph, "fell off the wagon and hit my shoulder bruising it so badly that I had to wrap my arm to my chest. Gordon's men fixed the wagon while I tried to help, and we started out again for Schenectady."

Lizzie pulled on Sam's sleeve and whispered, "What does the number twelve mean?"

Sam quickly explained, "Father scored the beams with numbers so he could take the house down and later put it back together here, matching the beam joints by matching the scored Roman numerals. We weren't born when he built the saltbox. Listen."

"Then the Nor'easter struck and we were trapped in Schenectady until the ferry captain could see well enough to run the river. Kaspar found us and offered to bring a sleigh across on the ferry and bring me home if there was a break in the weather." Joseph seemed to have trouble speaking as he looked at Kaspar. With a choke in his voice, "It's Christmas Eve."

Anne put her hand on her husband's sore arm.

Joseph cleared his throat and continued, "Gordon's men are happy to stay the night in Schenectady. They've had enough cold for one day; and the town is ablaze with candles, and doors are decorated for Christmas. There will be much feasting tomorrow. There's ice in the Mohawk, and it will only be days before the ferry will close. The men agreed to come with the wagon if the ferry is running."

Anne then needed to hear an answer to Francois's question.

"Joseph, why didn't you write? We didn't know if you were well or even if you had reached the house," she asked with tears in her eyes. "We have been so worried."

"I did write, Anne, but that is a long story. I have much to tell of my trip, but that can all wait until after Christmas." He pulled Anne close and kissed her hard again.

Kaspar interrupted. "I must head back to Schenectady before it's too late, and the ferry stops running tonight."

Joseph interrupted. "My good friend, the ferry may well be closed by the time you reach Schenectady and you will have to stay on the Glen side. You are welcome to stay with us the night."

Now Anne interrupted, "...and enjoy a Christmas feast with us tomorrow."

"Kaspar, you must stay for Christmas dinner tomorrow. Plus, I have a surprise in the barn I wish you to see," said Lucy with a sly smile that Lizzie mimicked.

"Well then, Miss Lucy, get your wrap, and we shall take a sleigh ride to the barn." replied Kaspar with a deep bow. "I'm sure Blitzen will find your barn a good place tonight."

Sam glanced at Thomas who looked to Francois who raised his eyebrows at Lizzie who hid her smile with her coat. Lucy buttoned her coat, put on her hat and mittens, and was escorted out to the sleigh on Kaspar's arm.

The night was clear and cold, and stars filled the black sky. Blitzen was ready to move and stomped impatiently in the snow. Kaspar helped Lucy into the sleigh, went to the other side, and easily joined her on the broad seat. He covered their laps with a heavy blanket. The family heard the sleigh bells fade as Blitzen headed down the hill. "I think they are taking the long way to the barn, Sam," said Thomas.

Sam smiled. Sometimes it's better just to listen.

Much later, after eating dinner and listening to Sam, Lizzie, and Thomas say their prayers, Anne and Joseph lay together like spoons under their winter quilt.

CHAPTER XXIX

Remorse

The children were still laughing and retelling the fun of Christmas day. There had been sleigh rides in Kaspar's fast sleigh, visits from Uncle Will and Aunt Nellie and the cousins, feasting and singing, and sledding down the back hill. Even Anne had gone sledding, and the children had laughed as their mother stood and brushed the snow from her jacket, laughing and happy again; her cheeks rosy with the cold and her eyes alive and sparkling as she looked to the top of the hill and waved to Joseph.

And Lucy had memories of her starry-night sleigh ride with Kaspar. She still could feel the thrill of the sleigh's speed and the cold air on her face and the near presence of Kaspar next to her warmed by the heavy woolen blanket. She had felt such excitement and such a rush of relief and happiness that her brother was home. Later, as they walked to the barn and unharnessed Blitzen from the sleigh, Kaspar had marveled at the beauty of Liberty. He thought her only the second most beautiful young filly in the barn as he looked at Lucy.

Lucy thought to herself that he had certainly improved his English since he moved to Schenectady. His sincere gaze brought a smile to her lips, and he had pushed her hair back from her face and gently kissed her. The memory of the night still made her pause and forget what she was doing.

The storm had delayed Gordon's men from departing from Schenectady. The January day was gray, and the Mohawk River ominous, but it was not snowing, and the roads had been trampled by local wagons. The men worried that as they got closer to Balls Town, the roads might be impassable, and they hesitated to leave the safety of civilization. Ice had started to form along the shallow banks of the river, and fingers of frozen water reached into the middle from sheltered coves. It might be just a few days before ice skimmed the river connecting the two banks. Then, until spring, the ice would only thicken. The air was bitter cold, but thankfully no wind.

The ferrymen, anxious to close up their business, encouraged and then told Gordon's men to board the ferry now or wait until spring. They couldn't guarantee a safe crossing much longer. The young men, still only partially convinced that a crossing was safe, reluctantly decided they would cross. Putting their fears aside and anxious to be home, they drove the two oxen pulling the heavy wagon onto the ferry. The weighted and now lowered ferry swayed and deflected the ropes. Water washed over the back ramp until the men pulled in the heavy planks. The oxen bellowed cries of alarm when the ferry swayed, but the wheels were well blocked, and the wagon didn't shift. The ferrymen knew their business and had carried loads heavier than this, but danger always lurked if a rope should break or an oxen bolt and break free.

As the broad river moved steadily beneath them, Gordon's men could only think of home. They had stayed in Schenectady too long and worn out their welcome. Christmas was over, and the tavern was now stripped of holiday cheer and empty. Men were doing inside work, and women had begun to ration their food to insure they would not run short before the roads were again open.

The crossing had gone well. As they drove the oxen up the ramp on the north side of the river, the men were relieved that this job would soon be over. The repaired wheel was holding up, and the roads remained frozen and firm. The trip had been a frightening experience, and the men were weary of being on the road. With Joseph no longer with them, they hurried the hungry oxen, pushing the beasts to move faster on the flat stretches. The oxen were not cold, but sweating and lathered from the heavy burden of the loaded logging wagon, and hungry. The men's stomachs rumbled, too, and their feet and hands were white with cold. They had thought they would be home long before Christmas and had brought neither warm hats nor gloves.

Thomas and Sam were looking for rabbit tracks, or any critter moving about in the south field, when Thomas spotted the wagon with Sam's spy glass. As he heard his younger brother's call, Sam ran to his side and told Thomas he was the best lookout he had ever known. Together they shared the spy glass and watched their father's oxen pulling the heavily laden logging wagon up their hill. Thomas was pleased with the compliment. Then added his own, "I know I have the smartest brother in the whole State of New York." Sam smiled. He knew he probably wasn't, but it was all right if his brother thought he was. The boys raced to the cabin to tell their father the men were coming.

As the wagon reached the top of the hill, the family, warmly dressed in their jackets, hats, and mittens, stood and cheered the men as the wagon pulled into the yard. Anne could see the young men were very cold and ran back to the cabin to fix bread and cheese and reheat the soup. Lucy stayed with her brother and watched. Joseph, too, could see the men's cold hands and asked them to drive the wagon up to the cellar's foundation and quickly come into the cabin.

Then to his son, Joseph said, "Sam, unhitch the oxen and get them to the barn. They are tired, thirsty, and hungry, but don't feed them quite yet. Let them drink first and take an old blanket and dry their sweaty necks. They may bolt for the barn, so be careful."

Sam did as he was told, and Francois went to help the boy. Thomas ran ahead and opened the barn door. But the oxen were so tired from the last pull up the hill that they barely walked to the barn. They could smell the hay, knew they were home, were gladly rid of the wagon, but they could not muster even a slow trot to their barn.

Joseph again invited the men in for a hot mug of soup, and soon all were in the cabin, listening as Gordon's men dipped the bread into the soup and burned their lips as they slurped the soggy, hot bread and broth. They were burning their throats while at the same time talking about the river crossing.

Joseph thanked Gus and Zach and said he would pay for the crossing and settle with the ferrymen. The trip had been longer and more dangerous than he had thought, and he thanked them for never wavering in their determination to bring the house timbers to Balls Town. The men looked at Joseph and nodded as still more bread was cut, and slabs of cheese followed the bread down to their hungry stomachs.

Sam joined Lizzie and Thomas as they sat by the table watching and listening, realizing that the trip had been a real adventure for the two. Lizzie poked her brother and whispered, "Sam, I wish they would slow down and talk a bit more. They're making a mess, and we're not hearing much about the trip."

Sam nodded in agreement and Thomas, who had heard his sister's whisper, boldly told her, "Can't you see they're hungry?"

The men had heard the children's comments. Warmer, with their hunger somewhat relieved, they did slow to tell about the crossing. The ice in the river now became huge chunks of broken ice floes swirling in black water. They exaggerated to the delight of the children and hidden smiles of the women.

Gus began his tale, "The oxen gave us quite a start. I held one with all my might, and Zach held the other during the crossing. They might have dove into the water when the ferry lurched hard to the left if we hadn't held them by the horns. They are brutes, and when hungry, they are hungry brutes." Everyone sighed.

Now it was Zach's turn. "The ferry almost drifted into a huge whirlpool by the landing. One kick from the oxen and the whole ferry might have been dashed to pieces careening into icy water." More sighing. "But Gus and I steadied the nervous critters until we reached the other side of the river, and the ferry ropes held and those ferry men are mighty strong," emphasized Zach, who winked to Joseph. He continued, putting the last piece of cheese in his hand back on the platter before ending the tale, "It was a rough crossing. The wind kicked up huge waves, and the river water chilled us to the bone with heavy spray. Our clothes did not dry until the last few miles. I thought I might be a frozen statue on Gordon's old wagon, with my hands frozen to the reins." More sighs from the children.

Thomas now gasped and looked at the men with new respect. Joseph cleared his throat and told Sam and Lizzie to go out to the barn to give the worthy oxen plenty of hay taking Thomas with them to help. The three children hurriedly and excitedly dressed in their warmest clothes, as Zach, Gus, and Lucy hid smiles behind their hands.

As soon as the children were out the door, the men laughed and then asked Joseph about the bundles. He answered that he thought they would be best stored in the barn. Zach and Gus put on their jackets and returned to the wagon. Lucy dressed again in her fur jacket and warm knitted hat and mittens, pushing her hair behind her ears and over her shoulders. She followed the men to show them where to store the bundles in the barn. The men quickly untied the paneling, doors, trim and shutters, making several trips to the barn, stacking the finished pieces in the empty horse stall next to Yankee. Zach stopped to look at Yankee.

"Is this your horse?" he asked.

"No, it's my brother's, but the foal is mine," answered Lucy.

"You look so familiar, and when I saw the horse, I remembered seeing you at the 4th of July race. You were standing by the horse with Kaspar and his horse. Was that you racing on Kaspar's horse?"

"Yes," said Lucy. *This will be a test*, she thought to herself. Lucy was now aware, but a little cautious of any young man's attention, yet eager to engage conversation with this good-humored fellow.

The words coming from Zach's lips were a surprise to Lucy. "You ran a good race. Of course, you were on a good horse, but you took the second creek jump well, and I couldn't keep up with you through the trees. Maybe this year I'll have better luck."

Lucy was speechless. Then a smile broke out, and her eyes revealed an inner happiness. Now Zach was surprised and quickly excused himself and went back for the rest of the doors and trim.

The family watched as Gus and Zach unloaded the heavy beams from the wagon and stacked them in front of the cold cellar foundation. The heavy roof tresses were left leaning against the maple tree. When the last beam was unloaded, Zach suggested that he would come back in a couple of days to get the wagon with Gordon's horses. Joseph agreed and thanked the young men again, shaking their hands awkwardly using his good arm.

Joseph had invited the men to come in and warm themselves before leaving, but the men were warm from work and declined, not because they weren't still hungry and knew Joseph's wife would offer them more food, but they were anxious to be home with their own families and ready to sleep in their own beds. They were exhausted.

The children had been watching as the men unloaded the last few house beams from the wagon. Lizzie and Lucy stood together and watched as the men ran down the hill towards home. Then Lizzie walked over to the beams with tears in her eyes and joined Sam and Thomas who were looking for the Roman numeral markings. Lizzie thought the beams looked just like the beams in the barn. She sniffed away a little sob, as she wondered out loud, "They look just like the beams in the barn. Sam, will the house look like the barn?"

Sam, still with his head close to the ground looking for his father's slash marks on the corners of the beams said, "I remember the house. It looked like a house. Don't worry; you won't be disappointed when father is through building the saltbox."

Lizzie just shook her head, shivered, and then ran to the cabin behind her Aunt Lucy.

January

This year Sam would be 10, Lizzie 8, Thomas 4, and baby Charles would celebrate his first birthday in March. The cabin seemed roomy. With Uncle Will married, and Jack, Jonas, Louisa, and Abby now living in Aunt Nellie's cabin, their three-room cabin felt empty. But the emptiness had lasted only a few days. After everyone spread out their books, clothes, and collections, the hooks and shelves were quickly filled again.

Aunt Lucy and Lizzie slept on the girls' side. Sam and Thomas slept on the boys' side and, on very cold nights, Francois joined the boys in Uncle William's old bed. But for most of the winter, Francois preferred sleeping in his den outside, under the honey locust tree. He told them when they had rearranged the cabin after their Uncle Will's wedding, "My first cup of coffee next to the fire always tastes best after a cold night on the ground. Trappers are hardened to cold nights. That's when we sleep the best!"

Sam tried hard to imagine being any colder than some nights in the cabin. On those nights he doubled up quilts with Thomas, and the brothers slept together. On really cold nights, they rearranged their bedding and Sam, Lizzie, and Thomas slept in the loft over their parent's bed. It was warmer near the ceiling when the fire was going. Baby Charles had his crib near the fire, but often woke up in bed with his parents. If the fire went out during the night, there was ice in the water pail, and nobody even thought of using the outhouse on very cold nights.

After the mid-January thaw was replaced with a blast of cold Canadian air and a heavy dump of snow, the split wood for the cabin fireplace was half gone. No one was splitting logs to replace the burned wood. William could no longer come to the hill to split firewood for his brother as the lane was closed with drifting snow, and Francois had not picked up the axe.

Francois had not offered to split wood. Joseph was worried. His shoulder was sore. He could barely move his lower arm without pain. The bruise from the falling beam was an ugly purple-blue color, but was turning yellow-green around the edges. Francois did once say that was a good sign. It meant the muscle was healing and the bruise shrinking. But Joseph only winced in pain when he moved his arm to pull on his shirt.

Francois knew Joseph should be moving his shoulder a little each day to help keep his arm and fingers healthy and strong. He did not cut down trees for Joseph nor split wood.

Anne said it was important for Joseph to keep his shoulder warm and to eat meat. She made hot broth for lunch everyday with onions and vegetables. Joseph did what he was told, but his shoulder still hurt. He could not chop firewood, hoist a pail of water from the well, or rollover onto his sore shoulder at night without waking up in pain. But when he did wake during the night, he stirred the fire, added a new log, and thanked God for his safe deliverance home. Tonight, with his family soundly sleeping around him and his split wood supply terribly low, he promised himself he would begin moving his arm more and bring in the water even if it hurt. *Next, I will swing the axe.*

The wind whistled down the chimney, and downdrafts scattered ash on the cabin floor. Joseph worried about the wind, and the glowing embers and flaming logs. The fire would be needed through the night to keep the cabin warm. The children and Lucy were sleeping in the loft, and the two side rooms had been closed off to keep the heat in the center of the cabin.

It was sure to snow again. Sam had just told his father, he could smell snow coming through cracks in the log cabin's north wall. Lucy added that the animals were all especially hungry; a sure sign there would be a storm. Sam was telling Thomas there would be good sledding on the back hill in a couple of days. Anne and Joseph were listening to the conversation, while Charles snuggled and pulled his mother's hair and ears, not at all sleepy. Francois, too, had reluctantly agreed that sleeping on the ground was not as good as sleeping on a wood floor in the cabin and had brought in his heavy bear skin blanket. It was still early, too early to be sleeping, but the cabin was too cold for sitting around the table, when Lucy asked the question that the family had been waiting to hear answered.

"Brother, what took you so long? Please tell us of your journey. We must hear about your trip."

Everyone was still. It took long minutes before Joseph responded. He seemed to need time to gather his thoughts, and no one said a word. Anne was glad that it was Lucy who had asked. She feared the worst and knew that her husband would not have delayed telling, unless there was bad news. She prayed that it was not about their family.

"Well," Joseph began, "the roads were hard and dry, and we made good time past Albany. Of course, oxen move at a slower pace than a horse, but they were steady. Gordon's men, Augustus and Zacheus, are just grown boys, much like Uncle Matt. In fact, they are all good friends and worked well together at the sawmill for Major Gordon. Gordon was willing to let them go for a few weeks when the Mourning Kill no longer flowed strong enough to drive the saw at the mill. They were eager for an adventure, but not eager enough to sign-up with Washington's Continental Army like Matthew. They are both in the militia and live on East Line Road. I know they probably ran all the way home when they left our hill. They're good strong boys.

"We camped beside the Hudson River most nights. There was little grass for the oxen to eat, even though the frost had not yet touched the banks of the river. There were so many people traveling along the road that the ground was bare; there was no firewood to be found. The road looks so different from when we came to Balls Town. It is much wider, and now the ruts are huge. Some of the holes have been filled with river rocks, but most have to be driven through very slowly. The oxen were the best choice to haul the wagon.

"Zach brought his fishing pole, and we did have some good meals, but most of what we ate was what you had packed in the wagon, Anne. And all of our fires were from our own logs. We rationed the hay, knowing we would need feed for the oxen on our return trip. We slept in the wagon, and the oxen were always tied close to the wagon at night. We trusted no one.

"There were so many families fleeing the Indians in the western Mohawk Valley. There had been a terrible Indian attack at Cherry Valley. Have you heard about it?" asked Joseph.

"No," said Anne. "We have not been to church, and William said nothing about it when he came to chop firewood. Surely Major Gordon would have called the militia if there had been danger to Balls Town."

"Yes. I'm sure he knew of the danger. It was south and west of here. We heard on the road that the local militias did their best, but took heavy losses. The Iroquois tribes may pay dearly for the attack made by but a few Indians and Loyalists. One night we stopped near the camped farmers. I could tell they had little in their wagons except their quilts and cooking pots. Most were going back to the towns and villages they had come from; I suppose hoping to find friends or family who would shelter and feed them for the winter.

"It took three weeks to reach Will's cabin and the saltbox. Traveling with oxen is not as fast as traveling with horses," Joseph repeated, "I couldn't believe how slowly the miles passed. We had gone through more than half of our food, and the oxen had too. I should have known how much food we would eat from our trip to Schenectady, but I did not plan well. Driving the oxen to Schenectady, now seems like a very short trip. We could have used twice the hay and feed. As we turned down Will's lane, I could see fresh wagon and horse tracks and wished I had brought my musket. Zach and Gus had brought theirs, hoping to do some hunting, so at least we had some arms. Passing through the woods, we reached the cabin and house. I was shocked with what we saw. There were people; wagons parked across our yard, children playing on the swings. They were surprised to see us drive straight toward them, and several men went for their muskets. Will's cabin was still standing, but people had pulled down the door and were prying logs from the cabin walls and loading them into wagons. The windows were broken and the cabin looked empty. Sarah's beautiful garden was a weed patch, as was yours, Anne. Even our young maple trees had been cut down, and there was neither a stick of furniture nor fence post to be seen, but men and women hurriedly scavenging for wood, any wood."

No one made a sound.

"I guess I was in shock, because it was minutes before I looked up behind the cabin at the saltbox. It was still standing, but people had also begun stripping the siding from the beams. My heart almost stopped beating as I saw a man rip one of father's shutters from the house. Had it not been for Zach and Gus warning me to stay calm, I might have fought him."

The family was now talking. The Indians' attack on the settlers had changed everything, Sam and Lizzie were whispering. Anne spoke to the children and asked if they were okay. They answered yes, and that Thomas had fallen asleep. Lucy urged her brother to continue.

"I had a letter all written and ready to be mailed saying we had reached the house and were now taking it down. But should I leave the house to this destruction, and where was I to find a Post?"

Anne interrupted again. "Thank God William brought the children north and stayed with us last year. Oh, Joseph, think what might have happened."

"What did happened next, Joseph," urged his sister.

"Lucy, if I hadn't been to Saratoga and seen the battle, I might have been more scared. But I knew these folks were just like us. I stood in the wagon and called them over, just as Major Gordon might have done. I explained that the saltbox was my house and that the cabin belonged to my brother. I told them that we had moved to Schenectady. Nobody knows were Balls Town is. They stopped and listened to me. I thought fast, Will's cabin was half gone. I told them that William would not be back, and that as his brother, I would give them his cabin. They could take every log. I told them that if my family were in such need, I would be doing the same as they were. They all seemed to relax a bit. I told them I came back for the beams of the saltbox and my father's doors, paneling, and shutters. The man holding the shutter let it drop. I did not mind if they stripped the siding from the house, in fact, that would make our work easier." Joseph paused, and no one spoke.

"For the next few days, more people came down the lane when they saw wagons filled with logs and siding coming from the house. We had a steady stream of people, now salvaging wood and broken shingles. Zach was good with the Beetle, and as soon as the beams were stripped, he pounded out the pegs at the joints. Both he and Gus climbed onto the skeleton of the house and worked from the top down, freeing the beams from the rest of the structure. It was hard work and dangerous, too. We did not let the sides fall, because the bents were too big, and the beams might have cracked. I think it's harder to take beams down than to have a barn-raising. I directed their work and lowered the pieces with the rope. Many times I was up on the main beam right alongside Gus while Zach was pounding. And the heavy beams sometimes did fall. We were not strong enough to lower them slowly."

The family collectively sighed with sad little groans.

"We used every foot of Gordon's and our rope. We worked as fast as we could, but there were often distractions and people asking questions, and we had to eat. Anne, we ate all of the food you packed, every last crumb. There was no time to cook or hunt. You can't imagine how good your breakfast here tasted on Christmas morning." Joseph paused.

He cleared his throat and continued. "We loaded the wagon as the house came down. The beams went on first. We then used the rope to tie up the panels and doors. Now out of rope, the oxen were free to wander about and search for food. Their hay was long gone; there was no grass. The oxen ate dried weeds – whatever they could find. We looked up once and thought they had been stolen. But after a short search, we found them behind Will's orchard, eating the rotting fruit on the ground."

Anne felt anger. *How could fruit on the trees be left to fall and rot? When had Joseph's sisters left the house? How long had the house been empty?*

"William asked me to dig some of his apple trees and bring them back, but I did not. I did find Sarah's and the baby's graves and said a prayer. I was so tired that I didn't stay long. I thought we might stop at her family's cabin, but we did not do that either. It was cold, we were hungry, and I didn't know if they had enough food for themselves, let alone three hungry men.

"Lucy, I kept praying as we took the house down, that I would find a note from our sisters. Patience and Susanna would have known I would come back for the house. But if they did leave a note, it might have been tucked under the siding which has now been burnt to keep some family warm this winter." Joseph paused. "I found mother and father's graves."

Joseph then paused a long while. Sam could hear his mother whispering to his father. No one said a word. But then they heard Joseph say, "I know I should have found a way to send you a letter. Please forgive me, that I made you worry. I'm sorry that I didn't think to make a better effort to get word to you. Please forgive me, Anne."

But her anger continued until it was spent. She told Joseph about her loneliness. She had been so hopeful for so many days. She had fired up her outdoor oven once and baked loaves of bread, thinking Joseph would surely come. Then she had cried, guiltily realizing how much wood she had used to bake bread. The wood pile was going down so fast with the cold wind. Then, still sobbing, Anne told how the wind had blown at night, and she had gotten up to add yet more wood to the fire, and not been able to sleep. How the baby had been fussy. Then Anne just cried in relief. Lizzie and Sam heard their mother's sobs and cried too.

Joseph thought, *I must not let my family down again. I should have gotten word to them. I was driven, thinking only of the house, desperately sad over seeing my parent's graves. I must work my arm and swing father's axe.*

After Anne's weeping had subsided, Joseph cleared his throat and began again. "I left my letter to you wrapped in elm bark, wedged between stones by Phebe's and Samuel's grave markers. If any of the family comes back to the house, they will find it and the cabin gone. They may look by the graves and know I had come for the house. I can only hope they find the letter addressed to you and come to us."

Lucy thought of her sisters, Patience and Susanna, and whispered a prayer for their safety. Lizzie snuggled close to her aunt, heard the prayer and joined in the "Amen."

Joseph was now speaking. "When we left, the wagon was very heavy. We had some hard rains, and the roads were muddy. The slow oxen were even slower. Days ran together. I thought it might be December. When we got on to the main road and found it was two weeks until Christmas, I panicked."

Joseph's voice weakened. "I pushed the oxen too hard. It was getting dark, we were going too fast, and the wagon wheel broke. We tried to repair it without unloading the beams. The beam fell off when the wagon tipped and hit my shoulder, pinning me to the ground. The rest you know. We made it to Schenectady, and Kaspar found us. He took us to his room, and we had a good night's sleep on his floor. The next morning was Christmas Eve."

"Oh Joseph," Anne's sobbing began again. The children could hear their mother and father whispering, this time with little sympathetic moans and groans.

"Riding in Kaspar's sleigh, coming home to you, seeing our little cabin tucked into the hill, I guess I wondered why I had gone for the house. We have everything we need."

Then to the surprise of everyone, Thomas sat up in the loft bed, his eyes were now wide open, and with his loudest voice announced, "Yes, Papa – and now we have a house!" Everyone laughed in relief, especially Joseph.

CHAPTER XXX

New plans

Mornings were spent outdoors. Sam and Thomas, bundled up against the cold, walked the hill before breakfast. The storm had left little piles of snow on their quilts when the wind pushed snowflakes through the cracks of the cabin's north wall. Today they would ask Lizzie and Aunt Lucy to sled with them on the back hill. A good cover of snow and the windblown drifts off the top of the hill had covered the stumps. But fun only happened after chores were done. Still, it was amazing to everyone how quickly the family did the chores and cleaned up the cabin. With only half as many people living in the cabin, there was only half the bread to bake, half the water to fetch, and half the clothes to wash.

But, there were more animals to care for, and Lucy, Sam, and Lizzie spent time each morning bringing water to the barn and feeding Yankee and Liberty, the two oxen, pigs, and three and a half cows; the calf would be born in April. Thankfully, the yearling lambs were still at McKnight's with the ewes and would come to the barn in the spring after sugaring.

Anne found time to sew and was already talking of setting up her quilting frame in the house. She would love to have Lydia, Nellie, and Molly come to quilt. On the next trip to Schenectady, she would see about buying muslin to mix with her sack cloth. If she could quilt with friends, they could sell their quilts just as she had done with her sisters. Her husband was swinging the axe. *Maybe he could start the house this spring.*

Lucy was happy for her free time to spend in the barn with Yankee and Liberty. She slipped a soft bridle on the little filly and led it around the barn. They ventured out on sunny days, and Lucy led her from one path to another, until the little horse knew where the cabin and the barn and everything, including the Liberty Tree, were on the hill. Yankee always trotted along behind. Lucy could hardly wait for spring. Lucy would be giving riding lessons to Lydia's children. Lizzie had asked for lessons, too.

Lucy walked back to the cabin with her brother. "Joseph, a few more horses in the barn would be a good idea. I plan to have a whole stable full of horses some day."

Joseph took no time at all thinking about his sister's plan. "That would require a lot of hayfields and oats and another barn just for the horses."

They heard horses coming up their lane. It was Zach, riding one of Gordon's horses with another tied and running alongside. Zach had come to pick up the lumber wagon to return it to the mill. He harnessed the horses to Gordon's wagon and readily agreed to stay for lunch.

Zach brought news with him. Farmers on East Line Road were talking of building barns, real barns with hay lofts, and houses. They had heard about Joseph's house. What they needed was someone to show them how to plan, measure, and make the joints so they, too, could have barn raisings and houses. Zach had told them about the Roman numerals, and how they had taken down the house and brought the beams to the hill.

Joseph was flattered that someone would need his advice on anything. He paused before he spoke. *He did know how to build a barn! And a saltbox!*

"I will meet with your neighbors. Maybe we could meet at the fort. Maybe some of the men could bring a log or a couple of their beams, we will need paper, the men need to bring their sharpening stones, as a dull axe blade will never work for the joints. We can draw plans, and then I will show them how to measure so that everything goes right at their barn-raising."

The children were listening to their father. Lucy was watching Zach. He had spoken directly and assuredly, gently persuading her brother to help his neighbors. Joseph had responded just as directly, hesitating, but thinking clearly. Lucy caught Zach looking at her several times and blushed. The looks and blushing did not go unnoticed by Sam and Lizzie. Sam immediately thought of Ben Franklin; these glances were beginnings, and Lizzie was already looking forward to the day a handsome boy looked at her and made her blush.

Anne could hear the excitement building in her husband's voice. This sounded like a wonderful idea. He had become too much company in the cabin, and it would be weeks before the fields were dry enough to plough. His shoulder was not yet strong enough to cut down trees, but he was chopping firewood and becoming a little grumpy. This would be a good project for her bored husband, and then she could get a project of her own going. She glanced at Zach who was now looking at Lucy.

Anne also had heard Francois speaking to Joseph about the wood pile. He said he had plans and cutting wood was not one of them right now. He had planned a trip as soon as the roads were clear and would take some of his pelts to Schenectady and sell them. He said he had plans for his money, too, and Joseph gathered it might be for a tannery and saddle shop somewhere north of their cabin. No one asked, but Sam overheard his parents one night talking about the new families buying land north of their farm. If Francois was thinking of a tannery, it might be where the Mourning Kill crossed the path north. Anne had laughed when her husband bragged, "Reverend Ball is selling land at Hop City." Anne decided the long nights had all the men planning. Working with the other men would be a good project for her husband. She was ready to quilt with her friends.

"Happy Birthday, Lizzie," said her father as he added three logs to the glowing embers.

The fire burst into flame, and soon the soft pine logs were sputtering and warming the cabin. The sun was just up, and it was a beautiful morning. Lizzie lay back on her bed. She was eight years old. "Today I shall wear my new dress and long stockings to dinner, Father, the dress I wore to Uncle Will's wedding."

Francois came into the cabin with frost on his whiskers and a heavy pail of water. "Happy birthday, Lizzie! Thanks to you, I will get to taste Lucy's creame cake today."

Anne had baked Lucy's Washington Creame Cake for the occasion. It had come hot from the oven with a golden top. She now understood how her oven worked; she knew the hottest and coolest places. She also knew to heat her oven by first burning rather large hard wood logs for bread or beans and split pine wood for thin cakes and puddings. The day before, she had baked two custard puddings and a soft, buttery apple cake with Lizzie's cake. Sam and Thomas had stood by the oven to warm their hands and smell the cinnamon as the apple cake baked.

"Mama, I shall want General Washington's cake for my birthday. Someday I'll be a general," bragged Thomas.

"If you're going to be a general, you had better hop out of bed and get dressed. You have a lot of schooling to learn," said his father.

Thomas began hopping around the cabin and almost fell on Charles, who now crawled around the cabin like a mouse. He was into every basket and had pulled over a sack of flour, spilling the precious wheat on the dirty floor. Anne rushed to her son, while reminding her husband that when they moved into their saltbox, she would have a proper kitchen with shelves for her dishes and cupboards to store her flour. Joseph put on his coat and went out to split wood. He still had not figured out how he was going to rebuild his house.

Anne inspected the seam Lizzie was stitching and said it was crooked. Lizzie's pot holder not only had a crooked seam, but one side of the pot holder was inside out. She had to rip it all out and start again. Lizzie was only sewing doll clothes and pot holders, but she had her own sewing basket on her shelf and was angry that her mother made her rip out the bad seam on her birthday of all days. Anne consoled her, "Let's put this away until tomorrow."

Lizzie put up her sewing and thought about her aunt's promise. Lucy had promised she would give her riding lessons in the spring. Her father had promised her a new book on the next trip to Schenectady. Her father had made a good teacher. Maybe not as much fun as last year when her cousins were here, but Joseph carefully explained everything. She could now recite her reading lessons to Thomas at night, and he was learning to read. She put on her coat and went out to the barn to see Liberty. Was Yankee's foal big enough to ride? Lucy said no, but the foal was getting taller. Lizzie thought, *maybe I will be more like Aunt Lucy and raise horses. I don't like sewing.*

Anne, spreading the creamy custard on the bottom layer of Lizzie's cake, could not wait for spring. "Ah, to open the door and have the sun shine into the cabin would be such a joy." Charles was ready for his lunch and started to fuss. "Just think Charles, a sunny cabin is coming in just another couple of months!" Anne laughed. "The house will be wonderful next winter. I must remind your Papa to check on our windows the next time he goes to Schenectady. Big windows, nine 'or nines I believe I heard him say. We shall hold him to nine over nines, and then we shall have enough light to sew a straight seam."

Joseph's arm was much improved, but after morning chores, he happily sat at the table with his children. They always started with their numbers, then a writing lesson, and Thomas insisted that they have a science project before reading. The *Chicken Almanack* had been fun, and he wanted to have a winter project. His father told him he would have to think of one.

The book of maps was always on the table during reading. Sam wanted to know where every country was and where the people in his books lived. Sam had drawn maps of Hop City, Balls Town, and the United States. Every time he looked at his map of the United States, he thought about his Uncle Matt in Georgia fighting with the Continental Army. Where was George Washington? He missed newspapers and the news from the musters. He asked to ride Yankee to the trading post, but his father answered no; it was too late in the day and, besides, it was his sister's birthday.

Anne had promised to embroider something on the school-girl jumper she was sewing for Lizzie. Lizzie drew a picture of Liberty, and Anne was embroidering the sketch of Yankee's foal across the bodice of the jumper while Joseph taught.

The snow was quickly melting off the hill. Lucy was cleaning out Yankee's stall and wearing her grubby old clothes. The clothes needed a good airing and soon, when the weather changed, a good washing.

Lucy was singing as she brushed Yankee's thick winter coat. The horse had started to shed, and the hair would make a fine stuffing for wagon seat cushions. This year she wanted a proper saddle for Liberty, and Francois had said she could probably sell seat cushions to buy a saddle; he would give her some of his animal hides. She had woven thin reeds into cushion slips and would tightly pack the horse hair into the cushions. Francois had helped her find good reeds. They had used Francois's snow shoes and walked far into the wood lot behind the orchard to where a shallow depression was always swampy. The reeds had been beaten down by the snow, but they were still strong and, best of all, plentiful.

The day she had been in the woods with Francois was the day Jacobus had brought another ham. Lucy still could not believe her bad luck, or was it good luck? She seldom thought of Jacobus. She talked to Yankee about male animals, and the horse only looked at her with understanding. Lucy wished the horse could talk. *Yankee, you had no problems capturing Blitzen's heart, but I shall not try to capture Jacobus's.* She found herself thinking of Zach. *He likes horses, and it sounds like he is going to race on the 4th of July. I wonder if Kaspar will race.*

Joseph tapped the maple trees, and the sap was flowing. That was a good indication that spring was coming at last, and everyone was happily pouring the pails of clear sap into the boiling pan. The procedure had an added twist this year; Thomas had found his science project. Each pail now had an alphabet letter scratched by the rim, and Thomas measured each pail's sap before it could be poured into the pan. This was slowing things down, but his father had agreed, making the dipping-ruler and adding the figures each day was a worthy school experiment. Joseph also could not believe his good fortune with his barn-building classes. He loved teaching the men and spent his free hours working out plans for all sizes of his basic barn and two houses. One problem that plagued him as he sat at the cabin table was the lack of light while he worked. *Windows...I need more light!*

> Sam's Almanack:
>
> *Today was my birthday. I'm now ten years old, and Mother made me an apple and hickory nut cake. The cousins and Uncle Will and Aunt Nellie came to celebrate and eat with us. Jack and I took a long walk after lunch. He said they are all doing well, but he misses us. Uncle Will is very busy planning what he should grow. He knows he must plant all the field crops and garden, but he wants to do something special, too. He's very excited and thinking of planting an orchard – a big orchard of three or four kinds of apples, then they would have apples, cider, and vinegar to sell. It would mean a lot of picking, but he has six children now, and Uncle Will told Jack he already has his pickers! Jack thinks there will be more brothers and sisters and they will need a house like ours! Jack misses school. He has not opened a book since he moved. SR*

Balls Town farmers were ploughing their fields; the days were long and exhausting. Now it would be a race for the Rues to clear one more field of stones and be ready to plant. The field of Timothy hay would grow without ploughing or planting, but the oat field must be sown and Indian corn planted. Anne promised to plant the corn in hills, just as the Indians had done. This would give them corn, beans, and squash; and Lizzie wanted the pumpkins in the hedge rows like the Indians had planted them, too. They had not seen the Indian boy or his mother all winter. Sam spoke a few times about where Lone Fox may be, but he quickly pushed back the longing to see his friend and now said nothing.

Zach unexpectedly knocked on the cabin door before daybreak. He was out of breath from running up the hill, but mostly breathless out of excitement. "Joseph! Joseph!"

Joseph was helping Lucy dole out oatmeal and was startled at the voice just outside their door. He reached for his musket. Then, recognizing Zachary's voice, he put his musket aside and opened the door. "Come in, my young man, come in and have breakfast with us."

"Oh, I had breakfast an hour ago," Zach quickly explained, "I shall be late for work if I stay too long, but I just had to tell you the good news. This Saturday the men from East Line Road are coming to build your house!

Joseph sat down. The family looked at the earnest young man. They had heard his message, but no words formed from their lips and their mouths hung open in surprise.

"It's true, it's true," continued Zach, now more formal. "I was sent to tell you of their decision. They are so grateful for the help you gave them in planning their barns, they wanted to give you something, but had no money. So I reminded them that your house was yet to be built, and they jumped on the idea, especially the men who want to build a saltbox. They are anxious to show off how well they can follow your directions, I think," concluded Zach.

"Tell your neighbors I accept their generous offer. What a wonderful offer!" Joseph repeated.

With that answered, Zach was out the door, but he quickly turned and stepped back inside the cabin, bumping into Lucy. They laughed. Then, Zach kissed her blushing cheek.

He turned twice as he ran down the hill, and smiled and waved his arms at the pretty young girl standing in the doorway waving back to him. He jumped the stone wall and yelled back to her, "I'm practicing for the race!" And then he stopped and turned back again shouting, "We begin the house on Saturday! I'll be back Saturday!"

Sam's *Almanack:*

> *We cheered and then Mother and Lucy were dancing, and then Father was kissing Mother, and then Lizzie was hugging me, and Thomas must have thought we all looked pretty silly, but banged the cooking spoon on the kettle and laughed, and Charles waved his arms and spilled his oatmeal on the floor, and then Lucy began and soon we were all singing* Yankee Doodle. *SR*

Washington Creame Cake

Cake part:

1 egg
½ cup sugar
¼ cup milk
¾ cup flour
1 ½ tablespoon powder
Pinch salt

Filling:

1 cup milk
½ cup sugar
¼ cup flour
Pinch salt
1 egg
½ teaspoon lemon extract

Cake: Combine cake ingredients in order. Hand mix until smooth. Bake in a small round tin until done. Filling: Mix first three ingredients. Beat in egg, add salt and lemon, beat until creamy. Let cake cool. Split into two layers and spread cooled filling between the layers.

Adapted from: Recipes from Historic Burnt Hills, New York, settled in 1763.
Recipe submitted by Mrs. Betty Seelye

Photo Gallery

Merci and Horton Rue

Picture thanks to the previous owner, Harold Rue. I visited with Harold Rue and his daughter in 1977. Harold said that in 1774, Rue land was "taken out," and a cabin was built 200 feet south of the present house. There was a sawmill and covered bridge behind the house, and a blacksmith shop by the driveway turnoff. East of the house was a sugarbush, still, and tavern, and charcoal pits. The Rues raised sheep and had looms for weaving the wool. There was a small orchard across Hop City Road opposite the saltbox.

The barn was huge with a hay loft and beautiful beams. The attached shed had stanchions for cows. There was a small shed at the road for the milk cans waiting for pick up and a chicken coop off to the right of the picture. Below: house under renovation, 1969.

Restoring the house and fireplace above.
Below, our daughters posing for their Christmas picture.

The house is barely visible but our garage and pool can be seen. The garage is most likely where the cabin stood. Below: swimming with cousins in the Mourning Kill at the bottom of the hill behind the house.

Cannons and cousins at West Point, New York.

Daughters visiting friends with growing piglets.

Harold Rue told me he remembered his grandfather owned a beautiful black horse. He said his grandfather drove his wagon to Schenectady to sell apples and pears, and then stopped along the way home, handing out bananas to children who recognized his horse and ran out to the road to greet him.

Hop City's Yankee Lady, our first Lab, playing with our youngest daughter.

A load of bricks from Schenectady to make a path to the front door.

Clowns and pumpkins!

Fun after a Nor'easter!

After school chore, bringing firewood from the barn to the wood box for our Franklin stove.

Ice skating in Ballston Spa.

Our home on Hop City Road., the renovated Rue saltbox.

Books I read to learn more about the historical background:

Books about the discovery of America:
A New World by Arthur Quinn
The Island at the Center of the World (Manhattan) by Russell Shorto
The Mayflower by Nathanial Philbrick

Books about patriots:
John Adams by David McCullough
1776 by David McCullough
Poor Richard's Almanack by Benjamin Franklin
Benjamin Franklin's Autobiography

Religious writers:
Writings on Pastoral Piety by John Calvin

Books about Native Americans:
The War (French and Indian) That Made America by Fred Anderson
Forgotten Allies (Oneida Indians) by Joseph Kirby Martin
Many Tender Ties, Women in Fur–Trade Society, 1670–1870 by Sylvia Van Kirk
Nature's Healing Grasses by H.E. Kirschner, MD
Turtle Meat and Other Stories by Joseph Bruchac
The Indians of New Jersey by M. R. Harrington

Books about the Battle of Saratoga:
Saratoga, Turning Point of America's Revolutionary War by Richard Ketchum

Diaries:
Growing Up in Cooper Country, diaries edited by Louis C. Jones
The Journal of Robert Treat of Orange, Connecticut edited by R.A. Mason
The American Revolution edited by John Rhodehamel
Domestick Beings compiled by June Spring

Regional books collected by the author:
Saratoga County Heritage edited by Violet B. Dunn
Schenectady Ancient and Modern by Joel Henry Monroe
Ye Olde Days, Ballston by Katherine Q. Briaddy
Burnt Hills – Ballston Lake by Girl Scout Troop 107
Ye Cohorn Caravan by William L. Bowne
Historical Booklet of Ballston Spa Area 1609–1959 sponsored by the Historical Society
Recipes from Historic Burnt Hills settled in 1763, compiled by the Women of Calvary Episcopal Church
Tales of Old Schenectady by Larry Hart
A Reverence for Wood by Eric Sloane
An Age of Barns by Eric Sloane